Willard
Christmas 92

Loose Cannons & Red Herrings

A BOOK OF LOST METAPHORS

BOOKS BY ROBERT CLAIBORNE

SCIENCE

TIME (1967)

DRUGS (1969)

CLIMATE, MAN AND HISTORY (1970)

ON EVERY SIDE THE SEA (1971)

THE SUMMER STARGAZER: Astronomy for Absolute Beginners (1975)

HISTORY AND PREHISTORY

THE FIRST AMERICANS (1973)

GOD OR BEAST: Evolution and Human Nature (1974)

MYSTERIES OF THE PAST, with Lionel Casson and Brian Fagen (1977)

LANGUAGE

THE BIRTH OF WRITING(1975)

OUR MARVELOUS NATIVE TONGUE: The Life and Times of the English Language (1983)

SAYING WHAT YOU MEAN: A Commonsense Guide to American Usage (1986)

LOOSE CANNONS & RED HERRINGS: A Book of Lost Metaphors (1988)

TEXTBOOKS

MEDICAL GENETICS, with Victor McKusick, M.D. (1973)

CELL MEMBRANES, with Gerald Weissmann, M.D. (1974)

Loose Cannons & Red Herrings

A Book of Lost Metaphors

ROBERT CLAIBORNE

W·W·Norton & Company   New York   London

Published simultaneously in Canada by Penguin Books Canada Ltd.,
2801 John Street, Markham, Ontario L3R 1B4.
Printed in the United States of America.
The text of this book is composed in 10.5/13×23.5 Century Old Style,
with display type set in ITC Clearface Bold.
Composition and manufacturing by The Haddon Craftsmen, Inc.
Book design by Margaret M. Wagner.
First Edition

Library of Congress Cataloging-in-Publication Data
Claiborne, Robert.
Loose Cannons to Red Herrings/Robert Claiborne.
p. cm.
Bibliography: p.
1. English language—Etymology—Dictionaries. 2. Metaphor—
Dictionaries. 3. English language—Terms and phrases. I. Title.
PE1583.C55 1988
422′.03—dc19 87-32599

ISBN 0-393-02578-0

W. W. Norton & Company, Inc.
500 Fifth Avenue, New York, N. Y. 10110
W. W. Norton & Company Ltd.
37 Great Russell Street, London WC1B 3NU

1 2 3 4 5 6 7 8 9 0

FOR PAUL BEALE, COLLEAGUE AND FRIEND.

CONTENTS

ACKNOWLEDGMENTS

So many people have made suggestions for this book that it would be impossible to list them. However, special thanks are due to my sister, Clara Claiborne Park, and her husband, David (both of Williams College), for giving me access to "The Park Family Twenty-Year Collection of the Deadest Metaphors and Clichés," which contributed several dozen entries—though I don't agree they're all clichés. (Others undoubtedly *are* clichés—but, just possibly, may be given a new **lease on life** by this book.) Also, to William Morris and the late Mary Morris, authors of *Morris Dictionary of Word and Phrase Origins,* which has contributed scores of entries—though I don't always agree with their etymologies.

The manuscript for this work was written on a Kaypro 4 microcomputer, using the Perfect Writer (Version 1.20) word-processing program, with Plu*Perfect and Smartkey II enhancements. The printout was made on a Silver-Reed EXP 550, linked to the computer through a Quadram Microfazer 64K buffer. The master list of metaphors from which I worked was alphabetized with SORT, a public domain program given to me by M.E. Thornsberry of San Antonio, Texas.

New York and Truro, 1986–87

INTRODUCTION

A metaphor, the dictionaries tell us, is a word or phrase used figuratively. That is, its original sense—almost always a concrete, tangible thing or action—has been transferred to something else—often quite abstract—that in some way resembles the thing originally referred to. Thus metaphors set up analogies between their literal and figurative senses; for example, when we speak of "the evening of life," we're drawing an analogy between the literal approach of night that we experience every day and the figurative approach of "death's dateless [endless] night."

Many people think of metaphors as a device of poets and other literary folk, and certainly they *are* widely used in poetry, and have been for thousands of years. More than twenty-five centuries ago, Homer sang of "rosy-fingered dawn"—the eastern horizon before sunrise, streaked with color as if a goddess had dipped her fingers in dye and drawn them across the heavens.

Nor was Homer by any means the first user of metaphors. Scholars who have studied the ancient Indo-European tongue, the earliest known progenitor of English and dozens of other languages, have reconstructed the phrase *wekwom texos,* "weaver of words."* This was the title given the tribal bards who, more than seven thousand years ago, chanted the songs and legends of our remotest linguistic ancestors, weaving words into poetry as their fellows wove thread into cloth.

---

*For more on the Indo-Europeans, and how researchers have reconstructed their lost language, see Chapter 2 of my *Our Marvelous Native Tongue: The Life and Times of the English Language.*

But metaphor also lies at the heart of language itself. Daily, and quite unthinkingly, we use such expressions as the *eyes* of a potato, the *head* of a hammer and the *foot* of a hill. You could argue about whether such terms are metaphors now, but they surely were once upon a time: a potato can't literally see with its eyes any more than a hammer can think with its head or a hill can walk—or hop—on its foot.

These and hundreds of other words and phrases are obvious metaphors, because both their literal and figurative senses are still current and we need not strain to see the analogies they draw. But English also includes hundreds of "lost" metaphors— words and phrases we still use figuratively, but whose original, literal senses have been obscured or erased by time and change. Thus the **aftermath** once meant the grass that sprang up after a farmer had mowed a field; today even farmers, if they use the term at all, do so figuratively, in the sense of anything that "springs up" after some notable event, as in "the aftermath of Watergate." (Words and phrases given here in **boldface** will be discussed at greater length in the body of the text.)

Many of these metaphors derive from events or legends now little known or forgotten entirely. How many people nowadays know the Bible well enough to guess why **sodomy** means whatever it does mean, or are familiar enough with Greek myth to explain why someone's **Achilles heel** is their vulnerable spot, or why prominent people often find themselves beneath the **sword of Damocles**?

Some metaphors are even more obscure because their original, literal sense was lost even before they became English; that is, they were borrowed from other tongues in which they were already being used figuratively. (English, which has borrowed far more words than any other tongue, is specially rich in such expressions.) It takes a Latinist or philologist to know that **investigate** comes from a word meaning to track an animal; only an Italian speaker could guess that an **alert** person was originally a sentry on a watchtower. And even some philologists don't know that **fink** comes from the German-Yiddish word for "finch" (the fink, like the finch, "sings"—to the cops).

Expressions of this sort are lost in the fullest sense: few of us even think of them as metaphors. Others aren't exactly lost but, you might say, mislaid. That is, we know they must be metaphors, since they clearly aren't meant to be understood literally, but we don't know why. If we say that something is for the **birds**, or that an actor got the **bird**—just what birds are we talking about? What acid is involved in the **acid test**? And why shouldn't you **look a gift horse in the mouth**?

Thus behind hundreds of everyday English words and phrases lie concrete images that can conjure up vivid human activities and encounters from the past. When we decide to **bite the bullet** and face up to something unpleasant but inescapable, we are unwittingly emulating the wounded soldier, enduring field surgery after Waterloo or Gettysburg, biting on a musket ball to keep from screaming; when we wonder how some deal or scheme will **pan out**, we face the same quandry as the "miner, Forty-niner," washing sand in a flat, metal pan in hopes of finding gold.

To people fascinated by the lore of words, lost metaphors are engrossing in themselves. But they are more than that: properly understood, they are a sort of hidden poetry that can heighten the colors and sharpen the meanings of words and phrases that we read or write daily, and thereby enhance our enjoyment of them.

Before telling you more about this hidden poetry, however, I must sound a warning: writing about the origins of words and phrases isn't the same thing as writing about, say, chemistry, because it doesn't—can't—limit itself to "hard" facts. Even the most authoritative etymological dictionaries contain a sizeable proportion of terms marked "o.o.o." (of obscure origin), or words to that effect; other derivations will be hedged with "probably" or "possibly."

Etymology, that is, inevitably involves a certain amount of guesswork—and people sometimes guess wrong. For example, the editors of one of the best-known American dictionaries guessed that the American woodpecker called the flicker derived its name from its "flickering" flight; bird-watchers know that the only flickering thing about the creature is one of its calls: "FLICK-a, FLICK-a FLICK-a."

Moreover, people who deal with word origins are, like the rest of us, sometimes seduced by a good story, so that they recount as fact what is, at best, colorful conjecture. Ernest Weekley, author of several books on words, jokingly ascribed such tales to a fictitious author, Ben Trovato—a gentleman of Italian extraction given to inventing colorful but inaccurate etymologies. (His name comes from the Italian expression *Se no e vero, e ben trovato*— loosely, "If it's not true, it's still a good story.")

Sometimes, too, one encounters two equally plausible etymologies for the same metaphor; in such cases, I've usually picked the most colorful—with due warning that Sr. Trovato may have been at work. Finally, some metaphors are *totally* lost, meaning that nobody can do more than guess where they came from; "like **sixty**" is one example. I've included only a few of these, since the constant repetition of "nobody really knows" or its equivalent would bore you as much as it would me.

Writing about lost metaphors also often involves grappling with the tricky question: "How lost is 'lost'?" The origins of many expressions in this book are "lost" to nearly everyone; **escape** is merely one example. Others, however, are well understood by sizeable minorities. If, for example, you've ever done small-boat sailing, you won't need me to instruct you on the literal meaning of **take another tack**; if you're a horseman or -woman, you probably know what happens when your mount **takes the bit in his teeth**.

The odds are that you'll encounter at least a few metaphors in this book that to you aren't lost at all; if so, remind yourself that what's old hat to you may be new and striking to others. For example, the origin of **sour grapes** was by no means news to *me:* I've known it since I was a kid. Nonetheless, I included it because I discovered that quite a lot of other people—some of them highly educated—don't know it. So should you find yourself at some point muttering, "Hell, *I* knew that!," congratulate yourself on being better informed than most—and go on to something you *don't* know. I guarantee you'll find it, whoever you are!

The metaphors that follow are, of course, listed alphabetically. This is clear enough when we're dealing with single words, but phrases can introduce complications; if, for example, you're looking for **clean as a whistle**, will you find it under "clean" or "whistle"? I've chosen, more or less arbitrarily, to list phrases under their first "significant" word: that is, their first adjective, noun or verb—in this case, "clean." Similarly, you'll find "in the bag" under **bag, in the,** but "holding the bag" under **holding.** This may seem inconsistent, but—take my word for it—any other system would have been equally inconsistent, albeit in different ways.

I've included some cross-references, though I've tried to keep them to a minimum. These (e.g., **scare something up**), refer you to some other entry (in this case, **beat the bushes**), where the metaphor will appear in *italics.* Words within entries in **boldface** (e.g., **cold deck** under **according to Hoyle**) refer you to other entries for more information.

I should be surprised if some readers don't feel moved to write me disagreeing with my conclusions, or suggesting alternative theories. While I'm always happy to get feedback of this sort, I'd urge such people, before taking pen (or typewriter, or computer) in hand, to make sure that their ideas square with the facts. The most authoritative source of facts on word origins and usage is, of course, the *Oxford English Dictionary (OED),* including its four-volume Supplement; other useful information can be gleaned from Craigie and Hulbert's *Dictionary of American English on Historical Principles* (also in four volumes).

A good example of what I mean is **chestnut** (tired joke), which is often credited to a line in a play from around 1800. But since the expression was described as a "new" slang term eighty years later (by which time the play in question was long forgotten), the theory doesn't hold up very well. The game of word origins is, happily, one at which any number can play—but before you start playing, make sure you know the rules!

Loose Cannons & Red Herrings

A BOOK OF LOST METAPHORS

abounding, abundant. From Latin *unda* (a wave), from which you might guess that "abundant" had something to do with what Shakespeare called "the multitudinous waves." Not quite: Latin *abundare* means "to overflow," like a boat swamped by a wave, or the waves themselves "overflowing" onto a beach. If something abounds or is abundant, it's present in overflowing quantities.

aboveboard. A board is a plank, of course, but it also was, and occasionally still is, a table ("the festive board"). If you're playing cards and notice that another player frequently drops his hands below the tabletop, pick up your chips and go home; he's probably up to something not aboveboard. An *under the table* payment—a bribe or off-the-record "commission"—uses much the same image.

absurd. Latin *surdus* means "deaf," but *absurdus* means "discordant" or "inharmonious"—presumably something that only a deaf person could stand. The word was applied to things that were intellectually discordant—didn't harmonize with reason. A person embracing an absurd idea is deaf to the principles of logic—or even common sense.

AC-DC. Nearly everybody knows that "AC" stands for "alternating current," and "DC," for "direct current," but few people under fifty know the original source of "AC-DC." DC was the first form of electric current generated commercially, at Thomas Edison's pioneering Pearl Street (New York City) power station. AC was adopted later, among other reasons because it could be transmitted much more efficiently over long distances.

Edison, however, stuck with DC: he considered electric power his own invention (which, in part, it was), and nobody was about to tell *him* what kind of current was best. So for years his companies continued to generate DC and propagandized against the new-fangled AC. Thus, when the sinister electric chair was introduced around 1890, the Edison companies were quick to point out that it used AC, not DC.

The competition between AC and DC continued for years; which of them you got depended on where you lived. And this posed problems: a lamp worked equally well on either kind of current, but a radio or washing machine didn't: plugging it into the wrong current would ruin the appliance, blow a fuse or both. I discovered this in 1942 when I rented my first apartment, in a DC neighborhood (New York's Greenwich Village)—and a damn nuisance it was.

Appliance manufacturers were naturally careful to label their products "AC," "DC" or (for gadgets that worked on either type of current) "AC-DC"—which was soon transferred to people whose sexual appliances could operate with either sex. DC and AC-DC appliances are long gone, but AC-DC people are still with us—though we more often call them "bi."

accident (noun). Latin *cadere* means to fall; *accidere,* to fall *on.* The word came into English as "accident," meaning "mishap"— still its commonest sense. And a mishap is indeed something that "falls on" or befalls you—sometimes literally, as when you accidently drop a hammer on your toe.

accolade. Originally, an embrace—throwing one's arms around someone's neck (*col* in French). Later, it became the formal ceremony (which included an embrace) by which one was dubbed a knight. If a play got "the critics' accolade," they embraced it.

according to Hoyle. In 1742, an Englishman named Edmond Hoyle wrote *A Short Treatise on the Game of Whist* (an ancestor of bridge), which for more than a century was used to settle arguments about the rules. In 1897, one Robert Foster greatly enlarged the book, including the rules of many other games; he titled it *Foster's Hoyle.* Ever since, "according to Hoyle" has meant according to the rules of the game, including such "games" as business deals. If a deal isn't according to Hoyle, then somebody is giving somebody a **fast shuffle**—or slipping in a **cold deck**.

ace (verb). Cops, crooks and crime writers sometimes speak of a person being aced or aced out, meaning killed. Some people believe the term derives from the tennis player's "ace"—a serve that can't be returned. The idea is plausible—a person who's been "aced" can't return his killer's stroke—but almost certainly untrue: the kinds of people who use the term don't go in much for tennis.

Much more likely, the ace in question is the ace of spades, which (as Kipling's Terence Mulvaney noted) has long been intimately connected with battle, murder and sudden death. Handing someone the ace of spades was equivalent to giving him the "black spot" described in *Treasure Island:* a message that he was due to be "terminated with extreme prejudice." Modern killers seldom bother with warnings; they just ace their victims.

Curiously, "ace out" has recently acquired an additional sense: to deprive someone dishonestly or unfairly of anything. Not long ago I heard the teenage son of a friend complain that she had aced him out of the family car—meaning that she was using it when he wanted it.

ace in the hole. As experienced poker players know, in the game of five-card stud (one card down, four up) a pair of aces will usually take the pot. If, then, a player has an ace showing and bets aggressively, his opponents need to decide whether he has another ace, in the hole (down), or is bluffing. In poker or any other game, an ace in the hole is a useful—often vital—thing to have.

Achilles heel/tendon. The *Iliad,* Homer's famous epic of the Trojan War, opens with the ominous words, "The anger of Achilles is my theme." His account of that anger and its fatal consequences, and of how Achilles at last overcame it and became a man instead of an arrogant, spoiled youth, make the poem, even after nearly three thousand years, one of the greatest ever composed.

Homer never explained why Achilles was such a brat, though his depiction of the hero's mother, the goddess Thetis, gives us a clue: she was continually fussing over him, in ways that prove you don't have to be Jewish to be a Jewish Mother. Later poets provided a further explanation: Thetis had dipped her infant son in the River Styx, thereby making him invulnerable. And invulnerable men who can lick anyone in the house are often arrogant.

Unfortunately for Achilles, he wasn't *quite* invulnerable: when his mother dipped him, she neglected to wet the heel she was holding him by. The god Apollo, who favored the Trojan side in the war, slipped this bit of classified information to Paris (whose womanizing had started the war); he thereupon shot an arrow into Achilles' heel and killed him. (Presumably the wound got infected, or the arrow was poisoned.)

Plenty of people who've never heard of Achilles nonetheless refer to someone's vulnerable spot as their Achilles heel. And the big tendon that connects the calf muscles to the heel-bone is still called the Achilles tendon.

acid test. For generations, jewelers and chemists have known that concentrated nitric acid won't dissolve gold but will dissolve base metals, or alloys such as brass. Accordingly, when a jeweler was offered gold by a seller whose looks he didn't care for, he'd give it the acid test: place a drop of acid on it to see what happened. If something passes the acid test, you know it's genuine.

For example, in 1918, President Woodrow Wilson declared that "The treatment accorded [revolutionary] Russia by her sister nations in the months to come will be the acid test of their good will." Since the nations in question—Britain and France—subsequently launched or financed half a dozen military expeditions against the Soviet government, their good will was evidently something less than pure gold.

adamant. A metaphor piled on a metaphor. In ancient Greek, *adamantos* literally meant "invincible"; then, metaphorically, the "invincibly" hard substances, steel and emery. Borrowed into Latin, it was transferred to the still harder diamond. In the seventeenth century, the metaphorically invincible diamond itself became a metaphor for hardness ("an adamant heart"). Someone who's adamant may or may not be hard-hearted, but is certainly hard-headed and hard-nosed—as hard to move or convince as a diamond is to scratch.

adroit. Literally, "on the right" (French *à droit*); an adroit person is a right-handed one. This is one of many metaphors slandering left-handed people; some others are *dexterous* (= right-handed), and *gauche* and *sinister* (= left-handed). Then we have the *left-handed compliment* and, most recently, "right-handed" meaning "heterosexual" ("only about sixty percent righthanded"—George V. Higgins).

In case you hadn't guessed, I'm left-handed.

affluent. Literally (in Latin), "flowing to"; we still speak of the affluent of a lake, meaning the waters flowing into it. An affluent person is one to whom worldly goods have flowed abundantly, and the same holds for an "affluent society"—though generally the goods have flowed far more abundantly to some than to others.

aftermath. Once upon a time, a math was a mowing of hay or grain, and the aftermath, the grass that sprang up afterward, which might provide either pasturage or a second hay crop. Today, of course, the "aftermath" means the events that "spring up" after some notable occurrence ("the aftermath of World War II").

alarm. When an **alert** sentry in medieval Italy spotted an enemy approaching, he cried out *All'arme!* (To arms!). It was borrowed into English, first as an actual call to arms ("Alarme! Alarme!"), later as the name of the call ("Ready to ride and spread the alarm/ Through every Middlesex village and farm"). Modern alarms rouse us to less martial and usually less alarming pursuits—often, to no more than the deadly daily grind.

albatross around one's neck. The wing of the albatross has what aeronautical engineers call a high aspect-ratio: it's very narrow in proportion to its length. The design makes the bird a superb glider; with the help of air currents over the waves, it can travel for miles with scarcely a wing-beat.

Old-time sailors, struck by the bird's ability to "fly" without moving its wings, credited it with supernatural powers, which made it a good-luck token—meaning that to kill one was bad luck. The poet Coleridge got hold of this legend and wove it into his famous poem, "The Rime of the Ancient Mariner"; as many readers will recall, the Mariner shot an albatross and brought a curse on his ship.

His shipmates, becalmed and dying of thirst, hung the dead bird around his neck ("Instead of cross, the alabatross/ Around my neck was hung"). So we speak of a disgraced public figure as having an albatross around his neck—though the consequences are seldom as serious as in the poem. Instead of suffering the Mariner's "nightmare Life In Death," he'll probably make a bundle out of his memoirs, and may even be rehabilitated into an elder statesman.

alert. In Italian, *erta* is a watchtower, and *all'erta,* on watch. If you're alert, you're watching out—though probably not for an enemy, just for whatever may come up.

all the traffic will bear. No connection with the traffic that bedevils motorists; the phrase comes from an earlier form of transportation. In the late nineteenth century, railroads were not burdened with meddlesome government regulations, and therefore charged shippers (especially farmers) every nickel they could squeeze out. One railroad tycoon summed up his policy as "all the traffic will bear"—that is, the highest rates that could be extracted without bankrupting the shippers and stopping the traffic entirely. This kind of thing doesn't happen nowadays, of course.

aloof. A major hazard of navigating under sail was (and is) to be caught on a "lee shore"—close to land, with a strong wind blowing shoreward and thus threatening to drive the ship aground. To escape from this situation requires careful ship-handling, and if anything goes wrong—trouble with the rudder, say—the ship may well be wrecked. (An old manual of seamanship, discussing how to escape from a lee shore, gave as its first principle: "Never allow your ship to be caught in this position.")

The helmsman trying to escape from a lee shore could not steer directly away from shore (i.e., directly into the wind); instead, he "luffed up"—steered as close to the wind as possible. If he carelessly let the bow of the ship fall away from its optimum course, the skipper would likely snap out "Aloufe!"—steer closer to the wind! Today even those of us who don't know port from starboard try to stay aloof from dangerous, or merely unpleasant, situations or people.

alpha and omega, the. Alpha and omega are the first and last letters of the Greek alphabet; that is, they're the beginning and the end—and, by implication, everything in between ("the alpha and omega of science").

amateur. Literally, one who loves (from Latin *amare*, to love); hence, someone who exercises his or her skill, in sport or the arts, for love, not for money. The word has acquired rather different connotations on either side of the Atlantic: to the British, an amateur sportsman is rather a nice thing to be (at one time, amateurs were "gentlemen" but professionals were merely "players"). In the U.S., where this sort of snobbery is less common, "amateur" often implies "inept," and we speak of an "amateurish performance."

ambiguous. From Latin *ambigere,* meaning, according to various accounts, either "wander about" or "drive (a vehicle) uncertainly." I prefer the latter, since it clarifies the modern sense: if someone makes an ambiguous statement, you're bound to be uncertain of what they're driving at.

ambition. In Latin, *ambitio* meant "running around"—what Roman politicians did in search of voters they could persuade, or buy. (One Roman historian noted acidly that a politician needed to make three fortunes in office: one to pay back the money he'd borrowed to buy votes, a second to put in the fix when he was later tried for misconduct, and a third to retire on.) Ambitious people in and out of politics still do a lot of running around.

Annie Oakley. Phoebe Anne Oakley Mozee (1860–1926), under the name of Annie Oakley, gave vaudeville exhibitions of sharpshooting—notably, as part of "Buffalo Bill" Cody's Wild West show. One of her tricks was to flick a playing card into the air and **riddle** it with holes before it fell to the ground.

In the vaudeville, theater and sports worlds, "comps" (complimentary tickets) had, and often still have, a hole punched in them, to prevent resale. According to Oakley herself, Ban Johnson, president of the American League, noted the resemblance between the comp and one of her shot-up playing cards, and from then on such tickets were "Annie Oakleys." The colorful term was later extended to other freebies such as a base on balls (English readers may need to ask an American what this means.) The metaphor is now, regrettably, almost extinct.

ante up. In draw poker, the ante is what everyone puts into the pot before (Latin *ante*) the deal; if you're told to ante up, you're being urged to come up with the required chip—to *chip in* your share of the expenses.

aphrodisiac. Aphrodite was the Greek goddess of love; an aphrodisiac, then, is a drug or food that supposedly makes one more susceptible to her enchantments. But "supposedly" is the operative word: such substances are as mythical as Aphrodite herself.

apple of someone's eye. In the days of Alfred the Great (ninth century), the apple of eye was the pupil, which was thought to be a solid, round body (later, the phrase sometimes meant the iris or even the entire eyeball). But almost from the beginning it also meant something precious, for reasons that escape me: why should the "apple" of the eye have been more precious than the eye itself?

apprehensive. This, like the last, is something of a puzzle. Latin *apprehendere* meant to seize, and the original meaning of "apprehend" was to seize something or someone physically (cops still sometimes report that they've "apprehended" a "perpetrator"). Shakespeare seems to have been the first to use "apprehend" to mean "expect" or "anticipate"—often, something unpleasant.

I'd guess that the poet, or one of his friends, took the "-pre-" in its literal sense: "before" or "in advance," (e.g., "precooked"). "Apprehend," they would then have reasoned, must mean to seize something *beforehand*. Certainly that's what an apprehensive person does: constantly seizes on dangers long before they happen—if, indeed, they ever do.

arctic. The Big Dipper, known in England as the Plough or Charles's Wain, is one of the most conspicuous star groupings in the northern sky. Moreover, it's conspicuous all year round in Europe and most of North America, and the farther north you are, the more conspicuous it is. The Dipper, part of the constellation Ursa Major (the Greater Bear), was itself long known as the Bear—in Greek, *arktos.* The arctic lands, then, are those far to the north, "beneath the Bear" (Kipling).

assassin. Terrorism in the Near East is nothing new; it dates back to at least the eleventh century, when the Crusaders were trying to steal Palestine from the Arabs (who'd stolen it from the Romans, who stole it from the Jews, who stole it from the Caananites, who probably stole it from somebody else).

During the First Crusade, a young Iranian student, Hassan ben Sabah, decided to start his own jihad (holy war) against the hated infidels. Seizing a mountain fortress, he set himself up as a sort of medieval ayatollah under the title *Sheikh al Jebal* (Chief of the Mountain), and organized what a later historian called "a company of most desperate and dangerous men."

These were fanatical killers, sworn to knock off anyone whom the sheikh fingered. Their first victims were Crusaders and other Christians, but later (the group remained active for several centuries) they began targeting fellow Moslems of other sects.

Their leader gave them strong incentives. According to Marco Polo, who passed that way during the thirteenth century, the sheikh would give them "a certain potion which cast them into a deep sleep, and when they awoke, they found themselves in a garden, all full of ladies and damsels, who dallied with them to their heart's content, so that they had what young men would have." The potion was hashish, and the killers became known as *hashishin,* Arabic for "hashish eaters."

Assassins, in and out of the Near East, are still with us. Some, like the original *hashishin,* are enthusiastic amateurs; others are professionals who work for gangsters or governments. Few of them use hashish—except, perhaps, recreationally—but the amateurs, at least, get just as stoned, on religious and political dogma.

astonish, astound. In Vulgar (popular) Latin, *extonare* means to strike with a thunderbolt (lightning), or stun. An astounded person is indeed *thunderstruck*—though an astonished one is startled rather than stunned.

atropine. This metaphor didn't just happen; it was invented. It harks back to the ancient Greek belief that everyone's destiny was determined by the three Fates: Clotho, who spun the thread of life and thus set the time of one's birth; Lachesis, who wound up the spun thread, thereby determining the course of one's life, and Atropos, who cut the thread.

When eighteenth-century botanists began classifying plants scientifically, they gave the poisonous belladonna the appropriate name of *Atropa;* later, the poison itself was christened "atropine." It's used in medicine, but in tiny doses; with a large dose— Atropos gets out her scissors.

attention. Latin *tendere* means "stretch" (the "ten-" is the same one we find in "tension"); *attendere* means "stretch toward." If you're paying attention to something, that's about what you're doing: stretching out your mind toward it.

Augean stables, the. The mythical Greek hero Herakles (Hercules), as one of his "twelve labors," was required to clean out the stables of King Augeus. The king had three thousand oxen— and the stables hadn't been cleaned in thirty years; Herakles did the job by diverting a river through the stables. People still sometimes describe the municipal politics of, say, Chicago or Boston as "an Augean stables," meaning that the, uh, dirt is piled yea high.

auspices, auspicious. Ancient Romans took the auspices (a sort of public-opinion poll of the Gods) by observing birds *(aues specere)*. A modern benefit performance "under the auspices" of so-and-so enjoys the favor of those local "gods"; an auspicious occasion, of course, is one favored by whatever gods are around.

ax to grind. This wonderful expression, often ascribed to Benjamin Franklin, was actually coined well after his death, by the humorist Charles Miner. He described how, as a boy, he encountered an agreeable stranger carrying an ax, who inquired if he could borrow the family grindstone. Young Miner naturally said yes. The man then asked him in aimiable tones if he was strong enough to turn the grindstone; Miner proudly said that he was, and offered to demonstrate. The smiling stranger, holding the ax to the stone, praised the boy's industry—but when the ax was ground, walked off without a word of thanks.

Thus, said Miner, "When I see a merchant over-polite to his customers, begging them to taste a little brandy . . . thinks I, that man has an ax to grind." It's a story worth remembering whenever you encounter some over-agreeable person who's eager to buy you drinks.

Bᵣ **babel.** If you know your Bible, you surely know this one; if you don't, you'll find the story in the eleventh chapter of Genesis. Briefly, at the time of Noah, "the whole earth was of one language. . . ." The people in the land of Shinar said to one another, "let us build us a city, and a tower, whose top may reach unto heaven"; the city was called Babel. (The name was probably inserted later, as a disguised crack at the Babylonians when they were giving the Jews a hard time.)

God took a dim view of this presumption, and accordingly changed the speech of the workers so that they all used different tongues. The result, obviously, was total confusion, with everyone talking at cross-purposes. Modern discussions of overambitious, high-tech projects sometimes turn into babel—even when the participants talk the same language.

Back to the salt mines! The custom of shipping dissidents to the chillier parts of Siberia was not invented by the Soviets; Russian governments had been doing it for generations. Some of these prisoners were set to mining salt, under miserable conditions—though rather less miserable than working outdoors in the Siberian winter.

In the 1890s, the miseries of Russian exiles were almost as well publicized in the West as they are today. "Back to the salt mines!" was probably first used in a play on the subject, but was soon picked up as an ironic U.S. catch phrase meaning, "It's time to get back on the job."

Like many catch phrases, it acquired variants—"back to the jute mill," or "the chain-gang," or "the old boiler factory." And we still sometimes use *Siberia* as the equivalent of "exile": when a cop has displeased his superiors and been transferred from a downtown metropolitan precinct to one in the **boondocks**, he's "sent to Siberia."

back up, one's. If you've ever seen two cats squaring off for a fight, you know this one without being told. Amid threatening howls, they arch their backs, which seem to rise still higher as their fur fluffs up. People with their backs up are spoiling for a fight; if you deliberately put their backs up, *you're* spoiling for one.

Sometimes cats with their backs up stop with threats, like some people. If not, they *make the fur fly*—literally: the battleground becomes strewn with tufts of fur.

backhander. Originally, merely a backhand stroke, or a blow with the back of the hand. But for close to a century the British have used it to mean a bribe or other payment given "with the hand behind the back."

backing and filling. Sailing ships couldn't sail directly into the wind (see **aloof**). Instead they would tack (sail) as close to the wind as possible (50–60 degrees), then take the opposite tack, with the wind on the other side, and thus in slow zigzags move along their chosen course.

However, tacking required plenty of "sea room"; in narrow waters such as a river, moving against the wind involved the laborious maneuver of backing and filling. The ship would tack to one side of the channel, then her yards would be hauled around and the wheel put over, so that the wind would push her stern-first to the other side. (This worked only with square-riggers, not with the fore-and-aft rigs used on nearly all sailboats today.) Then the yards would be hauled round again, the sails would fill and the whole maneuver would be repeated. Backing and filling was a slow and laborious way of getting somewhere (if the current was against you, often nowhere).

The metaphor owes even more to the involuntary backing and filling of a ship in the **doldrums**—the belt of light, shifting winds near the equator. The vessel would be carried forward for a while, then the wind would shift and she would be **taken aback**. This sort of thing could go on for days, with forward progress almost nil. A 1903 dictionary eloquently described a backing and filling policy as "shilly-shally, trifling, irresolute."

backlog. Before stoves were invented, the kitchen was sometimes the only room in the house that stayed warm in cold weather. Its enormous fireplace served for both cooking and heat—and was kept burning continuously.

To do this, you built your fire against an enormous backlog, up to two feet thick. At night, when the fire was let die down, the backlog would smoulder away, hour after hour; by morning it might be gone, but would have left enough embers to start a new fire. This was important: the paper and matches we now use to start fires were rare or non-existent.

Both the log and the word spread from pioneer America to pioneer Australia, Canada and New Zealand, and eventually became a metaphor in all three, as well as in Britain. A financial backlog is a warm and comfortable thing to have; so, for a businessman, is a backlog of orders. A backlog of work is less cheering—but a lot better than no work at all.

backstairs influence/information. Ambassadors and high officials who visited a king or powerful nobleman naturally entered by the impressive front stairway of the palace or castle. Secret agents and other "unofficial" visitors naturally used the back stairs—and their backstairs influence was often more potent than that of the officials ceremoniously received in front.

badger (verb). From the old "sport" of badger-drawing. The animal, which is both powerful and fierce, was placed in a barrel and a group of dogs were turned loose to "draw" it out with their teeth. They kept badgering the creature until they grew tired, or killed it.

bag, in the. Some call this expression no more than a variant of "all wrapped up," but I don't believe it. To a hunter, the "bag" is his game-bag, and a bird in the bag is a dead certainty. In Australian racing, a horse that's in the bag is also a certainty—to lose; similarly, in the U.S., a "bagged" legal case is one where someone has put in the fix.

"In the bag" also means "drunk"—maybe the same metaphor, but maybe not. The drunk, like the bagged horse, is certain to lose, if only his equilibrium, but he'll also move as clumsily and blindly as someone literally inside a bag.

bail out. Though nobody knows where the term came from, flyers have been bailing out of crippled planes for 50 years or more. The rest of us do the same from risky situations—and hope our parachutes will open.

baker's dozen. Some say this was a thirteenth loaf, given the customer in medieval times to make sure he was getting full weight (legal penalties for short-weighting were severe). This sounds unlikely: very few people would have needed—or could have afforded—to buy a dozen loaves at a time.

More likely, it was an extra loaf given by wholesale bakers to street peddlers, which provided their margin of profit. However the expression originated, it became a useful euphemism for the unlucky number thirteen, and for the "devil's dozen"—the thirteen witches supposed to make up a coven.

balk (verb). In Old English times, a ba(u)lk was an unplowed ridge between two fields; later, for obvious reasons, anything you might stumble over. It also means a heavy beam, though this may be a different word. But certainly if someone leaves a baulk across a road, vehicles will be balked.

balled up. Dictionaries tell us that it comes from the balling (compacting) of soft snow on the bottoms of horses' hooves, but I think this is **whitewash**: the snow (or the horse) didn't ball *up*, it just balled. More likely, "balled up" is a close relative of "bollixed up," in which "bollix" is a transparent "misspelling" of British "ballocks" (testicles); some Britishers speak bluntly of "making a ballocks" (mess) of something—which is then called a "balls-up." A "balled up" situation, then, is one so topsy-turvy that its figurative balls are up, not hanging down.

banal. From "ban," originally a public proclamation requiring people to do something (nowadays, *not* do something—"MAYOR BANS PUBLIC SMOKING"). The adjective "banal" meant something imposed by a ban, as when villagers were required to use the landlord's mill to grind their grain. Later, the sense shifted from something that everybody had to use to something that anyone *could* use. And if just anybody could use it, it was obviously commonplace and boring—banal.

bandbox (just out of a). The original bandbox was a lightweight, flimsy box used to hold ruffs and collars ("bands") so they wouldn't be soiled or crushed. Someone who looks as if (s)he is just out of a bandbox looks like (s)he's just been washed and ironed.

bandwagon, on the. Politics before radio, television and photo opportunities was a face-to-face business of hand-shaking, baby-kissing, mass meetings and parades. These last were led by a large horse-drawn dray carrying a band, and usually the candidate as well. As the parade passed through a city, the local ward-heelers would climb on the bandwagon to show their support—and advertise themselves. Today the literal bandwagon is long gone, but people still climb on it, from the same mixed motives.

bandy (words). Bandy was a game much like tennis (later, also a kind of field hockey). If two people are bandying words, they're batting them back and forth.

bane of someone's existence, the. The "bane" in this cliché meant "poison"; it survives in such plant names as "wolfbane" (the highly toxic aconite). If someone is the bane of your existence, (s)he's poisoning your life.

bankrupt. The bank you keep your money in comes from Italian *banca,* the bench or counter where Italian bankers (who invented modern banking) did business. Samuel Johnson, in his famous dictionary, cited a rumor that when an Italian banker went bust, his *banca* was ceremoniously broken *(rotta);* he was *banca rotta.* It's a nice tale—but *rotta* means not just "broken" but also (financially) "broke," so that "bankrupt" may not be a metaphor at all. What's certain is that if you're bankrupt, you're broke, whether or not your bench is.

barking up the wrong tree. When pioneers hunted coons or possums, they'd turn loose their hounds to find the creature and chase it up a tree. Gathered around the trunk, the dogs would bark to let their masters know where the quarry was. Sometimes, however, the hunters would find to their disgust that the dogs had gone off on a false scent and were barking up the wrong tree.

barmy. A thousand years ago, English households brewed their own ale, as a few still do. They called the yeasty froth that formed on the fermenting mash "barm," and used it to leaven bread and as a paste for the complexion. "Barmy" meant "frothy," whence the "barmy" person with frothy, fermented brains—a bubble-brain. The term may have picked up some extra head, so to speak, from the town of Barming, Kent, once the site of a well-known lunatic asylum.

In the 1920s, "barmy" reached the United States, where the word "barm" had dropped out of use. Some Americans then did what people often do when confronted with an outlandish word: turned it into one that seemed to make more sense—"balmy." No doubt they reasoned that balm makes your skin soft, balmy weather is "soft" weather, so a soft-headed person must be "balmy." I prefer the original metaphor and the original spelling.

barnstorming. When third-rate theatrical companies played small towns, they used whatever space was available, even abandoned barns. Often the performance was a **one-night stand**, meaning that the players would come and go almost as quickly as a thunderstorm. Barnstorming political candidates operate at a similar pace—though seldom in barns.

bats in one's belfry. I doubt that any active belfry was ever inhabited by bats: since the creatures have very acute hearing, the pealing of the bells would drive them bats. But bats *are* found in disused towers of various sorts, from which they sortie at twilight in fluttering, seemingly erratic flight. Since the belfry is the highest part of a church, someone having his top story aflutter with erratic notions might reasonably be said to have bats in his belfry; nowadays we usually clip the phrase to "batty" or just plain "bats."

battle royal. Originally, a nasty kind of elimination tournament for game-cocks, in which a dozen or more birds were pitted against each other (see **cockpit**); they battled it out until all but one were dead or disabled. Figurative battles of this sort are, happily, less bloody.

beam, on the. In the early days of aviation, a pilot navigating through cloud or fog could easily lose his way; in mountainous country, he might crash into a peak. Radio navigation did much to reduce these risks. Ground stations emitted beamed (directional) radio signals such that the pilot heard a series of dot-dashes in his earphones if he was to the left of the beam, dash-dots if he was to the right. And when the dots and dashes merged into a continuous buzz, he was right *on* the beam—dead on course. The system is now obsolete, but if you're on the beam, you're right; if you're off it, you're wrong or even crazy.

beam-ends, on one's. To a carpenter, a beam is a heavy timber; to a shipbuilder, it's a deck-beam—one of the side-to-side timbers or girders that support the deck. A ship on her beam-ends, then, is one forced so far over by wind and wave that one side of her deck is touching the water—in grave danger of capsizing. Alternatively, the ship might have rolled over on her beam-ends because she'd been left **high and dry** by the tide. Either way, if you're on your beam-ends, you're in bad shape.

bear (stock market). An old proverb mocks the man who "sells the bearskin before catching the bear." In the eighteenth century, when speculation in stocks became a popular pastime, some stock dealers would sell stock they hadn't "caught"—i.e., didn't own. They were called "bearskin jobbers"; later, "bears."

The idea, of course, was that by the time they had to deliver what they'd sold, the price of skins would have dropped and they could buy them cheaper than they'd sold them. But, if the price had gone up, they'd have to stand the loss, according to the maxim:

> He who sells what isn't his'n
> Must buy it back, or go to prison.

The bears were soon joined by "bulls"—speculators who worked the other side of the street: instead of selling stock in hopes of a drop in price, they bought it in hopes of a rise. Ben Trovato (see the Introduction) has suggested that these bulls hoped to toss the stocks upward with their horns; I'd guess that the word came from a staged fight between a bull and a bear—a type of "sporting" contest common enough in those days (see **badger**).

bear by the tail, a. I doubt that anyone ever managed to grab a bear by the tail; quite apart from simple prudence, the tail is very short. But if anyone did, they'd obviously be in a bad spot: holding on would mean being dragged through underbrush and banged into trees, while letting go would be worse. If you ever feel moved to jump into a situation impulsively, make sure you're not grabbing that hypothetical bear's tail. (See also **catch a Tartar.**)

beat around/about the bush. In medieval times, songbirds were considered fair game in England, as they still are in many places. Since shooting them (with a bow and arrow) was impracticable, the hunters would spread a net over bushes where the birds were roosting and then beat around the bush with a stick to make them fly into the net.

By the seventeenth century, the phrase had become a metaphor meaning, roughly, to engage in preliminaries; one saying mocked one who "bete around the bush whyles others got the birds." Later, the sense of the phrase shifted: people knowing nothing of net-hunting assumed that you were supposed to beat the bush itself, so that beating *around* the bush meant not getting to the point.

beat the bushes. Not, I think, a close relative of the previous phrase; more likely it comes from the American frontier. Game was usually plentiful there (far more so than in England); only occasionally did you have to get out and beat the bushes, hoping you could *scare something up.*

bedlam. A monument to the tendency of some Britishers to mumble, so that Greenwich becomes Grinnich, Cholmondeley becomes Chumley, and so on. "Bedlam" started as the Hospital of St. Mary of Bethlehem, which became Bethlehem Hospital, which was mumbled into Bethlem and, finally, into Bedlam.

Bedlam was one of the first hospitals in Europe to accept insane patients. For the lunatics, hospitalization was doubtless better than freezing and starving outside, but not much: they were sometimes "treated" by beatings, to drive out the evil spirits that supposedly possessed them. Other lunatics talked to themselves or screamed at their horrifying hallucinations—a bedlam indeed!

beef (complain). About all anyone seems to know about this word is that it derives from an earlier "cut a beef." Why this should have meant "complain," as "beef" still does, is a mystery; perhaps the "beef" was cut from the **bone of contention**.

beer and skittles. The original game of skittles resembled modern bar shuffleboard: the pins were knocked down by a wooden disc rather than a ball. Like its modern counterpart, it was closely associated with taverns; Englishmen who favored a relaxed lifestyle wanted nothing more than beer and skittles. English writers, however, have often warned that there's more to life than that.

bellwether. Originally, the ram leading a flock of sheep; now, anyone leading a group or trend. Kipling once referred to Prime Minister W. E. Gladstone as "the old bellwether," implying that his supporters followed him like sheep—and, even more nastily, that Gladstone, like most bellwethers, was gelded.

benefit of clergy, without. During the Middle Ages, the clergy could not be tried by ordinary courts but only in ecclesiastical ones—meaning that they could expect little or no punishment. This "benefit of clergy" applied not just to priests and higher ecclesiastics but to any "clerk"—in effect, anyone who could read. A person claiming benefit of clergy was handed a Bible or other book; if he could make sense of it, he was "saved by his book."

Ordinary folk naturally resented this privilege, and over the centuries it was gradually abolished; by the late nineteenth century, the phrase was obsolete except in historical writing. We owe both its revival and its modern sense to Rudyard Kipling, who titled one of his most powerful stories "Without Benefit of Clergy." It recounts the tragedy of Holden, an English civil servant in India, and Ameera, an Indian girl with whom he is deeply in love and who bears his child, but whom he, as a British official, cannot marry or even be seen with.

On the face of it, the phrase meant what it still means: an unmarried relationship, unblessed by the church. But Kipling used it in bitter irony: Holden, the civil servant, is a modern "clerk," but the "benefit" he gets from it is being unable to live openly with the woman he loves. The story ends with a savage contrast between the impersonal, six-word telegram with which Holden's "clerical" superiors shift him to a new post and the words of the dying Ameera—his wife without benefit of clergy: "I bear witness that there is no God but—thee, beloved."

berk. A bit of Cockney rhyming slang (see **bird, the**) that has spread widely among Britishers of all classes. It's short for "Berkshire Hunt," which rhymes with a very rude sexual term, which became an even ruder term for "woman," and then—in the rankest male chauvinism—for "damn fool." Few Britishers are aware of "berk" 's literal meaning, and many would be shocked if they were. (French has a very similar metaphor, *con*—literally, the same organ, but meaning "dumb" or "silly.")

berserk. The original berserker was a Viking warrior who fought wearing only a bearskin coat or, some say, a simple (bare) shirt— i.e., he was so enraged that he didn't bother to put on his armor. Either way, the berserker was a frenzied fighter, concerned far more with killing than with his own survival. Someone who goes berserk is as irrational as the berserker—and often as dangerous. Compare **run amuck**.

big shot. Often considered a modern version of "big gun," which for a century and a half has meant an important person. Alternatively, it may stem from the explosive "shot" (blast) used in mining and construction. Big shots, like big guns and big explosions, make a lot of noise—and require careful handling.

big wheel. The sense is the same as the last, but the source quite different. The original "big wheel" was a carnival ferris wheel; the human big wheel, however, may come from yet another source: the big wheel (flywheel) of the old stationary steam engine, which made the other wheels go round—which indeed big wheels are still doing.

bigwig. In British courts, both judges and attorneys (barristers) wear wigs; the custom dates from the eighteenth century. The lawyers wear short ones; the judge is the bigwig: his headpiece at one time lapped over his shoulders.

bikini. In 1946, the natives of Bikini atoll in the Pacific were evacuated from their homes so that the island could be used for a U.S. hydrogen-bomb test. Soon after, a diminutive bathing suit exploded on French beaches and was called *le bikini*—according to one account, because it revealed the most powerful forces known to man. If you don't believe this story, think up a better one.

bilge. To shipbuilders, the bilges are the lowest part of a ship's hull; to sailors, bilge is (or was) the stuff that collected in the bilges—seepage from casks of salt meat, rat droppings and similar fragrant stuff. To the rest of us it's garbage—utter nonsense.

bilious. For centuries human personalities were thought to be produced by the body's four **humors** (secretions): blood, phlegm, bile (choler), and "black bile" (melan choler)—a supposed constituent of the blood. Irritable, angry people supposedly suffered from an excess of bile, and were therefore called "bilious" or *choleric.* An abundance of blood (Latin *sanguis*) made for a cheerful, *sanguine* disposition; lots of phlegm produced the "cool" *phlegmatic* individual, while too much black bile made you *melancholy.*

Billingsgate. London, like many old cities, was once enclosed in defensive walls with gates. As it expanded, the walls crumbled away, but maps of central London still show Highgate, Moorgate, Aldgate and several others.

Billingsgate (possibly named for its supposed builder, one Billings) was originally on the bank of the Thames, and fishing boats unloaded there; it became the site of London's main fish market. The dealers there—especially the women *(fishwives)*—became known for their uninhibited language: an eighteenth-century writer defined "The Rhetoric of Billingsgate" as "Lying and Slandering." We even read of the "learned Billinsgate" of some philosophers and clergymen—something not unknown in modern academic life.

bird, the. The bird in question was a goose, and if you've ever confronted a gaggle of angry geese, you know they hiss. So do angry theatrical audiences. Nowadays, "the bird" means any form of jeering, including "the raspberry"—another originally theatrical metaphor. It comes from Cockney rhyming slang, a sort of private language in which "loaf" (loaf of bread) means "head," ("Use yer loaf!"), "titfer" (tit-for-tat) means "hat" ("keep it under yer titfer"), and so on. "Raspberry" was originally "raspberry tart," rhyming slang for the sound of the original raspberry—the rude noise better known in the U.S. as a Bronx cheer.

birds, for the. The problem of emission control didn't begin with the automobile: as recently as fifty years ago, when I was a youngster on the streets of New York, one could both see and smell the emissions of horse-drawn wagons. Since there was no way of controlling these emissions, they, or the undigested oats in them, served to nourish a large population of English sparrows. If you say something's for the birds, you're politely saying that it's horseshit.

birds and the bees, the. American schools have long been skittish about sex education—mostly at the insistence of parents, some of whom believe that if children aren't told about sex, the little devils won't think about it. Hah!

Schools that touched on sex at all carefully talked around it: the kids were told about the cute things the little birdies and bees do. Supposedly, they'd somehow apply these tales to human beings, but few of them did—fortunately, since human sex isn't much like bird sex and radically different from bee sex.

Nowadays, "the birds and the bees" may refer either to sex or to any information simplified down to the grade-school level. The phrase was immortalized in a famous line by Cole Porter: "Birds do it, bees do it, even educated fleas do it."

bite the bullet. Battlefields are unpleasant places, and before anesthesia were worse: the military surgeon amputated limbs or probed for bullets without benefit of pain-killers, so that the wounded soldier was given a leaden musket ball to bite on to keep him from screaming. (According to some accounts, the same custom was followed with soldiers who were "disciplined" by being flogged.) If you're biting the bullet, you're gritting your teeth and facing up to an unpleasant situation—though seldom as unpleasant as what the soldier faced.

bitter end. One might guess that this had something to do with the "end" of a bottle of wine, in which the last few mouthfuls had gone sour. In fact, it's a sailor's term: the bitter end is the part of an anchor cable or mooring line attached to the ship's bitts— stout posts bolted to the deck. If you've reached the "bitter end," you're at the end of your rope.

blackguard. Originally the humblest members of a royal or noble household: the scullions in charge of the (often sooty) pots and pans. Later, the upper classes transferred the term to criminals, or even the unemployed; given the state of English upper-class morals at the time (late seventeenth century), this was a clear case of the **pot calling the kettle black**. Today it means a cad or rotter, of any class.

blatherskite. The first half of this word is clear enough: "blather" is akin to "blow" and a blatherer is a blowhard. "Skite," by some accounts, comes from "skate" (the fish), but no one has ever explained why "skate" was an insult, since it was (and in many places still is) a valued food fish.

More likely, "skite" is the Scottish word meaning "shit." A blatherskite, then, is someone given to blowing shit—which indeed is what the word means, speaking roughly. (The "-skate" in *cheapskate* comes from the same source.)

bleeding heart. For thousands of years the heart has been deemed the seat of the emotions, no doubt because when we become excited or deeply moved our hearts beat stronger and faster. A specially distressing experience was said to pierce the heart—that is, would make it "bleed."

"Bleeding heart" had long been a nickname for various flowers, but around 1950 someone (I suspect a right-wing newspaper columnist) transferred it to people whose hearts bled for the poor and other unfortunates—that is, who believed they were in some sense their brother's keeper. (If it's a bad thing to be a bleeding heart, is it a good thing to be the opposite—presumably a "stony heart," since you can't get blood from a stone?)

The heart has given us several other metaphors, often based on the Latin equivalent, *cordis* (surprisingly, it comes from the same ultimate root as "heart"). A cordial greeting is a hearty or heart-felt one, while the cordial you drink warms the heart.

blink, on the. Yankee fishermen classified mackerel as "large," "second size," "tinkers," "blinks" and "spikes." According to some authorities, a fishing trip that pulled in too many small fish would be "on the blink"—unprofitable.

This theory sounds pretty fishy to me. I've eaten tinker mackerel—some may have been blinks, for all I know—and they're by no means on the blink, or unsaleable either. A more likely source is the blinking out of a candle or lantern; certainly if your car is on the blink, it's not unprofitable but out of order.

blood money. When Judas repented selling out Christ for thirty pieces of silver, he took the money back to the temple, threw it down and went and hanged himself. The priests couldn't return the money to the temple treasury, "because it is the price of blood"; instead they used it to buy "the potter's field, to bury strangers in." (In the U.S., *potter's field* has long been used to mean a burying ground for strangers, paupers and, sometimes, criminals.)

At certain times and places, "blood money" has meant money paid to the family of a murdered person—what we now call "victim compensation"—but its "normal" meaning is the price paid to an informer. One of Dashiell Hammett's early novels was titled *$106,000 Blood Money*—the reward offered for information on the perpetrators of a spectacular bank heist.

blow one's stack. When Mark Twain was piloting steamboats along the Mississippi, there was no Occupational Safety and Health Administration; sometimes pilots trying for a speed record would hang a wrench from the boat's safety valve, thereby increasing the boiler pressure and the boat's speed. This maneuver, or sometimes simple carelessness, could lead to a boiler explosion that would blow the boat's tall stack, superstructure, crew and passengers high in the air. Twain himself, in *Life on the Mississippi,* eloquently described the **aftermath** of such an accident, in which his brother was killed.

blow the gaff. Originally, "blow the gab"—criminal slang for "shoot one's gab (mouth) off." But it has, I think, picked up extra color from another metaphor, "gaff." The original fisherman's gaff was and is a heavy hook attached to a pole, used to haul in big fish—but the carnival worker's gaff is the gimmick used to "fix" a gambling device such as a wheel of fortune—and thereby haul in the suckers' money. No carney would blow this gaff to the rubes.

blue, out of the—see **bolt from the blue.**

blue moon, once in a. Some say this phrase derives from seeing "the old moon in the new moon's arms"—the bright sickle of the new moon edging the rest of the lunar disc, dimly illuminated by earthlight. But you can see this every month, weather permitting—a lot oftener than "once in a blue moon."

Others say that under very special conditions—ice crystals or dust high in the air—the moon really does look blue, though I've never seen it.

What's clear is that a "blue moon" was once deemed as ridiculous as one made of green cheese: a sardonic sixteenth-century rhyme averred that

> Yf they saye the mone is belewe
> We must beleve that it is true.

From which it would seem that the original "once in a blue moon" meant "never"—and, like many "nevers," ended up as "hardly ever."

blue-blooded. A loan-translation from Spanish *(sangre azul).* Of course everybody's blood is bluish after it's given up its oxygen and is flowing back to the heart—look at the veins on the back of your hand. Among the peasants, however, the blue veins were obscured by sunburn, in contrast with those of light-skinned aristocrats. Times change: many working people are now pale from staying indoors, while "blue-bloods" flaunt their tans.

bluestocking. Around 1750 a group of London ladies discovered that an evening spent in sober conversation was more fun than one spent playing cards and tippling. Many distinguished men of letters joined their gatherings, and some made a point of wearing "plain" clothing, including "blue" (gray) stockings rather than the black or white silk customary with evening dress.

Upper-class folk who preferred gambling and boozing to thinking sneered at these "bluestockings," as their modern counterparts do at "intellectuals." Soon the term was narrowed to women with intellectual interests—obviously eccentric if not downright unnatural. Nowadays, few of us are shocked by women interested in ideas, and the metaphor is, happily, moribund.

board(s), by the. The boards (planks) of a wooden ship have long been a metaphor for the ship itself: we *board* a ship, and sailors still speak of "inboard" and "outboard" (one version of a famous catch phrase runs, "Bleep you, Jack, I'm inboard!"). If the mast of a sailing ship was broken off by storm or enemy cannon, the captain had to decide whether to try and salvage it or simply let it go by the board—cut the ropes holding it to the ship and let it drift off. Which is about what happens to anything you let go by the board.

bohemian. The Gypsies were so named in English because they supposedly came from Egypt (see **gyp**). In France, they were called *Bohemiens* because they supposedly came from Bohemia (modern Czechoslovakia). In the nineteenth century, artists and similar loose types were christened *Bohemiens* because they lived "gypsy-like" lives, not over-concerned with conventional morals (Thackeray described his delightful but unscrupulous heroine, Becky Sharp, as "Bohemian by taste and circumstances"). This was a slander on the Gypsies, and, no doubt, on some of the artists.

boilerplate. See **cliché**.

bolt from the blue. I'd be very surprised indeed to learn that anyone was ever struck by a thunderbolt (lightning) from a clear, blue sky, rather than from a thundercloud. Something that comes as a bolt from the blue or *out of the blue* is almost as surprising.

bombast(ic). Bombast or bombace was once the cotton used to stuff quilted garments; then, inflated, pompous language ("the swelling bumbast of a swagging blanke verse"). In short, a bombastic speech is overstuffed.

bone of contention. Ever see two dogs with a bone between them? They have, you might say, a bone to pick with one another.

boondocks, the. Early in this century, U.S. troops were bringing "civilization" to the Filipinos; their methods were summed up in a popular army song, "Underneath the starry flag/Civilize 'em with a Krag" (Krag-Jorgensen rifle). The Filipino troops were mainly guerrillas, based in the mountains (*bandok* in one of the Philippine languages) and other remote places—to U.S. soldiers, "the boondocks."

bootleg(ger). Before World War I, outdoor workers, including farmers, cowboys and cavalrymen, typically wore calf-high or knee-high boots. The tops (legs) of these were convenient receptacles for personal belongings such as a pipe, a pistol or a flask. Unlicenced liquor sellers found the boot leg equally convenient for concealing their stock in trade. The advent of national Prohibition in 1920 made bootleggers big-business men, selling booze by the truckload rather than the bootload, but the name stuck.

bootstraps, by one's. Some styles of boot have cloth or leather straps sewn on or inside the leg, enabling them to be pulled on without assistance. Nobody, of course, can literally lift himself by his bootstraps, but some people do manage to elevate themselves with no help from anyone else.

After World War II, "bootstrap" acquired various technical meanings among electrical engineers—most recently in the computer field, where it means a short introductory program, usually built into the machine, that starts things going. When I insert a new disc into the computer I'm writing this on, I have to "boot it up," otherwise the machine won't work properly.

born to the purple. Well before the Christian Era, the Phoenicians discovered that the Murex shellfish could yield vivid dyes, ranging from crimson to a rich purple. But each mollusc yielded only a tiny quantity of dye, so that only the rich could afford purple, or even purple-trimmed, garments. The color became a symbol of the very highest social ranks—notably, the Roman and Byzantine emperors. The latter even built a small palace on the Bosporus, made of purplish marble, where their children could be literally "born to the purple."

brand new. Not from the cattleman's or manufacturer's brand, but the "brand" in "fire-brand": if something's brand new, it's hot off the (blacksmith's) fire. An older version is "fire-new" ("With a fire-new spoon we're furnished"—Browning).

brass hat. More than a century ago, British soldiers slapped the label "brass hat" on high officers whose caps were garnished with gold braid; soon it was applied to high civilian officials equally impressed with their own importance. During World War I, both British and U.S. soldiers used the phrase to express their justified contempt for the brass-hatted idiots who sent them up against machine guns. Nowadays, "the brass"—civilian or military—is just as self-important, and often just as incompetent, as the original brass-hats.

brass ring, the. When I was a kid riding the carrousel (merry-go-round) in New York's Central Park, I always tried for the brass ring. This, along with a couple of dozen iron rings, was contained in a hollow arm, so that you could reach out and hook a ring with your finger as you swung by. If you were skillful and lucky you'd grab the brass ring and get a free ride. Some people spend their whole lives grabbing for the brass ring, but unless they're very lucky they just get taken for a ride.

break, a good/bad. Supposedly, from the "break" at pool—the first shot that breaks apart the racked balls. A good break leaves the shooter with an easy shot; a bad one, with a hard one, or even behind the **eight ball**. Well, maybe. "Break" has long meant a breakdown or failure ("a break in the stock market"); later, it became the blunder that had precipitated the breakdown. Of course the blunderer would insist that his break was just an accident—"the breaks."

The "break" in "give me a break" may come from a quite different source: the break (collection) taken up among friends of a prisoner, to pay for his defense or help him after his release.

break the ice. A boatman seeking to move his craft along a frozen river or lake naturally had to break the ice first. When strangers get together, the social ice must be broken if the party is to get moving.

bring down the house. To actors, dancers and musicians, applause is music to their ears, and the louder the better. The ultimate tribute would be applause that literally brought down the walls of the theater—though with fans like that, who needs critics?

bring home the bacon. The phrase itself dates only from the 1920s, but its ultimate source is at least two centuries older: a 1725 dictionary of "canting" (criminal slang) terms defined "bacon" as "the prize, of whatever kind, which Robbers make in their Enterprizes." The bacon we bring home nowadays is more legitimate—usually.

bromide. Bromides (salts of bromine) were among the earliest sedatives; they were often used to induce sleep. People who utter bromides have much the same effect on their hearers.

brusque. Ultimately from Latin *ruscus,* a butcher's broom. If you dismiss someone brusquely, you're sweeping them off the premises.

bucket shop—see **watered stock.**

bugger. During the Middle Ages, Bulgaria was a center of heresy, and Latin *bulgarus* (Bulgarian) came to mean "heretic," as did its French equivalent, *bougre.* And as everyone knows, heretics, both religious and political, hold scandalous views on sex, engaging in unspeakable practices and unnatural acts such as buggery; they also, you might say, try to bugger up the natural order of things. (See also **sodomy.**) Curiously, both "bugger" and its French equivalent have become almost aimiable epithets, with "a good old bugger" paralleled by *un bon bougre.*

bulldozer. A double metaphor. During Reconstruction (1865–76), a "bull-dose" (a dose of a bullwhip) was dealt out to Southern blacks who insisted on voting, by terrorist groups such as the KKK. Soon anyone who dealt in coercion, by violence or even threats, was a "bulldozer." Later, the word was transferred to the tractor-mounted machine that can "coerce" just about anything in its path—earth, boulders, even small trees—whence the human bulldozer, who plows ahead with similar disregard for obstacles, human or otherwise.

bumpkin. From Dutch *boomkin,* small tree—hence, a country-man thought to possess the tree's intelligence.

bunk (nonsense). In 1820, during the debate on the Missouri Compromise, the Hon. Felix Walker, congressman from Buncombe County, NC, delivered a long and resounding oration with no relevance to the question before the House. Asked why he'd said so little at such length, he explained that his constituents expected him to make a speech and that was the speech he'd prepared; he was "only talking for Buncombe." Legislators and journalists alike quickly embraced "Buncombe" (soon respelled "bunkum") as the perfect word for windy nonsense. Though the word was eventually shortened to "bunk," the supply of it, in and out of legislative chambers, hasn't diminished in the least.

burke. An almost obsolete metaphor, but the story is too good to pass up. Two centuries ago, medical schools had few legitimate ways of getting cadavers for their students to dissect. Enter the "resurrection man" (such as Jeremy Cruncher in *A Tale of Two Cities*), who would surreptitiously "resurrect" recently buried corpses and sell them to anatomists.

During the 1820s, William Burke, an Edinburgh hoodlum, de-vised an even more certain way of supplying cadavers: instead of "resurrecting" corpses, he manufactured them. With a partner, one Hare, he suffocated drifters and other unfortunates and sold their bodies to a famous anatomy teacher, Dr. Knox.

Eventually, the secret leaked out, and Burke and Hare were

hanged (Knox, a man of consequence, wasn't even tried). The scandal was summed up in a famous verse:

> Up the close [alley] and doon the stair,
> But and ben [in and out] wi' Burke and Hare.
> Burke's the bully, Hare's the thief,
> Knox the lad that buys the beef!

"Burke" is occasionally still used to mean "suppress quietly and unceremoniously"—which is certainly what Burke and Hare did to their victims.

bury the hatchet. Many people believe this phrase comes from the peacemaking ceremonies of some Native Americans, in which a tomahawk was buried to symbolize the end of hostilities. But the earliest version, "hang up the hatchet," dates from the fourteenth century—long before anyone but a few Scandinavians knew about either America or its natives.

bush(ed). In America, "bush" once meant forest or wilderness, as it still does in Australia and New Zealand. If you got lost in that sort of country, you were "bushed"—and by the time you found your way home, would be thoroughly bushed (exhausted). The "bush" gets another twist in the "bush leagues," composed of semi-pro baseball teams from small towns out in the bush. A bush-league performance is inept, and to "bush" someone is to talk foolishly ("Don't bush me!"—George V. Higgins).

busman's holiday. Said to have originated in the days of horse-drawn omnibuses, whose busmen (drivers) gave careful attention to the teams they regularly handled. If extra-conscientious, they would even take a busman's holiday—ride the bus on their day off to make sure the substitute busman was treating the horses properly. Over-conscientious or overworked people still take such "holidays," though they may not know one end of a horse from the other.

butter wouldn't melt in someone's mouth. The phrase has been knocking about for more than four centuries, but no one has yet explained why it means "spurious innocence." There may be some remote connection with the Bible's description of an adulterous woman: "she eateth, and wipeth her mouth, and saith, I have done no wickedness" (Proverbs xxx, 20). Or it may simply mean that the person in question is pretending to be "cool" rather than "hot."

by and large. When a square-rigger was tacking into the wind, the helmsman would usually be ordered to steer "full and by"— that is, *by* the wind (as close to it as possible) while still keeping the sails *full.* This was called steering "small," and required both skill and close attention: if the course was too close to the wind, the ship would be **taken aback.** An inexperienced helmsman might therefore be told to steer "by and large"—by the wind, but not too close to it. If something is true "by and large," it's only approximately on course.

cadre. French *cadre* originally meant the frame of a picture, but *C* later also the "frame" of a military organization—its essential officers and non-coms—that could be filled by recruits when war broke out. Today, cadres can be civilian as well as military.

cahoots (with), in. Probably from Canadian French (source of many North American frontier words), in which *cahute* meant "cabin"; fur-trappers who worked as partners wintered in the same cabin and were therefore "in cahoot(s)." People in cahoots are still in the same cabin, so to speak; sometimes they end up in the same cell.

calculate. Long before the modern calculator, merchants did their sums on an abacus, a device still common in the Orient and the Soviet Union. Today it consists of beads, mounted on wires, that can be moved about to add or subtract, but the original abacus was simply a grooved board in which pebbles (in Latin, *calculi*) were slid back and forth. When you use a pocket calculator you're doing much the same thing, with electrons instead of pebbles.

The original Latin word has also passed into English as the physician's "calculi": the "pebbles" that some of us unluckily develop in our bladders or gallbladders.

came the dawn. This probably started life as a subtitle in a silent movie, perhaps announcing the dawn when the heroine realized she'd been betrayed the night before. Today, like some other erstwhile subtitles ("Meanwhile, back at the ranch"), it's used jokingly, to refer ironically to the slow dawning of enlighten-ment—or disillusion.

camouflage. In French, it means (among other things) the cos-tume and grease-paint with which an actor transforms and con-ceals his natural appearance. In World War I, the word was trans-formed into the "costumes" (fake foliage and the like) and painted patterns with which the natural appearance of military equipment was disguised, to conceal it from enemy eyes.

canard. In French, *canard* means "duck," and an old expression *vendre un canard a moitie* literally means "to half-sell a duck." Since nobody can half-sell something, its actual meaning is to swindle or make a fool of. Whence the modern English (and French) canard: an anecdotal swindle—an absurd (and usually slanderous) story or rumor.

One of the most effective such "ducks" in history was the rumor that the trademark of Proctor and Gamble (makers of Ivory soap and other washing products) was a picture of the devil (actually, it was the man-in-the-moon). P & G, despite months of investigation, failed to track down the source of the canard, and was eventually forced to devise a **brand new** trademark. When-ever you hear a wild tale about some public figure, institution or political movement, make sure it's not a wild duck that somebody's trying to half-sell you.

cancel. In Latin, *cancelli* means the bars of a lattice, hence the lattice of lines used to strike out *(cancellare)* part of a manuscript. A post-office cancellation machine prints a sort of lattice over the stamp, and we X-out, literally or figuratively, appointments or debts.

candidate. Another borrowing from Latin, in which *candidus* means pure white. Roman candidates for public office wore pure white togas, no doubt to assure the voters that they themselves were equally pure. We're still getting such assurances from politicians—and they're worth about what they were in Roman times. If somebody has to assure you he's not a crook, he probably is.

Canossa. Toward the end of the eleventh century, the Holy Roman Emperor Henry IV had a run-in with Pope Gregory VII: he appointed his friends, some of them laymen, to high church offices without His Holiness's leave. The pope angrily excommunicated Henry until he did penance. The emperor thereupon journeyed to the castle of Canossa, in central Italy, and stood outside it, in the snow, for three days before the pope annulled the sentence.

So, at least, runs the legend; modern historians believe the pope was more influenced by Henry's army than by his alleged penance. But we still read of someone's "Canossa" or "journey to Canossa"—a public and humiliating backdown. In language as in history, what actually happened is often less important than what people think happened.

canvass. For centuries "canvas" has meant a heavy cloth, used for sails, chair seats and the like. At one time, however, pieces of loosely woven canvas were used to sift flour—whence the modern canvassing that sifts faithful voters from doubtful ones.

Another meaning of "canvass," now obsolete, was "to entangle in a net"—a sense worth keeping in mind whenever you find yourself being canvassed.

capital (punishment). *Caput,* the Latin word for "head" (no connection with German *kaput*) has given us a whole family of metaphors via various languages. A *captain* is the head man of a ship or a military company; a *chief* (still the same word) is another kind of head man, and a *capitalist,* yet another. The *capital* of a country is the head city, and in *capital* punishment the malefactor loses his or her head, or its equivalent.

cardinal. Latin *cardo* means "hinge," and a Roman Catholic cardinal is one of the "hinges" that the church turns on. (The American finch called a cardinal isn't any kind of hinge; it was named for its color—the brilliant red of a cardinal's robes.)

cards, in the. If you've ever had your fortune told with cards, you know why this phrase means "fated" or "expectable." In the famous "Card Trio" in the opera *Carmen,* three Gypsy women dramatically tell their own fortunes in this way. The first learns she will marry an old, rich man—and inherit his fortune; the second, that she will find true love with a young bandit chief. But when Carmen takes her turn, she finds that what's in the cards for her is death. And, as she says (and as we see in Act 4), the cards don't lie.

career (noun). French *carrière* started off meaning "racecourse" (as it once did in English); later, it came to mean the course of one's life. If your career is running on the fast track, keep in mind the Biblical injunction that the race is not always to the swift.

carnival. During the Middle Ages (and still in some places), Carnival was the Tuesday before Ash Wednesday, when Lent began. Since in Lent you weren't supposed to eat meat, the day before it started was called, in Church Latin, *carne vale,* farewell to meat. In France, as in New Orleans today, the day was also called "Fat Tuesday"—Mardi Gras: a final burst of self-indulgence before the Lenten season. The modern traveling carnival (in Britain, "fair") is a pale echo of Mardi Gras, but still emphasizes fun, not fasting.

carpet, on the. Eighty years ago, only the boss was likely to have a carpet in his office; if you were called on that carpet the consequences were generally unpleasant. A hundred and fifty years ago, however, a carpet was a tablecloth, and "on the carpet" meant under discussion—as we'd say, "on the table."

carry coals to Newcastle. British readers can skip this one. For Americans, Newcastle, in northern England, was the center of one of Britain's rich coal areas; five centuries ago its coal was already being shipped to London for heating. Carrying coals to Newcastle is equivalent to shipping oranges to Florida or ice to Greenland.

carte blanche. If you know a little French, you'll guess that this means "white card"; if you know more than a little, you'll translate it correctly as "blank sheet" (of paper). When you give someone carte blanche, you're inviting them to fill the blank sheet with whatever they choose—giving them a blank check, in fact. We find much the same image in "Write your own ticket!"

castles in Spain. One of the oldest borrowed phrases in English: we took it over from French around 1400. At that time, much of Spain was controlled by the Moors, who did not love infidels; thus Frenchmen or Englishmen who daydreamed about building castles there were spinning foolish fancies.

cat and mouse. If you've ever seen a cat that's just caught a mouse, you know what this means. If you haven't—the cat often doesn't kill the mouse immediately; instead, it lets it loose, pounces on it, lets it loose and (eventually) kills and eats it.

Mother cats apparently do this as a way of demonstrating to their kittens the techniques of hunting; why other cats do it is a mystery. Presumably it's a form of play—for the cat, that is.

Shortly before World War I, some Englishwomen were fighting hard to get the vote, sometimes disrupting political meetings and trashing stores. The government (100 percent male, of course) jailed the perpetrators; the imprisoned women responded with hunger strikes. Concerned that the strikers might die and become martyrs, the government passed a law under which they could be released when they became dangerously weak—but could be pounced on again after they'd recovered their strength. The suffrage movement christened the law "the Cat and Mouse Act."

cat is out of the bag, the. There are almost as many theories on this as there are experts. One traces it to an ancient confidence trick, by which a **bumpkin** was induced to buy a cat in a bag, believing it to be a suckling pig; if he was cautious and insisted on seeing what he was buying, the cat was out of the bag.

Myself, I doubt that even the dullest bumpkin was ever stupid enough to "buy a pig in a poke" (bag)—especially since a cat in a bag makes distinctly un-piglike noises. A more likely source is the "cat" (cat-o'-nine-tails) used to punish sailors in the bad old days. Between floggings, it was kept in a cloth bag—and once it was out of the bag there was no time left for explanations or apologies.

catbird seat, in the. An old Southern expression, given national currency by Red Barber when he was announcing baseball games for the (then) Brooklyn Dodgers. The dictionary explanation is that the catbird typically sings from a high, commanding site—that is, if you're in the catbird seat, you're in just such a position.

The story, I fear, is **for the birds.** The shy catbird prefers to sing in seclusion; someone evidently confused it with its close relative, the mockingbird, which indeed favors high places. (One holds forth every July from the roof of my summer home.) In strict logic, then, "the catbird seat" should be "the mockingbird seat," but—languages aren't logical.

catch a Tartar. "Tartar" is an old word for an inhabitant of Central Asia—originally, one of the terrifying **horde** led by Chingis (Genghis) Khan; later, it meant a Turk. Figuratively, a tartar is an unpleasant, "difficult" person—though seldom a terrifying one.

To *catch* a Tartar, however, means something rather different: to "catch" (involve yourself with) someone who turns out to be more than you can handle—much the same thing as having a **bear by the tail**. As Francis Grose, a notable eighteenth-century collector of low language, explained it, an Irishman fighting against the Turks called out to a comrade that he'd caught a Tartar. "Bring him along then," said his friend. "He won't come," said Paddy. "Then come along yourself," said the friend. "Arrah, he won't let me!" The story sounds a bit too good to be true—but true or not, it's probably the true source of the phrase.

Catch 22. Since many readers will know the source of this— Joseph Heller's novel of that title—I was of two minds whether to include it. But it's one of the great modern metaphors, so if you don't know the story, read on. A young airman (the novel is set in Italy during World War II), having flown many combat missions, tries to get a medical discharge on the ground that he's gone crazy. No, says the squadron doctor: if you wanted to keep on flying, *then* you'd be crazy, and I could discharge you, but since you want to get away from the bullets, you're obviously sane— and have to keep on flying. And *that,* says the medico, is Catch 22.

The phrase immediately passed into the language because it sums up something basic about modern life: somehow or other, officialdom or "the system" always manages to write the rules so that "they" win and we lose.

cathedral. In Greek, *kathedra* means a chair; the term was later applied to the ceremonial chair or throne of a bishop. A cathedral church (later, simply cathedral) was thus the "seat" of a bishop. And when someone speaks *ex cathedra,* they're assuming the authoritative (and perhaps somewhat pompous) manner of a bishop or other high dignitary. Some professors are fond of making *ex cathedra* statements.

cat's-paw. Aesop told a tale of a monkey that found some chestnuts roasting amid the embers of a fire and persuaded a cat to pull them out; the monkey got the nuts and the cat got burned. Your modern cat's-paw or **fall guy** is seldom as innocent as the cat, but just as dumb.

caught with one's pants down. The basic idea is clear enough—but just how did the pants come to be down? Some say the person in question was answering a call of nature; my own guess—since the expression often implies an incriminating as well as an embarrassing situation—is that he was engaged in pleasanter pursuits. In either case, a famous remark of Rabelais applies: a man with his breeches down is in no position to right wrongs.

caustic—see **holocaust**.

chagrin. Originally, a piece of heavy, rough leather used to polish sword-blades and the like; then, the abrasive spiritual effects of rough experiences and, finally, the resulting spiritual soreness. If you're chagrined, you feel rather as if someone had gone over you with emery paper.

chairman. By one account, the original "chairman" was the one member of a committee or similar body who sat on a chair; the others sat on stools. I see the hand of Ben Trovato (see Introduction): "chair" has meant "seat of authority" since the early 1300s (compare **cathedral**), and a chairman (unisex "chairperson" or "chair") occupies that seat.

chalk it up to experience. In the old-time tavern, the host kept track of the drinks he served by chalking up a tally, on a slate or simply the wall, of who had drunk what; if you were buying someone a drink, you'd call out, "Chalk it up to me!" So if you chalk up something unpleasant or unprofitable to experience, you're saying that the experience gained will—hopefully—pay the bill.

chaperon. Originally a kind of hood; later, an older woman accompanying a younger, unmarried one, sheltering her "as a hood shelters the face." Some chaperons, however, may have acted as hoods in a rather different sense, by concealing the flirtations, etc., of their charges.

charm(ing). From Latin *carmen,* originally a song, then a chanted incantation like those of the witches in *Macbeth* ("Cool it with a baboon's blood/Then the charm is firm and good"). Though few of us believe in charms nowadays, a charming person can still bewitch us.

cheapskate—see **blatherskite**.

checkmate. Originally, from Persian *shah mat,* the king is dead. It quickly became a term in chess, indicating that one player's king was "dead" (captured), but nowadays means merely that the king is as good as dead. A player whose king is under attack ("in check"), and has no way of warding off the attack, whether by moving the king or interposing another piece, is checkmated. If somebody has you checkmated, you've lost the game.

chestnut. According to one account, its metaphorical sense, "a stale joke," comes from an old play, in which a comic character, recounting a well-worn tale, substitutes a cork tree for a chestnut tree. "But," protests one of his hearers, all too familiar with the story, "it was always a chestnut before." Neat but, I fear, an authentic Ben Trovato. The play dates from 1816; "chestnut" was described as "one of the latest slang terms" some sixty years later. The true source of the metaphor is still a mystery.

Chinaman's chance, not a. The Gold Rush brought tens of thousands of immigrants to California, not a few of them from China. The Chinese, like other immigrants from impoverished lands, were willing to work hard for little money, which was bad enough; worse, they weren't white. Labor leaders and politicians denounced "Chinese cheap labor" (see **euchre**); eventually, Chinese and other Oriental immigrants were barred, first from California and then nationally. The law wasn't repealed until after World War II.

Even before the legal bars against them, the Chinese had a thin time of it, especially in the gold diggings, where there was little law and even less order: their mining claims were "jumped," and if they protested they were lucky if they were just beaten up. In any conflict between a white man and a Chinese, the latter had a Chinaman's chance of winning.

chip in—see **ante up**

choleric—see **bilious**.

cinch, a. To the Mexican *vaquero,* a *cincha* was a strong strap, often made of braided horsehair, which passed around a horse's belly to hold the saddle in place. American cattlemen in the Southwest converted *vaquero* into "buckaroo," and *cincha* into "cinch."

A cinch—which naturally had to be buckled very tight—soon came to mean a firm grip on anything; eventually, a near-certainty. If something is a cinch, you can rely on its happening as confidently as the *vaquero* relied on his *cincha* when punching cattle.

Even more certain than a cinch is a lead-pipe cinch—probably from the old-time hoodlum's weapon that could be picked up on any building site. If a **thug** hit you with this blunt instrument, it was a lead-pipe cinch that he'd get your money.

circumstances. In Latin, things literally standing around *(circumstantia)* or surrounding something, whence a host of figurative meanings, most with the basic idea of what surrounds a thing or event rather than the event itself. Circumstantial evidence concerns the facts that "stand around" a crime—whether a person accused of a killing owned a gun, whether (s)he had a motive, and so on—as contrasted with eye-witness evidence of the actual killing. Contrary to what many people believe, circumstantial evidence isn't necessarily less reliable than eye-witness evidence; sometimes it's more reliable. Witnesses, after all, can lie, or be mistaken; circumstances generally can't.

claptrap. Originally, a piece of theatrical "business," or perhaps an ad libbed line, thrown in as "a trap to catch a clap" from the audience. Claptrap nowadays is commoner in politics than in the theater, but still, regrettably, often draws applause.

clean as a whistle. When I was a kid, somebody whose name I've forgotten showed me how to make a willow whistle. You cut a piece of willow, maybe four inches long and as thick as your finger, and gently tap the bark all around it. If you're careful and patient, the bark will be loosened enough to slide off in one piece, clean as a whistle (or *slick as a whistle*). (To finish the job, you notch the twig and the bark, slide the latter back on, and blow; if you've done everything right, you'll get a shrill, flute-like tone rather like that of the whistle's descendant, the recorder.)

cliché. In the early days of printing, illustrations were carved on wooden blocks, which were then inked and run through the press. With faster presses and bigger editions, wood wouldn't stand up; instead, the block was used to make a cast metal plate, called a cliché or *stereotype*. Since clichés were reused from time to time, some clever newspaperman transferred the term to stereotyped expressions that were also reused—too often.

Later, stereotypes were made of entire pages. These, once they'd been cast into metal, couldn't be changed without remaking the whole thing. The modern "stereotype"—a clichéd view of something (often, a racial or ethnic group)—is equally impervious to change.

Stereotypes used on rotary presses had to be cast curved rather than flat; printers called them "boilerplate," from their vague resemblance to the curved plates used by boilermakers. Later the term was transferred to syndicated editorial matter, circulated in the form of heavy cardboard "matrixes" from which the boilerplate was cast. Nowadays, "boilerplate" means the interminable, "standard" clauses of legalese used in insurance policies and publishers' contracts.

clod. Since the beginning of civilization, towns and cities have been where the action was: centers of new fashions and ideas generated by tens and hundreds of thousands of people rubbing elbows. Urbanites have therefore traditionally looked down on country folk—which is how a clod of earth became the human clod (originally, a countryman) with the brains and imagination of a lump of dirt. (Country folk, of course, have equally looked down on their urban cousins, as slickers given to nameless vices. I dare say both sides have a point.)

clone. In biology, "clone" has a very specific meaning: a group or colony of organisms with identical genes—hence identical for all practical purposes. In the figurative sense, as in "clones of the IBM PC" or "clones of Jerry Falwell," genes are out but the identity remains.

close—but no cigar. In the old-time country fair or carnival, the local lads were invited to exhibit their strength or skill by throwing baseballs at targets, pounding with a huge mallet to raise a weight, and so on; the prize was a cigar. Since these devices were almost always "gaffed" (see **blow the gaff**), the ambitious youths seldom won. Instead, the concessionnaire would encourage them to further efforts (at a nickel a time) with, "Close—but no cigar!" The phrase still means, "Nice try, but—sorry!"

cloud nine. Meteorologists classify clouds by the numbers. Number nine is the very tallest cloud, the cumulonimbus (thundercloud), whose top may reach 40,000 feet. If you're on cloud nine, you're feeling high indeed—but watch out for storms!

clout (political). None of the standard sources throw much light on this one. A literal clout is either a heavy blow or a piece of material used to patch or fix something. Somebody with lots of clout can certainly clout his opponents—but is also likely to be a good fixer.

clover, in. The various species of clover, including the common white clover you find on your lawn, are, like peas and beans, members of the legume family. Legumes are relatively rich in protein and therefore good for fattening cattle, which relish them. If you're in clover, then, you're both well nourished and happy.

clue. Literally, a ball of thread or yarn, often spelt "clew"; its figurative sense comes from the Greek legend of Theseus and Ariadne. Minos, king of Crete, each year exacted a tribute from the city-state of Athens: seven youths and seven maidens. They were taken to Crete and imprisoned in the Labyrinth—a bewildering maze of winding passageways—where they were eaten by a monster, half man, half bull, called the Minotaur.

One year Theseus, heir to the Athenian throne, volunteered to join the victims, believing he could kill the Minotaur. In Crete he attracted the attention of Ariadne, daughter of Minos, who fell in love with him. She gave him a ball of yarn, one end of which he tied to a pillar at the entrance to the Labyrinth and then unrolled as he and his companions passed into the maze. Having killed the Minotaur, he used Ariadne's clew as the clue to find his way out.

As Chaucer retold the story (I've modernized the language),

> With a clew of twine he entered in;
> The same way, he came out again.

Whence, of course, the clues by which real and fictional detectives find their ways through labyrinthine mysteries.

cockpit. Originally (sixteenth century), an enclosure where game-cocks are *pitted* against one another, but almost immediately it acquired the additional sense of any place where fierce contests were fought out.

The area along the present Franco-Belgian frontier has long been known as "the Cockpit of Europe," because of the many major battles fought there. These include Waterloo, which ended the Napoleonic Wars; Sedan, which ended the Franco-Prussian War of 1870, and the "second battle of Sedan"—the German breakthrough that smashed French resistance in 1940 and almost trapped most of the British army at Dunkirk.

The wild "Cockpit Country" in the mountains of Jamaica is full of "cockpits"—deep, enclosed valleys—which were the scene of many fierce fights between British soldiers and runaway slaves (Maroons). Some Jamaicans will tell you proudly that until slavery was abolished, the British government never managed to control the Cockpit, but was forced to concede a sort of autonomy to its tough inhabitants.

cocky. In Victorian times, the barnyard cock became a rooster, as the cockroach became a roach—in both cases, to avoid saying the dreadful word "c—k." But even delicate-minded folk continued to call people "cocky"—that is, having the seeming arrogant machismo of a crowing cock.

cold deck. Playing cards that have been used for a number of hands are naturally slightly warm. A skillful and audacious sharper will sometimes switch the warm pack for a new, cold deck, stacked to give him a winning hand. If somebody slips you a cold deck, they're conducting a bare-faced swindle.

cold enough to freeze the balls off a brass monkey. Some authorities on sailors' lingo claim that this metaphor involves a double pun: the "balls" were cannon balls, and the "monkey," a dished or indented tray, sometimes made of brass, on which the balls were stacked. In really frigid weather, the brass would contract more than the iron—enough to dislodge the balls; freezing seawater in the tray would have the same effect.

The only thing wrong with this engaging tale is that there's no evidence that "monkey"—which has a host of figurative meanings—was ever used in this particular sense. (Ben Trovato strikes again!) Much more likely, the phrase was elaborated from the nineteenth-century expression, "shaking like a monkey in frosty weather," which is clear enough: monkeys, as tropical creatures, would naturally suffer severely from cold.

cold feet. Though it's been used in the U.S. for a century or more, nobody has figured out where it came from. It may have begun as soldier's slang, from the response of some unenthusiastic private who, told to stand up and charge the enemy, tried to beg off on the ground that his feet were frozen. Anyone who's been in combat in chilly weather knows that sitting around waiting for something to happen is likely to give you cold feet, in both senses.

cold turkey. Heroin or morphine addicts deprived of their drug undergo withdrawal symptoms that include intense shivering; the skin develops large bumps resembling those on a plucked turkey. Equally unpleasant symptoms result from giving up other things cold turkey—tobacco, say, or a lover.

coldcock. If you've never encountered this slang term, it means to knock someone unconscious—often with the proverbial "blunt instrument." It's source is obscure; my own guess is that it refers to the piece of lead pipe once used for such purposes (see **cinch**), which was roughly the shape of a cock but—being metal—was cold, not warm.

colossal. In the Greco-Roman world, a colossus was any larger-than-life-size statue. The most famous of these—it was one of the Seven Wonders of the ancient world—was the Colossus of Rhodes, standing at the entrance of the principal harbor on that island. More than 100 feet (32 meters) tall, it was twelve years in the building, but was destroyed by an earthquake only sixty years later. Modern "colossal" and "super-colossal" films are equally impressive—and often even shorter-lived.

companion, company. A companion was originally someone with (Latin *cum*) whom you shared bread *(panis)*. The stockholders of a company also share "bread"—or hope to.

complicated, complex. From the same *cum,* with, plus *plicatus,* folded. A complicated thing is folded together, so that its nature isn't visible at first glance; a *simple* one is "without a fold"—completely open and understandable. See also **duplicity**.

conclave. Still the same *cum,* plus *clavis,* key. The original conclave was the assembly of Roman cardinals, held behind locked doors, to choose a pope; eventually, it became a rather pretentious term for almost any assembly or meeting. The Ku Klux Klan used to hold "konklaves," but these were not locked up—unfortunately.

congregation. This time *cum* is hitched to *gregis,* flock. A congregation is a flocking together and a church congregation, of course, is the priest or minister's flock.

Continental, not worth a. Revolutions seldom draw much support from rich people, meaning that they're usually short of cash. The American Revolution was no exception. The Continental Congress that headed it had next to no gold or other assets, nor even the power to levy taxes; it paid its bills by simply printing banknotes. As you'd expect, these "Continentals" depreciated until they were worth little more than the paper they were printed on. The metaphor is a useful reminder of what can happen when a government, by compulsion or choice, lives beyond its means.

cook someone's goose. Ben Trovato tells us that during the siege of a medieval town the inhabitants displayed a goose atop the walls, to demonstrate how well provisioned they were. But the besiegers succeeded in breaking into the town and burned it—thereby cooking the goose. A nice story—but the expression is modern, not medieval, and its true origin is surely much simpler: a goose (or any other bird) that's cooked is both done and done for.

"Cook" in such phrases as "cook the books" reflects the activities of some skillful (or pretentious) cooks, who can prepare a dish so artfully that no one can tell what it actually contains.

cool one's heels. During a long journey afoot, the feet may well become overheated, requiring a stop to let them cool. Eventually, the impatient pedestrian, anxious to continue on his way, became the impatient suitor or salesman, left to cool his heels outside someone's door or office.

copperhead. The copperhead, a handsome but poisonous snake of the eastern U. S., is related to the rattlesnake but, having no rattles, gives no warning before it strikes. During the American Civil War, the word was applied to Southern sympathizers in the North, who were deemed equally **insidious.**

cordial—see **bleeding heart**.

corn(y). Corn (in Britain, "maize") was cultivated by Native Americans long before Columbus, and has been a major U.S. crop since colonial times. "Corn-fed" has meant "rural" for generations; actors and vaudevillians transferred the expression to rural audiences, and then to the crude, rustic humor and old-fashioned melodrama that the hicks supposedly relished. Eventually, the stuff was called simply "corn." However, rural audiences don't always relish corn—witness the famous headline in the show-biz paper *Variety:* STICKS NIX HICK PIX (translation: "Small towns reject motion pictures on rural themes").

coup. We all know about the coup that overthrows a Third World government—often with the connivance of a First World ditto; it's short for French *coup d'état*—the "blow" *(coup)* that overthrows a state *(état).* The coup in "she scored a real coup" is the same word, but closer to the ultimate source, Latin *colpus,* a blow with the fist—in effect, a knockout blow. It may have picked up added color from the Native American custom of "counting coup" (so named by French trappers), whereby warriors could score prestige points (coups) by being the first to strike, or even touch, an enemy. See **feather in one's cap**.

coup de grace. Literally (in French), the "blow of mercy" by which a mortally wounded foe was dispatched. Whence, of course, any finishing stroke—which may or may not be "merciful" to the person who gets it.

Coventry. An account of the English Civil War by the Earl of Clarendon, a strong Royalist, tells of an incident at "Bromingham" (Birmingham), "a town so generally wicked that it had risen upon small parties of the King's [men] and killed [them] or taken them prisoners and sent them to Coventry" (an anti-Royalist stronghold).

This is one of what the *OED* calls "numerous ingenious conjectures" on the origin of the phrase. It's certainly ingenious, but not very informative, since "sending someone to Coventry" doesn't mean making them a figurative prisoner, but rather refusing to speak to, or have anything to do with, them.

Somewhat more plausible—but equally unproved—is the suggestion that at some unspecified time the inhabitants of Coventry, objecting strongly to having soldiers quartered in their houses, put the intruders "in Coventry."

coward. Almost certainly from Latin *cauda,* tail: a coward turns tail, or slinks off with it between his legs.

cows come home, till the. Cows put out to pasture come home—to be milked—at evening. Exactly how this fact of nature came to mean "until a very late hour" is unknown; perhaps via Jonathan Swift's remark to an idler: "I warrant you lay abed till the cows came home."

cozen. An archaic term for "deceive," whose source is interesting enough to make it worth reviving. It comes from French *cousiner,* which a 1611 dictionary translated as "to clayme kindred for advantage . . . as he, who to save charges in traveling, goes from house to house, as cosin to the owner of every one." If some stranger claims to be a long-lost relative, he's almost certainly trying to cozen you.

cramp one's style. Not, as I'd suspected, from a crowded dance floor, which might well cramp one's dancing style, but from literature: an early nineteenth-century writer complained that trying to compose something in inks of two different colors "cramps my style"; the same was later said of censorship.

craven. Ben Trovato derives it from Latin *crepitare,* to rattle—presumably referring to the chattering teeth of a craven person. Alas, the original sense was not "cowardly," but merely "defeated" or "admitting defeat." The modern sense comes from the expression "cry craven," equivalent to "say 'Uncle'." It's almost certainly a metaphor—but one whose source is well and truly lost.

crane. Years ago, I had business in Michigan—well outside my normal haunts. Finding myself with some hours to kill before my return plane, I asked some local people whether there were any interesting birds in the area. They told me that if I would drive out along such-and-such a back road, I might see a sandhill crane.

I did so, and eventually spotted two of the birds, in an old cornfield; presumably they were gleaning kernels left from the harvest. Tall and long-necked, they would slowly and deliberately dip their heads down to seize a grain with their bills, raise them just as deliberately to swallow, and repeat the process over and over. I saw then what some medieval construction worker must have seen when he gazed at the slowly rising and falling boom of a builder's hoist—and christened the apparatus a crane.

Interestingly, the same metaphor has been coined independently in several other languages; thus French *grue* means "crane" in both senses. When we crane our necks to see something, of course, we are figuratively emulating the crane—whose neck, however, is long enough so that it doesn't have to crane.

crawfish (verb). The crawfish or crayfish, like its cousin the lobster, can propel itself backward with a flip of its powerful tail. American politicians and others have been crawfishing—backing off from an earlier position—since before 1850.

credit, creed. One of the oldest metaphors we know of: it harks back to the ancient Indo-European tongue of perhaps seven thousand years ago (see Introduction). The Indo-European root *kerd-* meant—and is the ancestor of—"heart" (also of "cardiologist" and "cordial"—see **bilious**); the root *dhe-* meant "put." The compound *kred-dhe-* meant literally to put into one's heart—hence, to believe. A businessman who gives his customers credit believes in his heart that they'll pay, sooner or later, and your creed is what you believe deep in your heart.

creep(s). For over a thousand years "creep" has been applied to the crawling of insects, and for almost that long to an unpleasant sensation like that of insects crawling on the skin. Swift was the first to set down the expression "make one's flesh creep"—

nowadays more often "give one the creeps." A creep, of course, is a person who gives them to you.

crocodile tears. A fourteenth century teller of tall tales, writing under the name of Sir John Mandeville, claimed that crocodiles "slay men, and [then] eat them weeping" (language modernized). Two centuries later, the explorer Sir John Hawkins improved the tale: the crocodile's habit, he says, "is ever, when hee would have his prey, to cry and sobbe like a Christian body, to provoke them to come to him, and then hee snatcheth at them."

Lewis Carroll used a similar image in describing the Walrus and the Carpenter's fatal encounter with the oysters:

> "I weep for you," the Walrus said, "I deeply sympathize!"
> With sobs and tears he sorted out those of the largest size,
> Holding his pocket handkerchief before his streaming eyes.

During the Vietnam War, the caricaturist David Levine drew a savagely brilliant cartoon of President Lyndon Johnson weeping tears shaped like little crocodiles. (A second version showed a crocodile weeping tears shaped like little Johnsons.)

So far as I know, crocodiles don't weep at all—yet the legend may have a slight factual foundation. Marine turtles are now known to "weep"—secrete salty water from special glands near their eyes—to eliminate excess salt taken in when they drink. The females can be seen to do so when they come ashore to lay their eggs, whence the legend that they weep with the pain of laying. "Mandeville" may well have come across the tale and transferred it to the crocodile; it made a good story—and since none of his readers had seen the beast, nobody could call him a liar.

cross the Rubicon. Early in 49 B.C., Julius Caesar could look back on a highly successful nine years. As governor of Gaul (roughly, modern France) and commander of Roman troops there, he had forced the entire region to acknowledge the sovereignty of Rome; to ice the cake, he'd even invaded Britain. Now, on his way home, he had reached the Rubicon—a small stream that separated Cisapline Gaul (roughly, the Po Valley) from Italy proper.

According to Roman law, a provincial governor who entered Italy had to leave his troops behind. But Caesar had powerful enemies in Rome; if he returned without his army, they might well destroy him—yet if he brought it with him, it meant civil war. Finally, with the declaration *Alea jacta est!* (The die is cast!), he led his troops across the Rubicon and within a few years had made himself master of Rome—though his enemies did eventually destroy him.

Many of us at some time in our lives face a personal Rubicon: a decision that will radically change our lives, for better or worse. If we cross it, and are lucky, we'll come out of it better than Caesar eventually did.

crusade. The Middle Ages saw several European expeditions to "liberate" the Holy Land from the Moslems, who had themselves stolen it a few centuries earlier (see **assassin**). The liberators took as their emblem the Cross (Latin *crux*). Many crusaders were doubtless sincere religious fanatics, but many others were simply out for what they could get—as shown, for example, by their looting of the Christian city of Constantinople. Modern crusades against alleged social evils are often equally fanatical—and their leaders, often equally unscrupulous.

cry wolf. One of Aesop's most famous images. A shepherd boy, bored with watching his sheep, decided to liven things up by crying, "Wolf!" The villagers naturally turned out en masse to save their flocks, and were considerably annoyed to find that the boy had been having them on. Some time later, he pulled the same stunt, with the same result. Eventually, of course, an actual wolf appeared, and again the boy cried, "Wolf!" But nobody came, and he was eaten.

Ever since Aesop's day, unscrupulous politicians and journalists have been crying wolf: warning of urgent "threats" to the body politic; in my lifetime alone, they've denounced wolves enough to have eaten up the American republic several times over. Fortunately, the wolves were as fictitious as in Aesop's tale; unfortunately, their creators seldom suffered the shepherd boy's deserved fate.

cuckold. The European cuckoo (though not its American relatives) habitually lays its single egg in the nests of other birds, who feed the young cuckoo along with their own nestlings. For centuries, the cuckoo has been a **harbinger** of spring in northern Europe, and for almost as long has supplied a metaphor for a husband who has been "cuckooed" (cuckolded)—his "nest" has been invaded by another man, who may have left behind one of his own offspring.

One of Shakespeare's most delightful verses hails the advent of spring:

> The cuckoo, then, from every tree
> Mocks married men, for thus says he:
> Cuckoo!
> Cuckoo, cuckoo! Oh word of fear,
> Unpleasing to the married ear!

The cuckoo has given us another metaphor: it repeats its two-note call interminably, and thus sounds "cuckoo."

curfew. In medieval towns, with open fires used for cooking and heating and no fire departments, a fire left untended might get out of control and destroy the whole community. Accordingly, many towns adopted evening curfews (from French *couvre feu*, cover fire)—a bell or other signal at which all fires had to be extinguished, after which the populace could turn in for the night.

Modern curfews—orders to the population to stay indoors during certain hours—are often imposed by repressive governments or warring factions within a country. The incentive for obeying, however, is not fear of fire but fear of being fired on.

current, currency. The current of a river is flowing (Latin *currens*) water; an electric current is flowing electrons; current events are those flowing now, as contrasted with those already over the dam. And currency is the vital fluid that flows through the veins of commerce—and which, if we're not careful, flows all too quickly out of our bank accounts.

curry favor. This one is complicated, so watch closely. It comes from Favel, a horse in medieval legend that somehow became a symbol of dishonesty. To "curry Favel" became a metaphor for seeking favors dishonestly or by flattery. Later, when the original Favel was forgotten, people substituted "favor," which at least made a certain amount of sense. The expression makes even more sense if you happen to know that "curry" means to rub down a horse after exercise—to "stroke," as you might say.

curtains, that's/it's. In life as in the theater, when the curtains close, that's the end.

cut and dried. If you raise herbs in your garden, you know that when fresh they have a lot more flavor than after they've been cut and dried. Jobs or tasks that are cut and dried don't have much flavor either.

cut it—see **cut the mustard.**

cut of someone's jib, the. As sailors know, a jib is a sail set in the triangular area between a mast and the forward part of the deck or the bowsprit. Sailmakers of different countries cut jibs in distinctive ways, and experienced sailors could often tell the nationality of an approaching ship—i.e., whether it was friend or enemy—by the shape of its jib. If you don't like the cut of someone's jib, (s)he's somebody to steer clear of.

cut one's eyeteeth. A metaphor complicated by unconventional syntax: we speak of a baby "cutting" teeth, when in fact it's the teeth that are cutting the baby (i.e., its gums)—often evoking loud protests. The eyeteeth were the canines, lying more or less directly below the eyes. We cut our permanent eyeteeth around age 12, by which time we've clearly passed out of babyhood.

cut out of whole cloth. A difficult metaphor. "Whole cloth" originally meant a length of cloth as it came off the loom, as contrasted with pieces cut from it. "Cut out of whole cloth" was thus a term of praise, meaning a garment that wasn't pieced together out of whatever odd bits the tailor happened to have in his shop. But for over a century it's meant something quite different: completely false. The idea, I think, is that the story in question isn't, like many faked-up tales, a patchwork of truth and falsehood; rather, its whole fabric is false.

cut someone to the quick. The "quick" here has nothing to do with speed but harks back to its original meaning, "living" ("the quick and the dead"). If someone has cut you to the quick, they've cut through the skin into your living flesh.

cut the Gordian knot. Gordius, a king of Phrygia in Asia Minor ca. 400 B.C., tied the yoke of his chariot to a beam in a temple with a knot so intricate that nobody could disentangle it. Gradually, a legend grew up that whoever could unloose the Gordian knot would conquer not only Phrygia but all of the Middle East.

A few generations later, Alexander, King of Macedon, led his armies into Asia Minor. Hearing of the legend and seeking to boost the morale of his troops, he went to the temple and cut the knot with his sword; within a few years, he had indeed conquered all of Asia and even parts of India, thereby earning the historic title of "the Great." Ever since, anyone who finds a similar sharp and quick way out of seeming insurmountable difficulties is said to have cut the Gordian knot.

cut the mustard. Before the Pure Food and Drug Act of 1909, many foodstuffs were regularly adulterated—for instance, dried mustard was mixed with ground-up mustard hulls and a little coloring. Ranchers seeking to shave expenses often stocked their cookhouses with such junky supplies. The cowboys, in turn, began referring to "the proper mustard"—one with real bite; hence, anything of top quality.

This expression may or may not be the immediate ancestor of "cut the mustard"—to be of good quality; hence, successful or effective. At any rate, it makes a certain amount of sense: to say that someone can't cut the mustard, or simply can't *cut it* means that their skills or vigor are adulterated; they just don't have enough of what it takes—or, probably, much flavor either.

cuts no ice. To nearly all of us nowadays, ice is something you either slip on in the street or get, in cubes, from the refrigerator. But not so long ago, ice was literally cut (sawed) from the surface of frozen ponds; as a kid, I saw crews taking six-foot thick slabs from Bantam Lake, Connecticut, and storing them inside a thick-walled ice-house. It wasn't very skilled work, but exhausting and very cold. If something cuts no ice, it's thoroughly ineffectual or unimpressive.

cynic. Would you believe that this one is related to "canine"? Well, it is. A certain school of ancient Greek philosophers professed supreme contempt for worldly comforts; its most famous member, Diogenes, lived on the streets of Athens in a barrel. Their fellow citizens, feeling that they lived like dogs, called them *kynikos,* meaning "dog-like"—but also, perhaps, "cur-like."

Your modern cynic, who (in Oscar Wilde's famous phrase) knows the price of everything and the value of nothing, is dog-like only in the sense that he's perhaps more likely than most to be a son-of-a-bitch: the conviction that everyone is corrupt is a good excuse for being corrupt yourself.

cynosure. Another, but much rarer, canine metaphor: most people, if they know it at all, think of Milton's line, "The Cynosure of neighboring eyes"—i.e., the center of everyone's attention.

The word comes from Greek *kynos oura,* dog's tail; the original Cynosure was the constellation we call the Lesser Bear, whose "tail" has the Pole Star at its tip. Later, it meant the Pole Star itself, which is indeed the "center" of the heavens, since all other heavenly bodies appear to revolve around it. (The appearance— need I say?—is an illusion: the earth revolves, not the heavens.)

daisy. Everyone knows the daisy, whose bright blossoms dot ₵ **D** country fields in early summer. Europeans, but few Americans, also know that European daisies (known in the U. S. as English daisies), like human eyes, close at night and open when day returns, making the flower the "day's-eye."

Davy Jones' locker. Why sailors should have given the name Davy Jones to "the fiend that presides over all the evil spirits of the deep" (Smollett) is not clear. Some philologists, noting that Black West Indians refer to ghosts as duppies, suggest that "Davy Jones" may derive from "Duppy Jonah"—Jonah's ghost. Certainly sailors long used "Jonah" to mean anyone (or anything) that, like the original Jonah, was thought to mean bad luck aboard ship—which was why Jonah was flung overboard to be swallowed by the whale. However Davy Jones acquired his name, his locker is the ocean bottom, the final resting place of sunken ships, drowned sailors and anything else given the **deep six**.

dead as a doornail. Enormous amounts of labor—most of it unproductive—have gone into tracing this old expression (it dates from the fourteenth century). To understand it, you need to know that until fairly recently nails were hand-made, expensive, and therefore used only where absolutely necessary. Houses and ships were fastened together with hardwood pegs, called tree-nails.

One place where the costly iron nails often *were* necessary was in making doors, which are under repeated stress from being opened and closed. They therefore had to be either glued to-gether, requiring the expensive services of a skilled joiner, or, for the unskilled or do-it-yourself builder, nailed together. The nails were customarily driven all the way through the boards and clinched by hammering down the points. Since they then couldn't be re-used, they were "dead"—as a doornail.

decadent. From Latin *cadere,* fall. *Decadere* meant literally to fall away from something; a decadent person or society has fallen away from past virtue. (Compare **accident**.)

deception. Another Latinism, this one from *capere,* seize or take. *Decipere* meant "take away"; a deception is something that takes away our money—or our faith in the deceiver. As the late Marga-ret Schlauch noted, a child whose lollipop has been snatched away has been deceived both literally and figuratively.

decimate. Roman soldiers were a notoriously tough lot, partly because of the equally tough discipline they had to endure. Flog-gings were routine, but the ultimate disciplinary measure (as in cases of mutiny) was decimation. The members of the mutinous unit were lined up and every tenth man was hauled out of line and given the chop. "Decimate" has come to mean destroy or other-wise eliminate a large proportion (usually much more than a tenth) of some group; it's also sometimes used inaccurately (and pretentiously) to mean simply "destroy" ("the building was deci-mated").

deep six, the. Though this phrase sometimes means the grave, it doesn't, as you might think, refer to a deep "six by three" hole in the ground; it's from the sea, not the land. When a ship moved toward shallow water, the crew would take soundings with a lead weight attached to a line. The line was marked at specific inter-vals, as with a knot, a piece of calico, a strip of leather and so on. The marks were placed at one fathom (six feet or 1.83 meters), two fathoms, five fathoms and ten fathoms. If the line ran out to one of the marks, the leadsman would call out "Mark five!" or whatever the depth was; for depths between the marks, he'd estimate and call out "Deep four!" or "Deep six!"

But—why do we say "deep six" rather than one of the other "deeps"? I'd guess it had to do with the tides, whose rise and fall almost anywhere in the world is less—usually much less—than six fathoms. That is, something or someone thrown overboard in six fathoms at high tide would remain submerged even at extreme low water; if you give something the deep six, you've disposed of it permanently. During the Watergate conspiracy, one participant was told to give some incriminating papers the deep six; he dropped them in the Potomac River.

Incidently, Samuel Clemens, who'd been a steamboat pilot on the Mississippi, took his pen name from the leadsman's call for two fathoms—Mark Twain. ("Twain" is an archaic word for "two," as in "never the twain shall meet.")

delirious. In Latin, *lira* was a plowed furrow. A delirious person, then, is someone whose mind is out of the furrow—off the track, you might say.

Delphic. The temple of Apollo at Delphi housed perhaps the most famous oracle of the ancient world. One reason it was famous is that its priestesses phrased their predictions so ambiguously that they would be "right" whatever happened—as a much later English poet put it, "nonsense destin'd to be future sense."

A famous example was the oracle given King Croesus of Phrygia. Having made himself master of most of Asia Minor (and "as rich as Croesus"), he was tempted to take on the Persian Empire. When he asked the oracle's advice, he was told that if he went to war he would destroy a mighty empire; he did so, and indeed destroyed a great empire—his own. So we still read of someone giving a Delphic reply, or speaking in Delphic language.

denigrate. Latin *niger* meant "black" (as you might guess, it's the ultimate source of "Negro"); *denigrare* meant to blacken someone's name or reputation—in effect, to throw mud at them, which is what "denigrate" still means. The "blackening," by the way, had nothing to do with anyone's skin color; it referred to dirt, not ethnicity.

dependent. From Latin *pendere,* hang. A dependent clause in grammar "hangs" from the main clause of the sentence; a dependent person hangs from or on someone else—often like the proverbial millstone. And if you say, "That depends," you're saying that it's still hanging—up in the air, in fact.

derrick. Around 1600, one Godfrey Derick or Derrick was a famous London hangman (legend credits him with some three thousand executions). Soon "derrick" was transferred from the man to the gallows on which his clients were hoisted; later, some maritime wit applied the word to a **crane** used to hoist heavy objects aboard ship. Today, Godfrey Derick and his sinister derrick are long forgotten, but the anonymous sailor's gallows humor lives on.

despicable, despise. From Latin *despicere,* look down. A despicable person is one you look down on—or should.

desultory. Some Roman acrobats displayed their skill by leaping back and forth from one galloping horse to another; they were called *desultores,* leapers. If you read a book in a desultory fashion, you're leaping from one passage to another.

deuce, the. An old-fashioned expletive widely considered a euphemism for "the Devil." But "deuce" has long meant a two at cards or dice; if you throw a deuce ("snake eyes") at craps, you immediately lose your stake, and might well exclaim, "The deuce!" The German equivalent, *das Daus,* has the same double meaning.

deus ex machina. Ultimately from Greek *theos ek mechanes,* a gimmick often used by dramatists who had **painted themselves into a corner** (see **paint . . .**). That is, when the plot had become so embroiled that no dramatic resolution seemed possible, the playwright would bring some god *(theos)* down from heaven to straighten things out; the *mechanes* was the crane used to lower the "god" onto the stage.

The dramatic device is ancient, going back to Homer. In the *Odyssey,* the returning Odysseus regains his kingdom by killing off the suitors who, during his long wanderings, had been trying to grab off both his wife and his realm. As Homer and his audiences well knew, such a massacre would normally have set off a series of blood feuds that would have kept Ithaca in turmoil for generations; accordingly, the poet brought in Athena as a peacemaker.

The modern *deus ex machina* is anything that comes in the nick of time to unscramble a complicated situation—often, by implication, in a rather improbable way.

devil and the deep sea, between the. The "devil" in question was the outermost seam on the deck of a wooden ship. If you're between the devil and the deep sea, you're in imminent danger of going overboard—though the modern sense is closer to "between a rock and a hard place."

devil to pay, the. The phrase is sometimes elaborated with "and no pitch hot." Fanciers of sailors' lingo claim that the "devil" (see previous entry) also meant the *lowest* seam on a ship's hull—i.e., right next to the keel. Shipyard workers who had to "pay" (caulk) this seam, with oakum and hot tar (pitch), would have had to lie on their backs cramped under the hull, with the grave risk that some of the tar would drip on them—certainly a devil of a job.

There are two problems with this ingenious tale. First, there's no good evidence that "devil" was ever used in this sense; second, the earliest examples of the phrase say nothing about pitch. A much more likely source is the legendary pact with the devil, which got Faust into such trouble: if you had the devil to pay—or *hell to pay*—the price was your soul. The pitch may have been a later, sailors' addition—or simply a reflection of the well-known fact that the devil dealt in hot pitch, burning brimstone (sulfur) and similar uncomfortable substances.

devil's advocate. In Roman Catholic proceedings to canonize someone, a prominent participant is the Devil's Advocate: a churchman charged with bringing up all the arguments *against* sainthood—that is, doing the devil's job of **denigrating** a potential saint. Figuratively, it means someone who takes pains to bring out the arguments against a particular theory or proposal.

When I was in college, I got a good deal of perverse pleasure out of playing devil's advocate—arguing against propositions that "everybody knew" were true; as a result, some people considered me eccentric or plain disruptive. I still think I had a point: years of experience with ideas of the "everybody knows" variety have taught me that they're nonsense as often as not. Yet people continue to swallow them—until somebody comes along who's devilish enough to challenge them.

dexterous—see **adroit**.

diaphragm. Ultimately, from Greek *phragma,* fence. The human diaphragm is the thick muscular partition that fences off the lungs from the alimentary organs; the contraceptive diaphragm fences off the sperm from the egg.

die is cast, the—see **cross the Rubicon**.

different drummer, a. To explicate this metaphor, I can do no better than give its original source—a passage from Thoreau's *Walden:* "If a man does not keep pace with his companions, perhaps it is because he hears a different drummer. Let him step to the music which he hears, however measured or far away."

Good advice—so long as you remember that getting out of step with the crowd may get you trampled.

dilapidated. Ultimately, from Latin *dilapidare,* literally to scatter stones asunder, hence to destroy. The English word has moved toward a more limited sense: *partly* destroyed, run down. If you think of the Parthenon in Athens, still standing though many of its stones are scattered asunder, you'll have a good picture of what "dilapidated" means.

disaster. Literally, an *ill-starred* occurrence—one caused by the supposed malign influences of the stars (Latin *astra*) or planets. Most natural disasters are indeed "in the stars" or, as we say, "Acts of God" (what a nasty thing to say about God!)—but other catastrophes are man-made, so that we must say with Cassius, "The fault, dear Brutus, is not in our stars but in ourselves."

disgruntled. Logically, there should be a verb, "gruntle"—and, surprisingly, there is, though it's now obsolete or all but: it means (or meant) to emit a low grunt. According to the author John Moore, his pigs did this when they were contented, so that "disgruntled" would logically mean "discontented."

I don't find his logic convincing, because "gruntle" is an intransitive verb: pigs can gruntle but not *be* gruntled. But "gruntle" also meant a pig's snout, which would make "disgruntled" equivalent to having one's nose out of joint.

disseminate. From Latin *semen,* seed (later, also the male "seed" that fertilizes the female). *Disseminare* meant to scatter seed abroad; if you're disseminating ideas, that's what you're doing with them, hoping they'll land on fertile soil.

dissolute, dissolve. Ultimately, from Latin *solvere,* loosen; you solve a knotty problem by "loosening" it, so that its difficulties are dissolved—loosened away. The same thing happens when you dissolve sugar in water—quite literally: the bonds that link the sugar molecules into crystals are loosened, so that they can move freely through the fluid. And a dissolute person, of course, is one who has loosed himself from the constraints of morality—a loose fellow, in fact.

distaff. Literally, a stick with a bundle of flax or wool on it, from which the fibers were drawn out and twisted (spun) into thread. Hand-spinning has probably been "woman's work" ever since it was invented some 8,000 years ago: it's a job you can do at your own pace, while keeping an eye on the baby. And throughout most of human history and prehistory, women *had* to tend the babies, because only women could feed them. People still occasionally speak of the "distaff [female] side" of a family, but the phrase is almost as obsolete as the distaff itself.

dive (noun). On land, though not in the water, a dive is a low drinking place. Originally it was literally low as well—located in a cellar, into which thirsty patrons would "dive."

dog days. Sirius, the "Dog Star" (it's part of the constellation Canis Major, the Greater Dog) is the brightest star in the heavens. It was also, from ancient times, a sign of important events—though partly by coincidence. It happened that in Egypt the annual flood of the Nile, on which Egyptian agriculture depended, began in early July—just about the time when Sirius rose in the east just before the sun. By watching for this "heliacal rising," the Egyptian priests could "predict" the flood, enabling the peasants to prepare for it—and fortifying their own prestige.

To the Romans, the dog days were the uncomfortably hot days of July and August. According to some accounts, they believed that the weather was caused by the combined "heat" of Sirius and the sun, but I doubt they were that naive: Sirius was (and is) most prominent in the sky during the fall and winter—not notably hot seasons, even in Italy.

Due to the phenomenon called the precession of the equinoxes, the "Dog Days" have lost their connection with the Dog Star, whose heliacal rising now occurs in late August, not early July. But the expression is still current, as in a famous film about a couple of tragicomic bank robbers—*Dog Day Afternoon.*

dog and pony show. In circus lingo "dog and pony show" is a rather contemptuous term for a small circus—one with no acrobats or wild beasts but supposedly only dogs and ponies doing tricks. The phrase is sometimes used outside the circus world to mean an equally unimportant "circus"—a symposium in which there is much talk about very little, or an advertising "presentation" designed mainly to impress the client.

dog in the manger. Another of Aesop's contributions to the language; his fable concerned a dog who lay in an ox's manger, preventing the animal from eating the hay—which, of course, the dog itself couldn't eat. In the words of a fourteenth-century English poet, which I've translated rather freely:

> Though it is not the way of dogs
> To feed on hay, he would prevent
> The ox that came into the barn
> From eating what *he* did not want.

Whence the human dog in the manger, who operates on the principle of "I don't want it but you can't have it."

dogooder. Literally, someone who wants to do good to others, but actually an unpleasant epithet. It seems to involve two ideas: first, that trying to "do good" (especially for poor people) is unrealistic—meaning, usually, that the speaker simply dislikes the idea—and, second, that dogooders are more concerned with feeling virtuous than with doing good.

Some people certainly do good mainly to feel good, but personally I don't find that bothersome: if someone wants to do me some good, (s)he can feel as virtuous as (s)he likes. I've sometimes wondered, too: if it's bad to be a dogooder, is it good to be a "dobadder"? Compare **bleeding heart**.

doldrums, in the. The original "doldrum" was a dull or sluggish person, but sailors soon used "in the doldrums" to describe the state of a ship "almost becalmed . . . her sails flapping about in every direction with the eddying winds" (Marryat). Which pretty well sums up the situation of someone whose life or career is in the doldrums. See also **backing and filling**.

done to a turn. When houshold ovens were a lot less common than they now are, meats were typically roasted on a sort of rotisserie—a spit turned in front of an open fire. Some spits were even connected to a sort of **treadmill**, run by small dogs—turnspits—trained for the purpose. And when the roast had turned exactly long enough, it was done perfectly—to a turn.

donnybrook. Donnybrook was (and is) a suburb of Dublin once famous for its annual fairs—which in legend, at least, invariably ended in a free-for-all. The Donnybrook Fair is long gone, but political—or even scholarly—meetings still sometimes end in donnybrooks.

double cross. Since the early nineteenth century, "cross" or "the cross" has meant dishonest, as opposed to **on the square**. If one "cross cove" (crook) crossed another, it was obviously a double cross.

double in brass. Theater and dance-band musicians have long used "double" to mean "play two different intruments" (not simultaneously, of course): a musician who "doubled in brass" was a string or woodwind player who could also play the cornet, trumpet or trombone. Nonmusicians broadened the phrase to mean doing—or trying to do—two different jobs. I spend most of my working time writing books, but also double in brass as a lecturer and medical editor.

draconian, draconic. Around 620 B.C., the Athenian lawmaker Drakon introduced what was said to have been the first written code of laws in Greece. A later Greek writer described it as "written in blood": practically every crime was punishable by death. Within a generation or so the code was much softened, by Solon, but nearly twenty-five centuries later we still speak of draconic or draconian legislation or government.

dragoon. Originally, a sort of carbine which, like the legendary dragon, "breathed fire"; then, mounted soldiers armed with the weapon. Louis XIV of France used such troops in persecutions *(dragonnades)* of his Protestant subjects; English Protestants denounced him for dragooning their co-religionists. If someone's dragooning you, they may not be breathing fire but are unquestionably coercing you.

draw a bead on. The bead in question was the one on the front sight of the frontiersman's rifle, and to draw a bead was, obviously, to set one's sights on, literally or figuratively. Nowadays we're more likely to say **zero in on**.

Draw it mild! What you might say to an English pub-keeper if you wanted a mug of "mild" ale—but more often, what you might say to an English friend if (s)he's spinning a tale a bit stronger than the truth.

draw the long bow. An uncommon metaphor nowadays; few of us use bows and arrows. Medieval bowmen, like modern sharpshooters (and fishermen in all ages), went in for tall tales about their feats, often involving the bending (drawing) of a prodigiously long and powerful bow.

drop of a hat, at the. In *Life on the Mississippi,* Mark Twain described a quarrel between two vocally aggressive raftsmen, one of whom finally threw down his hat as a way of challenging the other. As it turned out, neither one was ready to fight at the drop of that or any other hat; they talked a lot tougher than they acted.

ducks and drakes. Literally, a game common in Britain and (though not under that name) in the U. S.: skipping flat stones over water. If you read that someone "played ducks and drakes" with his money, just imagine him with a handful of silver dollars or 50p coins, skipping them over the surface of a pond.

dunce. The fourteenth-century philosopher Duns Scotus was anything but a dunce, but one of the most brilliant scholars of his time. A couple of centuries later, however, he came under attack from disciples of the new, humanistic learning, who denounced his ideas as silly hair-splitting—and his remaining adherents as Dunses.

duplicity. Latin *plicare,* fold (the two words are related, though they don't look it) has given us many English words, some of them metaphors (see **complicated**). A duplicated document is, of course, literally two-fold; a duplicitous person is figuratively so: (s)he is two-faced, a double-dealer or, in English slang, a twicer.

Dutch courage/treat. Long wars, like other major social events, leave their traces in language—often as expressions imputing despicable traits to the enemy. Well before the Christian Era, the Punic Wars produced both "Punic [Carthaginian] faith" and, on the Carthaginian side, "Roman faith," both meaning **duplicity**. Five centuries of perennial conflict between Britain and France begot to take *French leave* (go AWOL), whose French equivalent is *filer à l'Anglais*—"go traveling English style." And "French" still refers to various unspeakable practices and unnatural acts.

Though the Anglo-Dutch wars of the seventeenth century lasted only a generation, they produced a specially rich crop of national insults. "Dutch courage" was poured out of a bottle—probably of Dutch *genever* (gin), since "genever courage" meant the same thing. (Wherever their courage came from, the Dutch had plenty of it; they beat the English several times.) A "Dutch treat," with everyone paying their own way, is not much of a treat and a "Dutch bargain," not much of a bargain. Less common are "Dutch comfort" (well, things could be worse) and "Dutch feast" (where the host gets drunk before the guests), ending in the boozy uproar called a "Dutch concert."

Dutch uncle, like a. Unlike the last group of expressions, this one comes not from the Dutch of Holland but from the Pennsylvania "Dutch" (actually, Germans—*Deutch*). They were and are deeply religious, and correspondingly strict with their kids; presumably a Dutch uncle would be even stricter with a niece or nephew. But the expression has softened over the years: nowadays, to talk to someone like a Dutch uncle means little more than to give them a sharp—and much needed—talking to.

dyed in the wool. Dying something "in the wool"—i.e., before the wool is spun and woven into cloth—yields, or once yielded, a much more permanent color. If someone is a "dyed-in-the-wool" conservative (I never heard of a dyed-in-the-wool radical), his opinions are ingrained and fixed, impervious to fading—and, quite possibly, to reason.

earmark(s). For centuries, British and American farmers identi- **E** fied their livestock by notching their ears in distinctive patterns. Earmarking of this sort was still current in Mark Twain's day: one of his villains seeks to revenge himself on a woman by notching her ears "like a sow." Today we earmark money for some special purpose, and say that someone "has the earmarks" of a crook or whatever.

easel. The beast of burden known as the ass (in Dutch, *ezel*) was considered a model of patience if not intelligence. The Dutch painter's *ezel* bore its burden—a stretched canvas or wooden panel—even more patiently.

eat crow. Various elaborate, circumstantial and not very plausible tales have been adduced to explain this metaphor. I'm more inclined to cite the simple fact that a crow will yield little meat, and tough to boot; it's something you eat only under dire compulsion. Frontiersmen may have, as some say, hazed tenderfeet by making them literally eat crow while the rest of the company dined on more savory game—but evidence is there none.

eating/living high on the hog. The lower parts of a hog—pig's feet, pig's knuckles and sow belly—can be tasty but aren't very meaty. If you're living high on the hog, you're dining luxuriously on the "high" cuts: ham, loin or shoulder.

eavesdrop. In medieval times, houses seldom had gutters to carry off rainwater. Instead, they were built with wide eaves to carry the dripping water (the eavesdrip or eavesdrop) well clear of the walls, thereby protecting their mud or clay surfaces. (An ancient custom forbade building a house less than two feet from a neighbor's boundary, lest his land be damaged by the eavesdrop.) Eavesdroppers, then, stood under the eaves, an excellent place to hear what people were saying inside the house.

ebullient. From Latin *bullire,* boil; an ebullient person is bubbling over with high spirits.

egregious. Literally, "out of the flock" (Latin *ex gregis*), and thus outstanding. For nearly three centuries, it could mean either outstandingly good ("an egregious artificer in wood") or outstandingly bad ("egregious impudence"). But for the last hundred years or so it has meant *only* the latter—perhaps, as the late Margaret Schlauch roguishly suggested, because an English gentleman was not supposed to stand out from the flock.

eight ball, behind the. From one version of the American game of pool (something like British snooker). In "Chicago" pool, the object is to pocket all fifteen balls, in sequence, *except* the eight ball; if that is pocketed or even touched, the shooter loses his turn. An unskillful player may leave himself behind the eight ball: that is, with the eight ball between him and the next ball to be pocketed. If you're behind the eight ball, you are, as the English say, "snookered."

emancipation. In ancient Rome, a purchase was not considered complete without the *mancipatio:* physically taking hold of the object—or person—purchased. (A similar custom in medieval England involved giving someone a piece of turf from the land he had purchased or been endowed with; he was then "seized" of the land.)

A Roman father "owned" his children, having the power of life or death over them. However, when a son came of age he could be formally released from his father's authority by the *emancipatio*—literally, letting out of one's hand: the father would formally take his son's hand and then release it. Much later, Lincoln's Emancipation Proclamation let the slaves out of their masters' hands—though not permanently out of their clutches.

equivocate, equivocal. Literally, to speak with two voices (Latin *equus vocare*). Someone who equivocates is speaking in two voices—out of both sides of his mouth, in fact ("White man speak with forked tongue!"); an equivocal statement is phrased—usually on purpose—to mean, or imply, two contradictory things.

escape, escapade. This takes us back to the bad old days of the declining Roman Empire, when law and order were in short supply. Literally, *excappare* meant to slip out of one's cloak (cape); one imagines a traveler on a dark road, feeling the clutch of a robber on his shoulder, slipping out of his cloak and—escaping. We find the same idea of flight in "escapade"—a flighty piece of conduct.

euchre (verb). The game of euchre (a variety of whist) is little played nowadays, but in the Old West was second only to poker in popularity. Its rules provided that a player who failed to take at least three tricks was "euchred," with the opponents getting a bonus in points. Just a few high cards could make the difference between winning and being euchred, so that skillful sharpers with a few aces up their sleeve could easily euchre suckers out of their money.

An unforgettable euchre game was recounted by the writer Bret Harte. The scene was Gold Rush California; the players, "Truthful James," Bill Nye and Ah Sin, the "heathen Chinee." Sin claimed he didn't understand the game, and accordingly, said James, "the cards they was stocked in a way that I grieve/And my feelings was shocked by the state of Nye's sleeve"—which was full of high cards. Yet the "heathen" won pot after pot. Finally Nye exclaimed: "We are ruined by Chinese cheap labor!" Grabbing Ah Sin, he found even more cards concealed in *his* long sleeves—no less than twenty-four packs, "Which is putting it strong, yet I state but the facts." Ah Sin made no profit from out-euchring the two crooks; you might say he didn't have a **Chinaman's chance**.

expedite—see **impede**.

explode. Roman audiences who didn't care for an actor's performance would *explodere* him: clap and hiss so loudly that he had to go off-stage. "Explode" still means to go off, with a loud noise.

extravagant. Originally, to wander (Latin *vagare*) outside the usual path; later, to wander outside the bounds of reason—which applies whether you're talking about an extravagant statement or extravagant spending.

F *c* **fabian.** When the great Carthagenian general Hannibal invaded Italy during the Second Punic War (218–201 B.C.), he beat the Romans time after time. The climax came at Cannae, where he

succeeded in encircling an entire Roman army and destroying it
almost to the last man. But Rome raised another army, with
Quintus Fabius Maximus in command. Recognizing that another
lost battle would mean total defeat, Fabius engaged in what we'd
call guerilla warfare: breaking his army up into small detachments,
he harassed Hannibal's supply lines and foraging parties, while
avoiding the main Carthagenian force.

Some Romans sneered at these "cowardly" goings on, and
nicknamed Fabius "Cunctator" (the Delayer). But he persisted,
and eventually his strategy paid off, albeit with some help from
the Carthagenian home front, where Hannibal's political enemies
dragged their feet on sending reinforcements and supplies. At
last, Hannibal was forced to leave Italy; Fabius had won one of the
decisive "battles" of history.

During the nineteenth century, English writers began using
"fabian" to mean any strategy—in war or politics—which avoided
all-out confrontation in favor of continual pressure against an
opponent. The term acquired even wider currency with the forma-
tion of the Fabian Society in 1889. This group of social reformers,
led by Sidney and Beatrice Webb, explicitly rejected the social
revolution urged by other leftists in favor of slow, piecemeal
reform.

The Fabians' policy paid off, though even more slowly than that
of the original Fabius: "victory"—a major improvement in the
conditions of the average Britisher—took nearly sixty years. And
it was still far short of total victory: Britain's economy is still being
managed (or mismanaged) by much the same sort of people who
were running it a century ago.

face the music. The explanations devised for this common
phrase range from a nervous singer who must literally face the
music (orchestra) below the footlights, to a cavalryman being
"drummed out" of his regiment, who supposedly was set backward on his horse so that he would face the music of the drums
as the animal trotted away. All are ingenious—and none are really
convincing.

I suspect the true explanation is much simpler: "music"—

pleasant sounds—has long been used ironically to mean highly unpleasant ones, especially the military "music" of enemy fire. The same irony would apply to a loud-voiced reprimand from a parent, mate or boss—a kind of "music" we all have to face from time to time.

fag(got). One of the most obscure metaphors—if indeed it is one—in English. The original sense of "fag(g)ot" was a bundle of sticks. But since Elizabethan times the word (if it's the same one) has also been a term of abuse for a woman; Joyce's *Ulysses* has "That old faggot Mrs. Riordan." It's not hard to see how this word was transferred from women to womanish men—but how did it get applied to women in the first place?

A competing theory assumes that the original homosexual term was "fag," not "faggot," referring to the practice in English "public" (private) schools of having younger boys act as fags (servants) to older ones; sometimes they supplied sexual as well as menial services. The problem with this theory is that both terms were first used among American hobos and similar types, who would hardly have known either the customs or the vocabulary of upper-class English schoolboys.

Whatever their source, "faggot" and "fag" now have highly unpleasant overtones. Since I believe that what other people do in bed is none of my business, I avoid both terms.

faint-hearted. From the ancient theory that the heart is the seat of the emotions (see *cordial*); more specifically, of courage. Faint-hearted people in a dangerous situation don't put their hearts into dealing with it; that is, they have no heart for it.

fair game. A hunter's term, the "game" being the animal or bird being hunted. When someone is fair game, it's open season for people to take potshots at them.

fall guy. By one account, the original fall guy was a wrestler who deliberately "took a fall"—as commercial ("exhibition") wrestlers are still doing. Well, maybe. In British criminal slang, "fall" has meant "be arrested" since the 1880s (it derives from the much earlier figurative sense, a descent from moral elevation, as in "Adam's fall"). A fall guy, then, was someone paid or framed to "fall" for a crime; as Sam Spade explained it to the Fat Man at the end of *The Maltese Falcon*, "he's not a fall guy unless he's a **cinch** to take the fall." The modern fall guy takes the blame or "carries the can" for any kind of misconduct or blunder.

false colors. To sail under false colors—under some other flag than one's own—was long considered a legitimate trick in naval warfare, so long as you *showed your true colors* a few seconds before opening fire. This sounds to me like typical military logic: it's O.K. to kill somebody, so long as you do it "honorably." I doubt that it makes much difference to the victims. Sailing under false colors is now deemed dishonorable; when someone shows his true colors, he reveals himself as the enemy he always was.

fanatic. Latin *fanum* meant "temple," and in some Roman temples, priests would be overcome with religious frenzy to the point of mutilating themselves. Modern religious and political fanatics are equally frenzied, but generally do more damage to other people than to themselves.

fast shuffle. Cards that are slightly sticky, from being played with, tend to cling together; unless they're very carefully shuffled, certain sequences will crop up time after time. Unscrupulous players take advantage of this fact and give the cards a fast shuffle, so as to disturb their sequence as little as possible. Sharpers in other fields of endeavor do much the same thing; in either case, sew up your pockets.

fate. Originally, an altogether neutral term, from Latin *fatum,* "(what is) said"—hence, an oracle or prophecy. But even in Roman times the word acquired the more sinister sense of calamity or even death—perhaps because the latter is, after all, the ultimate fate of us all. From the Victorians we get the "fate worse than death" suffered by many innocent heroines seduced by villains. Personally, I think death is worse.

fat's in the fire, the. Any cook who's ever spilled liquid fat or cooking oil into an open flame knows this one: the fat itself is done for—and unless you move fast, the house may be too.

feather in one's cap, a. Originally the feather was the mark of a fool, perhaps playing on the idea of "feather-brained." Its later sense, a mark of honor, may have been influenced by the custom of some Native American tribes, in which warriors who performed some daring deed were entitled to wear an eagle feather in their headbands. See **coup.**

featherbedding. Few of us have ever slept in a feather bed—a thick, soft mattress stuffed with feathers, and thus a cozy place to be in chilly weather. Legend has it that workers on the Rock Island railroad once complained to their boss that the bunks in the cabooses were too hard. Since *he* didn't have to sleep on the bunks, he snapped, "Whaddya want, featherbeds?"

Be that as it may, the word for sixty-odd years has meant the practice of creating soft, cozy jobs, requiring little or no work. But only, it seems, if the jobs are created in response to union pressure: if a boss contrives a soft job for his brother-in-law, that's not featherbedding but **nepotism.** Some say the jobs are created merely to let the union keep on collecting dues from its members, but they must be people who've never been unemployed. "Featherbeds" are created to keep union members working—which is one of the reasons people pay union dues.

federal case. Civil cases in the U.S. federal courts are usually more important than those in state or local courts, because they involve larger sums of money. And both civil and criminal federal cases are usually harder to fix. So if someone insults or injures you in a minor way—don't make a federal case of it.

feeling one's oats. To a horse, oats are a high-energy food, compared with the grass or hay it mainly feeds on. A horse that's just had a good feed of oats is full of pep and maybe a bit obstreperous; so are you, if you're feeling your oats.

feet of clay. As many readers will know or suspect, a Biblical metaphor. It comes from a dream of the Babylonian king Nebuchadnezzar, which was interpreted by the Jewish prophet Daniel. The king had dreamed of a mighty statue with a head of gold, a breast and arms of silver, a belly and thighs of bronze—but feet of iron and clay. And a great stone "smote the image on its feet," so that the entire statue came crashing down.

We need not go into Daniel's interpretation of the dream, which makes little sense unless you know a good deal about politics in the ancient Near East (interested readers will find the details in Daniel ii, 36–46). What stuck in people's minds was the noble image based on insecure foundations, which inevitably brought it down.

The metaphor has been applied to many public figures who, like Humpty Dumpty, had a great fall. But note that it properly means only people of real nobility brought down by some tragic flaw, as Shakespeare's Caesar was toppled by his ambition. I would not, for example, describe Richard Nixon as having feet of clay. Like Caesar, he was able, hard-working and ambitious, but to call him noble strains credulity: the "clay" in him—total unscrupulousness—was not just in his feet but in his heart.

fiasco. In Italian, it means "flask" or "bottle," but *far fiasco* ("make a bottle") was theatrical slang for "make a mess" (of a performance), perhaps from the mess caused by an actor dropping a wine bottle on stage. Certainly a smashed *fiasco,* with wine splattered over stage, performers and even the front rows of the audience, is a fine image for such fiascos as the Bay of Pigs or Contragate.

fiat money. In Latin, *fiat* means "let it be done"—hence, in English, a decree. Fiat money is what you get when the government decrees that a piece of paper is money, without backing it with gold or silver. Such money is often assumed to have little purchasing power, like the **Continental** currency of the American Revolution, but in fact nearly all modern money, including the coins and bills you have in your pocket, is fiat. How much it's worth depends on how prudently the government that prints it conducts its, and the nation's, affairs.

fiend. In Old English, *feond* was an enemy; then, the ultimate Enemy (the literal meaning of "Satan"); eventually, anyone acting in a satanic, "fiendish" or even obsessed manner—there are crossword puzzle fiends as well as sex fiends.

fifth column(ist). In 1936, when the fascist and mercenary troops of General Franco were advancing on Madrid in four columns, one of his generals boasted that there was also a fifth column inside the city—sympathizers who would rise up when the fascists approached. There were certainly Franco sympathizers in Madrid, but their military impact was minimal: the Spanish government lost mainly because it was outnumbered (thanks to troops supplied by Mussolini) and outgunned (thanks to munitions, planes and pilots supplied by Hitler, and the British-French-U.S. embargo, which prevented it from buying arms).

The supposed "fifth column" did, however, supply a perfect excuse for groups on the Republican side (notably, the Communist minority) who wanted to suppress their political enemies—which they promptly did, as "fifth columnists." Some very likely were, but all were people the Communists preferred to see in jail or dead.

A few years later, it was the French generals who needed an excuse. When the Nazi blitz defeated France in a few weeks, the French naturally wanted to know how come; the generals blamed the Nazis' fifth column. It was largely imaginary: the real culprits were the generals themselves, who (as any military historian will tell you) had fouled up in every conceivable way, in preparing for, planning and fighting the war. "Fifth column(ist)" isn't much used these days, but if you hear it, the odds are that the speaker is setting up an excuse for his or her own misfeasance or malfeasance.

filch. In sixteenth-century thieves' slang, a filch was a rod with a hook on one end, with which a petty thief could "hook" valuables from a merchant's stall. Petty thieves are still at it, but their filching now operates on the principle that hands were made before hooks.

file (papers). From Latin *filum,* thread (also the root of "filament"). Medieval bureaucrats filed papers by threading them on a length of string.

filibuster. A word with a long and disgraceful history. It started life as the Dutch *vrijbuiter,* who became the English freebooter (his "booting" had nothing to do with boots but a lot to do with booty). The Dutch word also passed into French and thence into Spanish, as *filibustero,* with much the same meaning.

In the 1850s, the term was transferred to such adventurers as William Walker, who (as recounted in a recent motion picture) mounted expeditions to bring the blessings of democracy to Mexico and Nicaragua—bloodily, and (it was hoped) profitably for his backers, who included the railroad magnate Cornelius Vanderbilt. Before the film, few Americans north of the border had ever heard of Walker; Nicaraguans have never forgotten him.

Almost immediately the term was readopted into American English, as "filibuster"—meaning to conduct a similar "freebooting" operation against a legislative majority, by using obstructive tactics and interminable oratory. These filibusters are less common than they once were, but the William Walker variety has been revived in Nicaragua.

fill the bill. Probably from a theatrical bill (poster); a star actor "filled the bill" when his or her name—in enormous type—was the only one that appeared.

fine fettle, in. The original Old English *fetel* was a belt or strap. Later, to "fettle" something meant to figuratively belt it up—put it in order. "In fine fettle," then, is equivalent to "well-belted"— as we'd say nowadays, really together.

fink. Back in 1926, some amateur etymologist speculated that this was a distortion of "Pink"—an operative of the Pinkerton detective agency, notorious for its strike-breaking activities. It took sixty years for the right explanation to break into print.

The fact is that "fink" originally meant (and among crooks still means), not a strikebreaker but an informer, who "sings" to the cops or the boss. The word comes from German-Yiddish *Fink* (finch), a family of songbirds. Most melodious of the finches is the canary—which is also another word for "fink."

fire (dismiss). If you fire a gun, you discharge it; if you fire someone, you discharge them—with almost the speed of a gunshot.

first water, of the. The best diamonds are completely colorless—water-white—and, of course, flawless; the gems were once classified as "first water," "second water" and so on. Something that is of the first water may not be as valuable as a first-water diamond, but is the best of its kind.

fish or cut bait. Modern commercial fishermen use nets, but even a century ago some of them also used hooks, baited with cut-up bits of squid, "trash" fish or pork rind. Aboard a fishing schooner, there was no room for idlers: you either fished or cut bait.

fishwife—see **billingsgate**

fit as a fiddle. A violin that's been properly strung and tuned is "fit as a fiddle"—ready for any piece the fiddler cares to play.

flag something down. Most of us flag down a cab from time to time, but not with a flag. The term comes from the actual flag once used to signal a train to stop—sometimes in an emergency, but often at a "flag stop": a station where even slow trains stopped only on signal.

flash in the pan. Here we must get a bit technical. The old-fashioned muzzle-loading musket or pistol was cumberously charged with powder, wadding and bullet; it then had to be primed. That is, a small quantity of fine powder was poured into the pan—a concave piece of steel adjacent to a small hole at the butt end of the barrel.

When the piece was cocked and the trigger pulled, a flint would snap down, striking a spark from a steel plate above the pan; the spark set off the priming powder, which in turn set off the powder in the barrel. If, however, the main powder charge had gotten damp, or the spark for some reason failed to reach it, all you got was a showy but useless flash in the pan. See also **half-cocked**.

flatfooted. A football player is expected to be on his toes—literally and figuratively—while a play is in progress; that is, ready to move in any direction. If he isn't on his toes, he may be caught flatfooted.

flea in one's ear. I've never had a flea in my ear, but am sure it would be as unpleasant as it clearly is to my cat, on the rare occasions when she gets one. If someone puts a flea in your ear, the brusque rebuke it refers to is probably even more unpleasant.

fly in the ointment. To us, an ointment is medicinal, but at one time it was more likely to be a perfumed cosmetic. Now picture a jar of delicately perfumed ointment with a large, buzzing fly stuck in it, and you have a perfect image for the not-so-hidden flaw—whatever is rotten in Denmark.

fly off the handle. Modern ax-heads are made so that they stay attached to the handle at all times. In the old days, however, the head of a vigorously wielded ax might literally fly off the handle, sometimes with disasterous results to bystanders. A person who flies off the handle can be equally dangerous.

fly the coop. The phrase may come either from a chicken escaping from its coop or a criminal escaping from the "coop." Either way, it means to depart hastily and unceremoniously.

forced draft—see **supercharged**.

fourflusher. At straight (five-card) stud poker, a hand with four cards of the same suit showing looks impressively like a flush (five of a suit)—a powerful hand. But if the down card is of a different suit, you have a worthless fourflush. A fourflusher, then, is someone with an impressive "front"—but worthless when it comes to a showdown. See also **ace in the hole**.

French leave—see **Dutch courage**.

fritter away. Fritters are, of course, a sort of pancake, usually containing cut-up bits of fruit, vegetables or meat, but also small bits of anything. If you fritter something away, you're dispersing or wasting it bit by bit.

Fritz, on the. Hans and Fritz, the Katzenjammer (literally, "headache") Kids of the old comic strip, had a talent for embroiling Der Captain and other innocent bystanders in messy and embarrassing situations—putting things on the Fritz (out of order), you might say. I don't know whether the expression actually derives from the comic strip, but nobody has come up with a better explanation.

full as a tick. The bloodsucking "insects" (actually, they're related to spiders) called ticks range from perhaps a quarter-inch long to the size of a pinhead—but that's before they've fed. If a tick fastens on to you unnoticed, it will bloat itself with blood to several times its normal size. So we sometimes say of someone who's consumed an improbable quantity of liquor that he's full as a tick.

funk(y). "Funk" originally meant thick tobacco smoke or any powerful stink, whence, we're told, the funky jazz that is both powerful and down-to-earth. I'm not really sure about this—but if you imagine a crowded bar or nightclub, whose funk combines tobacco smoke, cheap liquor and sweat, you'll have a pretty good idea of the ambience of funky music.

gadabout, gadfly. The "gad" in both expressions is akin to *G goad* (prod), and a gadfly was originally a stinging fly that goaded cattle into irritability—sometimes to the point of stampeding. Human gadflies can be equally annoying, but, unlike their insect equivalents, may serve a useful purpose: goading their more bovine fellows into thought or action. A gadabout is someone who moves erratically from place to place like a gadfly—or as if pursued by one.

gag (joke). A puzzling metaphor. It comes from the theater and means a joke, but originally not just a joke but one not in the script—as we'd say, an ad lib. Just possibly, this sense derived from another kind of gag: something thrust into someone's mouth to silence them. Perhaps some eighteenth-century player, victimized by a colleague's promiscuous ad libbing, may have complained that (s)he'd been "gagged."

gall (effrontery). Originally, a sore or blister, perhaps produced by some venomous substance; then, the mental soreness produced by a venomous tongue; finally, the unbelievable effrontery that induces a mixture of soreness and reluctant admiration at the possessor's chutzpah.

galluses. An all but obsolete word (you'll find it in *Huckleberry Finn*), meaning what Americans call suspenders and Britishers, braces. Like **derrick**, it's a bit of literal gallows humor: "gallus" is a variant of "gallows," and galluses suspend pants as the gallows suspends its, uh, client.

galvanize. The Italian scientist Luigi Galvani (1737–98) discovered how to produce electricity by chemical action—that is, he invented the battery. He also discovered that if an electric current was applied to the nerve of a dissected frog's leg, the limb would twitch spasmodically. If someone is galvanized, they react almost as if they'd received an electric shock.

"Galvanize" also means to coat with metal by means of a galvanic (electric) current. Ironically, however, the commonest "galvanized" material—iron or steel coated with zinc—is not produced galvanically: the object is simply dipped into molten zinc.

game not worth the candle. Before the invention of gas lighting, cards and other gambling games were often played by candlelight. High-stakes players finding themselves in what we'd call a penny-ante game might well complain that the game was simply not worth the (price of) the candle.

gantlet, the. For centuries, soldiers were sometimes punished by being forced to run the gantlet—that is, between two lines of their fellows, who would strike at them with sticks or knotted ropes; the experience was always painful and occasionally fatal. The modern author or performer forced to run the critics' gantlet will find the experience hardly less painful, though only to his or her self-esteem.

"Gantlet" is sometimes misspelled "gauntlet," which is a completely different word, meaning a heavy, over-the-wrist glove.

garble. Surprisingly, its original meaning (from Arabic *gharbala*) was to sift; hence, to purify. But by the seventeenth century it had come to mean "sifting" information maliciously—putting together selected bits to distort the meaning. Nowadays, the malice has dropped out, and the information is merely muddled.

gargantuan. In the first Book of *Gargantua and Pantagruel,* by the erudite, anti-clerical, bawdy and scatalogical—in short, *Rabelaisian*—French physician Francois Rabelais (?1494–1553), you can read of the birth, upbringing and "horrific" deeds of his eponymous giant. Even as an infant, Gargantua required the milk of seventeen thousand nine hundred thirteen cows, while the bulge of his codpiece, says Rabelais, was six feet long, and the rest of him in proportion. In every way, he was gargantuan—far bigger than life-size. And if you read of someone with a gargantuan appetite, just remember those herds upon herds of cows.

gauche—see **adroit**.

gerrymander. The practice of juggling the boundaries of legislative districts to maximize the strength of one's own party dates back to the early days of the American Republic. Around 1800, the political boss Elbridge Gerry presided over a notably biased redistricting of Massachusetts. An opponent, examining a map of one of the new districts and tracing its bizarrely twisting boundaries, muttered "It looks like a salamander!" "No," said another, "a Gerrymander!"

American politicos still gerrymander when they can. While writing this book, I happened to see a map of new electoral districts in the Boston area: four out of seven were gerrymandered (one was actually split into three pieces—one on the far side of Boston Harbor, one in Boston itself and the third several miles up the Charles river, in Cambridge). Both the word and the practice have also crossed the Atlantic to Britain.

get someone's goat. Nobody seems to know how this expression came to mean "annoy." My guess would be that it has to do with the he-goat's notorious irritability; if you get someone's goat, they may, like the animal, charge you and perhaps knock you down.

Another possibility, though a remote one, is suggested by the old image of the Devil, who had a goat's horns and cloven hooves. Perhaps getting someone's goat was equivalent to raising the devil in them.

get up on the wrong side of the bed. Like **adroit**, a slander on left-handed (or in this case, left-footed) people. Originally, it was "get out of bed the wrong way" or "on one's wrong side"— that is, with one's left foot first. This was supposed to foreshadow a bad day, and someone who inadvertently did it would naturally be in a bad mood.

ghost walks, the. The term—meaning payday—certainly originated in the theater, but after that you have the choice of several circumstantial stories. The ghost is usually the most famous specter in English drama, that of Hamlet's father. According to one account, the phrase refers to Horatio's suggestion that the ghost had returned to tell of hidden treasure—something that irregularly paid actors would have had much on their minds.

An even better story has Hamlet declaiming the line: "I will watch tonight; perchance 'twill walk again." *Ghost* (off-stage): "Not unless we get paid, it won't!" More prosaically, it's quite possible that in some small companies the manager doubled as the Ghost—a very short part—and would, hopefully, "walk" (hand out the pay envelopes) after the curtain was rung down.

ghost writer. Some literary craftsmen, like some ghosts, are invisible: they get paid (sometimes even well paid) for what they write, but the "author" on the title page gets the credit. In politics, "ghosting" has become routine: few political figures write their own speeches or public statements, even if they have the skill— which few do.

ginger up. An old phrase from the seamier side of horse-racing. Unscrupulous trainers would sometimes "ginger up" a horse by inserting a preparation of powdered ginger into the animal's rectum; the burning, stinging sensation would make it run faster. If you try to ginger someone up, that's what you're figuratively doing. The British "ginger group" has the same source: it means a small group of energetic militants that ginger up a larger political body.

give one's eyeteeth. The eyeteeth—the canines, just below the eyes (see **cut one's eyeteeth**)—are very deeply rooted; if you're willing to give them up for something, you must want it very badly indeed.

give someone a wide berth. The berth here is not the bunk that sailors sleep in, but a related maritime term meaning the area in which a ship anchors. In the bad old days of piracy and privateering, a predatory craft might take advantage of a dark night to send its crew in boats and seize some vessel anchored nearby. If you found yourself in harbor with a suspicious-looking ship, you made sure to anchor well away from her—give her a wide berth. Whence the wide berth we prudently give to predatory or suspicious-looking people.

go into a tailspin. If you like World War I flying movies, you've certainly seen a tailspin: a plane goes into an involuntary dive with the tail rotating (spinning) around the plane's axis. Unless the pilot was both skilled and quick, the tailspin would end in a crash; much the same can happen to people who go into a tailspin.

go the whole hog. Charles Funk, following a suggestion by the *OED*, explains the phrase by citing a verse by the English poet Cowper. I'm not convinced: the expression apparently originated in the U. S., and among people unlikely to have known the rather obscure poem in question.

A more likely (but unattested) origin is from an anecdote about an unenterprising thief who made off with only a ham when he could have taken the whole hog. Whatever its origin, going the whole hog is the opposite of unenterprising—or half-hearted.

go to pot. An animal that goes to pot is stewed up and eaten—finished, in fact. So is anything else that goes to pot.

go to seed. Gardeners know that if you don't harvest lettuce in time it will go to (form) seed, or "bolt," thereby becoming inedible; so will some other leafy crops. If you let a house or a business go to seed, you'll end up with something equally useless. And a person who's let himself go to seed looks—*seedy.*

go to the dogs. Somewhat the same sense as the last, but here the image is of bones tossed into the street for dogs to fight over. If a person goes to the dogs, (s)he may not be literally gnawed by curs but will likely end up in the street.

goad (verb). Originally (eighth century) a stick with a spike at one end, used to stimulate oxen to maximum effort; much later, to use such a stick, literally or figuratively. If somebody tries to goad you into something, make sure you don't react as automatically as the ox. See also **gadfly**.

goldbrick (noun and verb). A favorite trick of the old-time con-man was to peddle a goldbrick, resembling those found in bank vaults, but actually gold-plated lead. Supposedly it was stolen, meaning that the sucker could be induced to buy it "cheap."

The U.S. Army shifted the term to the human "goldbrick," whose conspicuous outer show of activity (goldbricking) is designed to dazzle the eyes of authority, thereby allowing him to goof off in comfort. Some years ago, I myself coined the phrase "goldbrick generality"—a rhetorical device, used by many writers on pop sociology and psychology, in which a glittering verbal surface conceals a leaden lack of substance.

goon. The immediate source of this rather muddled metaphor was a creature in the comic strip "Popeye"—monstrous looking but (as it turned out) quite aimiable if not over-bright, which is how the word is often used today. But a goon is also a thug—often part of a goon squad; I suspect this sense may have arisen from Arabic *ghoum* (fighter, thug). Certainly I've heard the word pronounced that way.

goose hangs high, the. There's no very good explanation of this one; the least implausible is that it started life as "the goose *honks* high"—that is, the weather is fair and the (migrating) geese are operating at height.

Gotham (New York City). The American writer Washington Irving was the first of many to take exception to the supposed know-it-all attitude of us New Yorkers. He christened them "Gothamites," after the legendary Three Wise Men of Gotham (an English town) who went to sea in a tub ("If the tub had been stronger, my tale had been longer").

In another version of the story, however, the Gothamites, facing the prospect of a visit from the king, played the fool deliberately, to avoid the heavy expense of entertaining him and his court. That is, they were foolish like a fox—which, I think, could be fairly said of many modern New Yorkers.

graft(er). No connection with the horticulturist's term for joining a shoot of one plant onto another; it comes from a nineteenth-century crooks' term meaning "to pick pockets"—which is pretty much what the grafting politico did and does to the taxpayers.

grain, against the. Carpenters, professional or amateur, know that the grain of a plank—the arrangement of fibers within it—almost never runs exactly parallel to the surface. If, then, you're smoothing the wood with a plane, you must go with the grain rather than against (or across) it, or end up with a rough, splintery surface. If something goes against your grain, it roughens your feelings—to the point where you may leave splinters in anyone who rubs up against you.

grain of salt, with a. Said to be a translation of Latin *cum grano salis,* but no classical writer is known to have used the phrase.

The most likely explanation is also the simplest: if you take someone's statement with a grain of salt, it evidently needs some
seasoning before you can swallow it.

grandstand (verb)—see **play to the gallery**.

grapevine, the. During the Civil War, the telegraph, a relatively
new invention, was extensively used to transmit both news and
military orders. In the Mississippi Valley, however, the troops
often moved through thinly settled country, where the nearest
thing to a telegraph wire was a wild grapevine. "News" circulating
in camp had therefore arrived on the "grapevine telegraph"—
eventually, just the grapevine. See also **poop**.

grass widow. Originally, an unmarried woman "widowed" by
her lover's desertion (especially if she was left with a child),
perhaps because she'd taken a roll in the grass or, as we'd say,
the hay. Nowadays it means a divorced woman, or merely one
whose husband is away. (A grass widower means a man in similar
circumstances; his traditional attitude is summed up in the old
catch-phrase, "My wife's gone to the country; hooray, hooray!")

graveled. Its older figurative sense (perplexed, confounded)
may derive from a ship that had been "graveled"—run hard
aground. Its more recent meaning rather sums up the feelings of
someone who has fallen onto a gravel-covered surface: both annoyed and sore.

gray eminence. A direct translation of French (and also English)
eminence grise, a phrase originally applied to Père Joseph, 1577–
1638, a grey-robed Capuchin friar who was the confidential agent
of Cardinal Richlieu, prime minister to Louis XIII of France.
Through confusion between Joseph and his master, both phrases
have come to mean the power behind the throne, which Richlieu
certainly was (he eventually became virtual dictator of France)—
and Joseph, equally certainly, was not.

grease someone's palm. No elaborate explanations needed here: "grease" has for over a century meant the bribe money that, like grease in machinery, makes things run smoothly.

greased lightning. A flash of lightning has long been a metaphor for anything fast or sudden ("quick as a flash"). And, since a greased wheel moves faster than an ungreased one, greased lightning moves even faster than ordinary lightning.

Greek to me. During the Middle Ages, as for centuries thereafter, any educated Englishman or -woman knew Latin, but only a minority also knew Greek. A major reason was that Greek uses its own alphabet, so that before even starting to learn the language you have to learn the letters. If something is Greek to you, you can't even begin to make sense of it.

The phrase itself comes from Shakespeare's *Julius Caesar,* where Casca, speaking of some side-remarks in Greek by the orator Cicero, says that "those who understood him smiled and shook their heads, but . . . it was Greek to me."

green-eyed monster, the. Another Shakespearian metaphor, this one from *Othello,* in which Iago hypocritically warns his master against jealousy, "the green-eyed monster which doth mock/The meat it feeds on." The "monster" he had in mind was the cat, often green-eyed, which "mocks"—plays **cat and mouse** with—its prey, as jealousy mocks its victims with alternating hope and despair before consuming them.

greenhorn. Immature fruits and young twigs are green; so, figuratively, are, immature people. A greenhorn may originally have meant a young ox with "green" (immature) horns; in the seventeenth century, it was transferred to new army recruits and soon to newcomers to any trade. In America around the turn of the century, it was applied to new immigrants—often by earlier immigrants only a year or two off the boat.

grenade. Soldiers, like other occupational groups, have always coined their own private (no pun intended) slang. Thus Roman troops called one type of catapult *onager* (wild ass), presumably because of the kick it could deliver to the enemy. Much later, Spanish soldiers transferred *granata* (pomegranate) to a hollow iron sphere, filled with gunpowder, that could be hurled at the enemy; it looked something like a pomegranate—but God help anyone who tried to eat it. The "British Grenadiers" of song and story were originally equipped with these weapons.

In World War I, Allied soldiers coined another fruity metaphor, christening the Mills bomb or grenade a "pineapple"—also from its shape. During the 1920s, the word was transferred to bombs of any sort used by gangsters. See also **hoist with his own petard**.

grit (courage). By some accounts, from the "grit" (pebbles) found in the craw of a chicken, which serves to grind up the grain the bird feeds on; a gamecock with insufficient grit would be ill-nourished and therefore a poor fighter. But the word may be merely a contraction of the obsolete phrase "clear grit"—though why this should have meant "courage" is anyone's guess.

groggy. For centuries, the British navy has provided its personnel with a daily ration of spirits—usually rum. Admiral Edward Vernon (1684–1757), noting that straight rum did not improve the battle-readiness of his men, ordered that in future it should be mixed half-and-half with water. Vernon's nickname was "Old Grog," because he favored a cloak of the coarse material called grogram; his watered-down beverage was promptly christened "grog." A groggy person looks or feels as if (s)he has overindulged in grog.

groove, in the; groovy. If the needle of a record player is not firmly in the groove of the record, the music sounds terrible. To jazz musicians of the thirties and forties, music—eventually, anything—that was "in the groove" was first-class. The phrase was soon contracted to "groovy," but both expressions are now out of fashion.

grueling. Gruel has for centuries meant a sort of thin soup made of oatmeal, often used to feed invalids—later (because of its cheapness), to feed prisoners. Whence, probably, the expression "give someone his gruel"—give him his deserts or punishment. A grueling contest or experience, then, is almost as punishing as a spell in jail, at hard labor.

gull (deceive). Here we have the choice of two equally plausible tales. A gull is not only the common sea-bird but also, in some parts of England, a young, unfledged bird, especially a gosling, and therefore a young, easily deceived person (compare **gunsel**). To gull someone is thus to make a gull of them.

But another "gull," akin to "gullet," meant to swallow or guzzle—whence, perhaps, the "gull" who was willing to swallow any sort of lie. On the historical evidence, either explanation is credible; indeed, both words may have been twisted together into a single crooked metaphor.

gung-ho. Originally (1930s), the motto of left-wing Chinese cooperative groups, meaning "work together." Lt. Col. (later, Gen.) Evans Carlson, USMC, like some other U.S. officers during World War II, admired Chinese leftists because they fought the Japanese vigorously, as the rightists, under Chiang Kai-Shek, seldom did.

As commander of the Marine "Raider" Batallion, operating behind the Japanese lines, Carlson emulated the cooperatives by organizing "gung ho" meetings at which problems could be threshed out and orders explained. Eventually, the men began calling themselves the Gung-Ho batallion. In time, the term spread throughout the armed forces, in the sense of energetic and zealous.

World War II was "the Good War." The Vietnam War, by contrast, was anything but good to many Americans, including some of the young men drafted to fight it. In their mouths, "gung-

ho" became an uncomplimentary description of the professional
soldiers ("lifers") who, as the draftees saw it, were all too eager
to mix it up with the enemy; you could get killed that way. In
short, it's good to be zealous, but bad to be overzealous—and the
difference between the two often depends on where you happen
to be sitting.

gunsel. In German and Yiddish, *Gansel* means "gosling," and
thus an inexperienced youth (compare **gull**). The word was
picked up around 1900 by U.S. hobos and crooks, but soon acquired the special sense of a youth accompanying an older man
as a sexual partner.

Enter now Dashiell Hammett, the first great writer of "tough-
guy" crime fiction. As a former professional detective, Hammett
had an unrivaled knowledge of cops-and-robbers lingo, which he
naturally used in his writings. But his sometimes uninhibited language led to collisions with strait-laced editors, like the one who
changed "get an erection" in the hardcover edition of *The Thin
Man* to "get excited" in the paperback.

Hammett revenged himself by throwing linguistic curves past
the editors. A notable one was his use of "gunsel" to describe
Wilmer, the undersized gunman employed by Casper Gutman,
"the Fat Man," in *The Maltese Falcon.* The editors, and nearly
everyone else, thought it was merely a fancy term for "gunman";
Hammett knew better and, chuckling to himself, had Sam Spade
snarl to Gutman "Keep that gunsel away from me!"

The ultimate joke, according to the writer and editor Ellery
Queen, came when life imitated art: real criminals began using
"gunsel" to mean—gunman. By such devious twists and turns do
some words acquire their meanings.

gyp. During the Middle Ages the Rom, a people of northern India,
began migrating into the Middle East and thence into Europe;
they reached England some time after 1450. In France, they had
been known as *Bohemiens,* from their supposed homeland in

Central Europe (see **bohemian**); the English, for some reason, thought they came from Egypt and called them Gypsians or Gypsies.

In England and elsewhere, the Rom had a thin time of it. Clannish, with their own customs and language (Romany), they were also "persons of no fixed abode," often with no visible means of support. Accordingly, they were classed with other "vagabonds" and "beggars" and encouraged to keep moving—the more so in that they were widely believed to support themselves by stealing pigs and poultry, and by what we'd now call confidence tricks, including "faking up" rundown horses to make them look saleable.

The accusation was not, I think, altogether unjust. As late as the 1930s, the writer Joseph Mitchell quoted an American Gypsy "king" (i.e., the head of one of their tribes) as saying that, "To a Gypsy, there's two kinds of property—lost, and not lost. Anything that ain't nailed down is lost." And I've been personally gypped by a gypsy who'd adapted his ancestors' skills in horse-faking to used-car-faking.

Were the Gypsies' thieving ways caused by their mistreatment by non-Gypsies, or vice versa? I'd guess it worked both ways. Impoverished, rootless people, of any nationality, easily take to crime—and, conversely, are almost automatically treated as criminals by more settled folk. And if you treat someone like a criminal, (s)he'll likely live up—or down—to your expectations. Whatever the source of the problem, it left a permanent record in our vocabulary.

hack writer. The original "hackney" was an ordinary riding **H** horse, as opposed to a draft horse or war horse. But from the fourteenth century on, it also meant a horse kept for hire. Whence the "hackney" or "hack" writer, who hires out to write anything that will pay. Naturally (s)he produces "hack work," notable more for its quantity than its quality. Still, the hack in his or her garret, like the hackney in its stable, works hard for an often meager living.

hair of the dog that bit one. An old legend—endorsed by many physicians as recently as the 1700s—held that the bite of a mad dog could be cured by binding some of the animal's hair to the wound. Doubtless the treatment often "worked," because the dog was only mad (angry), not mad (rabid).

The figurative sense dates from the sixteenth century, when a sufferer from hangover is made to say, "I pray thee, let me and my fellow have/ A hair of the dog that bit us last night,/ And bitten were we both, to the brain aright." Today, doctors have rejected both "hair of the dog" theories; the best cure for the "morning after," they say, is not to get bitten the night before.

hairy. When a cat confronts another cat, or a dog, the hair on its back and tail will often fluff up; the trait may originally have evolved to make the threatened animal look more formidable. I know of no evidence that our species possesses such a trait, but some people claim that in some situations their hair *feels* as if it were standing on end—in short, a hair-raising or hairy experience. See also **horrible**.

The word is also occasionally used in a very different sense: a hairy joke is one so old it has whiskers on it.

halcyon. In Greek legend, the *halkyon* (kingfisher) was said to make its nest and brood its eggs on the ocean around the winter solstice, during a spell of calm, cloudless weather. The myth is long gone—kingfishers, like other birds, breed on land—but we still speak of "halcyon days" or "halcyon weather."

half-cocked. The flintlock pistol or musket, after being loaded and primed (see **flash in the pan**), had to be cocked, by drawing back the part of the lock holding the flint until it was caught by a spring, which was released by pulling the trigger. Some models, as a supposed safety feature, could be placed on half-cock: the flint was pulled part-way back, locking the trigger.

The purpose of this mechanism is puzzling: surely the safest way of handling a loaded weapon is not to cock it at all! Hardly less puzzling is the metaphorical sense; does "go off half-cocked" mean that the half-cocked piece, because of some defect, went off anyway and hit the wrong target, or did it perhaps refer to an over-excited shooter, pulling away at the half-cocked (locked) trigger with no result? Either way, the phrase means to start something without adequate preparation, producing a **fiasco**.

ham. According to theatrical legend, actors of the lowest and worst-paid grade removed their makeup with lard (ham-fat) instead of cold-cream; one of them is said to have been memorialized in a nineteenth-century song, "The Ham-Fat Man." Well, maybe; "ham" has long been short for "ham-handed" or "ham-fisted"—clumsy. The radio "ham" was originally a student operator—hence, a ham-handed one—but nowadays is any amateur operator, who may be as expert as any professional.

hand over fist. A sailor seeking to pull in a long rope quickly didn't just yank at it but went at it hand over hand—first one hand, then the other. Soon mariners began speaking of one ship overtaking another "hand over hand," as if the pursuing vessel was hauling itself forward with a rope. Some unknown Yankee wit of the early nineteenth century then transferred the phrase to making money fast, meanwhile changing it to "hand over fist"; perhaps the idea was that hauling in the dough requires a tight fist as well as busy hands.

handwriting on the wall. The fifth chapter of the Book of Daniel tells of the great feast held by Belshazzar, king of Babylon, for his nobles, wives and concubines. Their scandalous activities included drinking from the sacred vessels stolen from the Temple in Jerusalem, and praising their heathen idols "of gold and silver, bronze, iron, wood and stone." But suddenly, "the fingers of a man's hand appeared and wrote on the plaster of the wall of the king's palace" the words MENE, MENE, TEKEL, PARSIN.

None of the king's wise men could interpret the mysterious words. Belshazzar called in Daniel, who declared they meant that the king had been "weighed in the balance [scales] and found wanting," and that his kingdom would be divided between the Medes and the Persians. Rather surprisingly—few kings or governments welcome bearers of bad news—Belshazzar dressed Daniel in costly garments and appointed him number three man in the kingdom. Too late: that very night the invaders marched in and the king was slain.

How much of this actually happened is anyone's guess. The Jews of that day were a small nation who were repeatedly being clobbered by one or another of the powerful kingdoms and empires that surrounded them. If one enemy clobbered another for a change, they were naturally delighted—and proclaimed that they knew all the time it was going to happen. Anyway, when you read that the writing is on the wall for someone (or something), you can be sure that they (or it), like Belshazzar, are for it.

hang fire. As we've already seen, an improperly loaded or handled firearm might go off **half-cocked**, or produce merely a **flash in the pan**. Under certain circumstances, it would do something worse: hang fire, with the priming continuing to sputter away without setting off the piece. This was dangerous: the gun was still loaded, and might go off at any time. Nowadays the phrase is less ominous: something that's "hanging fire" may or may not "go off" (come to fruition), but is unlikely to injure anyone.

hang out one's shingle. The modern doctor or lawyer usually has a shiny brass plate at the entrance to his office. On the frontier, fancy nameplates were expensive and hard to come by; accordingly, the young professional setting up in practice would have his name painted on a shingle and hang it out as a sign he was open for business.

harbinger. The original harbinger was simply an innkeeper (from French *auberge,* inn). Later, he was the advance man for an army or royal party, pushing ahead to the next town or castle to arrange lodgings. Eventually, a harbinger became anyone or anything that foretells the arrival of something. In England, the cuckoo (see **cuckold**) is the harbinger of spring, which, according to legend, begins when "the old woman lets the cuckoo out of the basket"; in eastern North America, the robin is the advance man.

harrowing. In a freshly plowed field, the surface is deeply furrowed and full of dense clods. To prepare it for sowing, it must then be smoothed with a harrow. The traditional harrow was a heavy wooden frame set with dozens of iron teeth; if you can imagine having such a frame hauled over you, you'll have a pretty good idea of what a harrowing experience is. As Kipling once wrote:

> The toad beneath the harrow knows
> Exactly where each tooth-point goes;
> The butterfly upon the road
> Preaches contentment to that toad.

hassock. Originally, a firm clump of matted grass—the tuffet that Little Miss Muffet sat on. Whence the firm cushions, sometimes stuffed with straw or hay, that we sit on or (in church) kneel on.

hat trick, the. In the game of cricket, the bowler (equivalent to the pitcher in baseball) seeks to "take wickets" from the batters—something that I won't try to explain to American readers. Suffice it to say that a bowler who takes three wickets with three successive balls has done something very remarkable, equivalent to a "perfect game" (no runs, no hits) in baseball.

A bowler who performed this extraordinary feat was (and for all I know, still is) rewarded with a new hat—i.e., he's done the hat trick. The phrase has since been used to describe a hockey player who scores three goals in one game, or a jockey who wins three successive races. In 1986, when my third book in a row was picked as a Book-of-the-Month Club alternate selection, I was able to inform my friends that I'd done the hat trick.

haul someone over the coals. In the bad old days of religious persecution, heretics who refused to recant were burned to death—in sixteenth-century slang, "fetched over the coals." Nowadays, if your boss hauls you over the coals he won't kill you, but he'll certainly make things hot for you—and you'll probably feel burned up.

havoc. Originally, a sort of military command: when a town was captured, the cry of "Havoc!" meant, approximately, "Stop fighting and start looting." The result, of course, was—havoc.

hawk from a handsaw, (know a). In one of literature's most famous quotations, Hamlet, apropos of his supposed insanity, declares, "I am but mad north-northwest; when the wind is southerly I know a hawk from a handsaw." The traditional explanation for this puzzling metaphor is that "handsaw" was a misprint for "hernshaw," a young heron; if you could tell a hawk from a heron (its prey), you evidently had at least some of your wits about you.

Equally plausible is a more recent explanation, that "handsaw" meant a saw and "hawk" meant what it certainly meant a century after Shakespeare: the square board, with a handle underneath, on which a plasterer holds the stuff he trowels onto a wall. Naturally, anyone could tell this hawk from the carpenter's tool as easily as a hawk from a heron. Since it makes sense either way, take your pick.

haywire. Hay compressed into bales is held together with loops of soft iron wire. When the bale is opened—often by chopping the wires with a hatchet—the wires retain their angular, looped shape. Opening several bales can easily produce a tangle of haywire full of sharp ends pointing every whichway. A person who goes haywire often goes every whichway—with plenty of sharp points to prick the unwary bystander.

hazard. In the thirteenth century and thereafter, hazard was a dice game, something like modern craps. Playing it was a hazardous occupation—a real crap-shoot, you might say.

heathen. Christianity began as primarily an urban religion; people in rural districts continued to worship older gods. The Latin word for countryman was *paganus*—whence, of course, *pagan;* the Germanic tongues had a similar word, something like *khaithanaz,* "dwelling in the heath" (wilderness)—whence "heathen."

heckle. The original verb meant to straighten and disentangle the fibers of flax or hemp, by drawing them through a heavy, sharp-toothed iron comb; later, it took on the additional sense of "scratch." A speaker who's being severely heckled may well feel as if he's being scratched with such a comb.

hectic. In medieval times, a "hectic" fever meant one with face flushed and skin dry—characteristic of tuberculosis. Nowadays, hectic activity of any sort is—feverish.

hedge (a bet, etc.). To hedge a piece of ground is to surround it with a hedge or fence, as for defense. Hedging a bet—betting on both sides of the proposition—"defends" you against losing, at least to a degree. In fact, if you're lucky enough to get the right odds, you can win something whatever the result.

Hedging a statement is another kind of defense: if you say something *may* be true, you're defending yourself against the possibility of its turning out to be false. Some academicians employ double and even triple hedges: *"It appears that* these findings *are consistent with* the view that the proposition *may be* true."

Here the hedges are so dense that they obscure what the writer is trying to say.

hell to pay. See **devil to pay**.

hem and haw. A sixteenth-century speaker stalling for time would hem ("Hmmm—uh") and hawk (clear his throat). People confronted with inconvenient questions are still doing it, literally or figuratively, though now they hem and haw.

hermaphrodite. The Greek god Hermes originally personified the male principle (he was sometimes commemorated by a phallic pillar); the goddess Aphrodite (Roman Venus) was his female counterpart. A hermaphrodite, then, combines physical traits of both gods. In the late eighteenth century, sailors applied the term to certain types of ships: a hermaphrodite brig was square-rigged on the foremast, fore-and-aft rigged on the mainmast—though I have no notion which mast was "male" and which, "female."

hide one's light under a bushel. A bushel is, of course, a measure of volume, equal to a little over 35 liters. But it also once meant a bushel measure or basket, which is the sense we find in the fifth chapter of Matthew: "Nor do men light a lamp and hide it under a bushel, but set it on a stand, and it gives light to all the house." Able but unassertive people are sometimes advised not to hide their light under that bushel.

hidebound. Cattle that have been underfed too long become hidebound: their skin clings so tightly to their backs and ribs that it cannot be raised with the fingers. Hidebound people cling to their convictions as tightly as the hidebound cow's hide clings to her emaciated carcass.

high and dry—see **beam ends**.

high horse, on one's. In medieval times, great horses or high horses were those specially bred to carry the weight of a man in armor. They were therefore ridden only by people of rank, such as "the Emperor and his cardinals on high horse" (John Wycliffe). To get up on one's high horse, then, is to assume, with no good reason, the air of some exalted personage.

high muck-a-muck. The Chinook jargon was a lingua franca or trade language, partly based on Native American tongues, used in the U.S.-Canadian Northwest and Alaska. In it, *hiu muckamuck* meant "plenty to eat"—which is one of the perks that go with being a high muck-a-muck.

high noon. Not just the middle of the day, but noon precisely— the moment when the sun (if you go by sun-time) is highest in the sky. Also, of course, a crucial confrontation, from the film of that name in which Gary Cooper was scheduled to confront the Bad Guys at high noon.

hipped (obsessed). In the eighteenth century, this slang term was spelt "hypt" or "hypp'd" and meant afflicted with hypochondria. The person who is hipped on something is as obsessed with it as the hypochondriac is with his or her imaginary disease. *Hyped up* has nothing to do with hypochondria, but rather derives from the condition of a racehorse that has received a hypodermic of some stimulant.

hit the fan. A euphemized version of a metaphor known to almost everyone; its source is an elaborate anecdote whose details I don't remember, but whose punch line was, "Where were you when it hit the fan?" Just imagine the state of a room, and its occupants, when a large mass of "it" is hurled into an electric fan.

hoax—see **hocus pocus**.

hobby. From "hobby-horse," at first a type of real horse, then a wicker horse worn in the old English sport of morris dancing (thought to derive from a primitive religious rite). Subsequently, it also meant a prostitute (presumably because she could be "ridden" by anyone), then a toy horse ridden by a child. A hobbyhorse or hobby is something you "ride" as a child rides its toy horse: for fun, not for money. (Compare **amateur**.)

Hobson's choice. Traditionally, from Tobias Hobson (d. 1631), keeper of a Cambridge livery-stable, who required his customers to take whatever horse was nearest the door. But a 1617 quotation refers to "Hodgeson's choise, to take such privilegese as they will geve us, or else goe without." So maybe it was a different stable, and a horse of another color. Or perhaps the man who wrote "Hodgeson" merely misheard the name.

hocus pocus. The original Hocus Pocus was a seventeenth-century conjurer, whose patter, beginning "Hocus pocus, tontus talontus," was described as "a dark composure of words, to blinde the eyes of the beholders." Subsequently, the phrase came to mean any kind of trick or deception (it may be the ultimate source of *hoax*), but now more often refers to elaborate, meaningless talk ("he gave me a lot of hocus pocus"). Hocus Pocus may have been parodying a phrase in the Latin mass, *hoc est corpus* (this is the body [of Christ]), but this is mere conjecture.

hoist with his own petard. Hamlet, chortling over his plan to "catch the conscience of the king" by means of a play, remarks that " 'tis the sport to have the engineer/Hoist with his own petard." This famous metaphor—actually, a double metaphor—requires a bit of translation.

Hamlet's "engineer" did not, of course, drive a locomotive; he was a military engineer, in charge of constructing and destroying fortifications and the like. One of the tools of his trade was the petard—a charge of gunpowder in a metal container—which could breach a wall or blow in a gate. The petard itself is a concealed metaphor: it comes from Italian *petardo*, a type of artillery, but literally, "farter"—a bit of soldier's humor like **grenade**.

The engineer hoist (blown up) by his own petard was in much

the same situation as the man in the Bible who "diggeth a pit" and "shall fall therein."

hold a candle to, not. If you've ever strolled along a backcountry road at night, you have some idea of what nightime city walking was like two centuries ago: with no street lamps, the only illumination was what leaked from people's windows (usually curtained or shuttered) and that of the moon, if any. The best you could expect was stumbling over a pile of garbage or worse (see **rain cats and dogs**); still worse would be an encounter with a footpad, who'd give you the choice of "your money or your life." Worst of all—he might take both.

Accordingly, people who had to go afoot after dark would, if they could afford it, take with them (or hire) a "linkboy"—a menial carrying a torch or candle. And if someone wasn't worthy to hold a candle, (s)he was even lower than that menial.

hold your horses. If you're driving a team of horses and they start going too fast, you hold them back by hauling on the reins. Few of us have ever driven horses, but we still advise our fellows to hold them if we think they're going too fast.

holding the bag. As early as the sixteenth century, "give someone the bag" meant to leave them abruptly ("give your masters the bag"). Later, it was "give them the bag to hold"; still later, "leave them holding the bag." Exactly what the bag was is not clear; most likely, a money bag, which an absconding servant or apprentice would "give" his master—empty.

The phrase may have picked up added color from a practical joke popular among cowboys and such around the turn of the century, and still not uncommon in boys' summer camps. A tenderfoot or **greenhorn** would be invited to take part in a nightime snipe hunt. His fellows would lead him by a circuitous route to some remote spot, give him a gunnysack, and instruct him to hold it open while they drove the snipe into it. They would then return to the ranchouse or campfire and spend the evening carousing, while the sucker was left (literally) holding the bag.

holocaust. When the Greeks sacrificed an animal to their gods, they often burned only part of it, consuming the rest themselves or giving it to the priests. But a really important sacrifice was *holokaustos*—wholly burnt.

In English, "holocaust" took on the sense of a total destruction or massacre; a nineteenth-century English historian claimed that the medieval French king Louis VII made "a holocaust of thirteen hundred persons in a church." *The* Holocaust, of course, was the Nazis' massacre of millions of Jews, Poles, Russians (both POWs and civilians), Gypsies and homosexuals, most of whom were also literally burned up completely.

We find the same Greek root in "caustic" (literally, burning): caustic criticism is the kind that really burns you up.

Homer nods. The poet Homer, great as he was, sometimes contradicted himself. Thus Paris, whose seduction and abduction of Helen started the Trojan War, is sometimes named Alexander; Troy is sometimes named Ilium. Again, the *Iliad* is supposed to take place in the tenth year of the war, yet at one point Helen, sitting beside King Priam on the city wall, points out to him various heroes on the other side—including Agamemnon, the commander-in-chief, who after ten years of fighting would surely have been known to every Trojan.

The Greeks don't seem to have been bothered by these contradictions; to them, the Homeric epics were semi-sacred. But the Roman poet Horace noted that "Homer himself has been observed to nod" (doze off)—meaning, of course, that even the best and brightest of us sometimes goof through inattention.

homeric. Homer's heroes (see **Achilles heel**) were all larger than life; so is anything described as "homeric." "Homeric laughter," however, refers not to the heroes but to the gods, whose "unextinguished laughter shakes the skies."

honeymoon. A sweet word, but with a touch of cynicism at the core: the love of a newlywed couple was as delicious as honey—

but was destined to wane like the moon (though not, one hopes, quite so quickly). Presidents and other important officials often enjoy a "honeymoon" immediately after they're elected: everybody "loves" them, not caring (or daring) to criticize them. Sooner or later, however, the honeymoon is over: the opposition plucks up its courage and starts doing what an opposition is supposed to do—oppose.

hoodwink. An Elizabethan writer speaks of "the Hoodwinke play . . . in some places called the blindmanbuf." As almost everyone knows, the game involves blindfolding one participant who must then grope about to catch the others. Someone who's been hoodwinked has been "blindfolded" by some trickster who leaves him groping about—often for his lost money.

hook, line and sinker. Nowadays, sport fishing has gone high-tech: rods of resin and carbon fiber, intricate mechanical reels, and a whole battery of lures to inveigle the fish into taking the hook. In my boyhood, however, all you really needed was a pole, a line, a hook baited with an angleworm or "nightcrawler," and a lead sinker to carry the hook to the bottom. A really greedy fish— often some species of sucker—would swallow hook, (part of the) line and sinker together. The human sucker who greedily swallows the con man's tale ends up like the fish: firmly hooked—and cooked.

hook or (by) crook, by. A real Ben Trovato pseudo-metaphor. Several writers have related it to a supposed medieval law permitting peasants to gather firewood in royal forests, but only dead branches they could pull down "by hook or by crook." But its earliest recorded use (late fourteenth century) had nothing to do with firewood; the phrase meant much what it does today: by fair means or (more likely) foul. And not surprisingly: "crook" had meant "deceit" since 1200.

The "hook" may have been added simply for the rhyme, or meaning "theft"—akin to its later sense of "steal." This would have given the phrase the precise meaning "by outright theft [hook], or by deception [crook]."

In *windfall,* by contrast, the firewood connection is clear: windfalls originally were (and sometime still are) blown-down boughs and trees, which, unlike living timber, could be appropriated by anyone. The term expanded to cover fruit blown down by the wind, requiring little or no effort to gather—which is about what you get if you're lucky enough to get a windfall.

hook, on one's own. Though the phrase has been in use for well over a century, nobody seems to have a clue to its origin. My guess would be among New England fishermen, who in the nineteenth century used both nets and "trawls" (long lines with hooks attached at intervals), but also fished with single lines—on their own hook.

hooker. The word, which dates from the 1840s, isn't quite a metaphor, since it literally means a woman who "hooks" her customers off the streets. But it took on a certain metaphorical color during the Civil War, thanks to General Joseph Hooker, who briefly headed the Union's Army of the Potomac. He won a well-deserved reputation for both military ineptitude and personal misconduct; the diplomat Charles Francis Adams called his headquarters "a combination of barroom and brothel." Hooker was quickly demoted to his former divisional command—and Washington punsters christened the city's flourishing red-light district "Hooker's Division."

horde. For centuries during the Middle Ages, the Central Asian nomads known as Mongols terrorized Eastern Europe, pillaging settlements and massacring the inhabitants without regard to age or sex. Their word for "encampment," *ordu,* transformed into Polish *horda,* was eventually applied to any Mongol army. These "hordes" of mounted archers were seldom very numerous, but moved so fast that they appeared so, since they seemed able to attack several places at once. Whence the modern "horde": an enormous and often destructive mass of people ("the Nazi hordes") or even insects ("hordes of locusts").

horns of a dilemma, on the. To the Greeks, a *dilemma* was merely an ambiguous proposition. To late medieval scholars, it became an argument or question that forced a person to choose between two equally unpalatable alternatives; a well-known modern example is "Have you stopped beating your wife?" The horns came from an earlier, synonymous term, a "horned question," which, like the scholars' dilemma, forced the respondant to "run on the sharp point of the horn" whichever way (s)he answered.

horrible. Latin *horrere* meant to stand on end; a horrible sight is one that figuratively makes your hair do so (see **hairy**). However, like many powerful adjectives, this one has been downgraded over the centuries: a horrible cold and a horrible bore are both unpleasant, but hardly hair-raising.

horse's mouth, from the. Originally, of course, a racetrack expression: a tip from a jockey was perhaps reliable but one from the horse itself was—supposedly—a dead certainty. I wish I had a dime for every dollar that's been lost on tips straight from the horse's mouth.

hotbed. Originally (and still) a gardeners' term meaning a covered bed of earth, heated by decaying manure, in which seeds or seedlings can be given an early start in spring. It came to mean any place favoring the rapid growth of anything, especially anything undesirable: an eighteenth-century writer called theaters "the devil's hotbed." When I attended Antioch College in the 1930s, some of the more dim-witted locals considered it a hotbed of "free love"; alas, it wasn't.

humor. Originally, one of the body's "humors" (fluids), whose proportions were supposed to determine people's individual temperaments (see **bilious**). From "temperament" was but a step to "mood"; we still speak of someone as in a good or a bad humor. Soon "humors" took on the sense, not just of moods in general but of personal oddities or caprices—whence, after this long journey, the modern sense of anything amusing, as oddities often are.

hyped up—see **hipped**.

hysteria. To physicians in ancient Greece, hysteria was supposedly a "female complaint," and was therefore diagnosed as a disorder of the female's distinctive internal organ, the womb *(hystera)*. The original sense of the word survives in "hysterectomy"—surgical removal of the womb.

We now know, of course, that hysteria has nothing to do with the womb. But oddly enough, it *does* seem, for unknown reasons, to be considerably commoner among women than among men; the masculine "counterpart" may be the much more serious disorder called sociopathy or anti-social personality. At any rate, both conditions run in families—and the same families: female members are often hysterics; males, often sociopaths.

I ⌐ **iconoclast.** In the eighth century A.D., Christians became embroiled in a struggle over whether "images"—paintings, mosaics and sculptures—should be allowed in churches. Pope Gregory the Great, like most churchmen in Western Europe, considered such religious art a positive good: "What those who can read learn by means of [religious] writing, that do the uneducated learn by looking at a picture." Since few people could read in those days, he had a point.

Many leaders of the eastern Church, however, claimed that religious images were all too reminiscent of the idols worshipped by **heathens**, and cited the Fourth Commandment: "Thou shalt not make unto thee any graven image, or any likeness of anything that is in the heavens above or the earth beneath or the waters under the earth." And it was they who got the ear of the Byzantine emperor Leo III, a religious zealot who had already forced all Jews and Moslems in the Empire to undergo baptism.

In 726, Leo decreed that all paintings and other images should be removed from churches; Gregory promptly excommunicated him as a heretic. Leo's son and successor, Constantine V, went further, ordering that the images be physically destroyed; he and his supporters were called (in Greek) *eikonoklastes,* "image breakers."

A century or so later, another emperor reversed the official line, and the images were restored, but the struggle helped engender the later schism between Eastern and Western churches. Much later, "iconoclast" was applied to English Puritans who also objected to "heathen" images and destroyed them when they got the chance—notably, during the English Civil War.

Modern iconoclasts break popular "images," attacking long-held beliefs or superstitions in terms that often win them the secular equivalent of excommunication.

ill-starred—see **disaster.**

impasse. A French *impasse* is what we call a dead-end street or blind alley; if you've reached an impasse, that's where you are.

impede. From Latin *impedire,* to place fetters on the feet *(pedes)* of a slave or prisoner. If you were fettered you were impeded—and if you're impeded, you're figuratively fettered. *Expedite,* as you might guess, comes from a related verb meaning to remove the fetters; when we expedite a project or operation, we "unfetter" it so it can move along more quickly.

incubus. From Latin *incubare,* lie upon—specifically, a demon that in medieval times was thought to lie on people in the night, giving them nightmares. Male incubi could impregnate their female victims, and that's how witches were born. If you call someone an incubus, you're saying that they're weighing you down, like the proverbial millstone.

inside track. As horse-players and footracers know, the inside track on a circular or oval course is the shortest track; a horse or runner on the inside track has an automatic advantage—perhaps a decisive one.

insidious. Latin *insidiae* means "ambush." If someone attacks you insidiously, they're sneaking up on you; the same goes for an insidious disease.

insult. From Latin *insultare,* to leap upon (compare **desultory**). If someone leaps upon you, they're likely to injure you physically; if they insult you, the injury is purely emotional—though perhaps just as painful.

inveigle. In Old French, *aveugler* meant "to blind." If someone inveigles you into doing something unwise, they've done so by blinding you to its morality or its consequences—unless, of course, you've blinded yourself, as people often do.

investigate. Huntsmen in ancient Rome, like hunters today, were forced to track *(investigare),* or seek the traces of, the animals they pursued. A *vestige* of something is a mere trace, and when a detective investigates a crime, (s)he's trying to track down the criminal.

irons in the fire, too many. The old-time blacksmith heated iron in his fire (forge) until it was soft enough to hammer into shape. If he had too many irons in the fire, none of them would get hot enough to be worked.

itching palm. The physical itch we all feel on occasion was long ago expanded to include psychological "itches"—uneasy, often irritating, cravings. Our fingers may itch to be doing something—and an itching palm can only be soothed by the application of money.

ivy league. The older U.S. universities and colleges—Harvard, Yale, Princeton and Columbia, for example—frequently have ivy-covered buildings. The "Ivy League," comparable to the various leagues of organized baseball, originally referred to the athletic teams of those institutions; subsequently, "ivy league" has been applied to certain styles of dress and even of personality ("a real ivy-league type").

jackass. The donkey or ass—the first beast of burden to be domesticated—is proverbially both stubborn and stupid, and in most countries where the animal is known, "ass" or its equivalent is used to characterize people with the same supposed traits. In the U.S., however, "ass" has another meaning, and "jackass"— literally, a male donkey—has been substituted. (A female ass, by the way, is a jenny.)

jackpot, the. Almost everyone knows the immediate source of this metaphor: the slot-machine (a.k.a. fruit machine, a.k.a. one-armed bandit), in which hitting the jackpot means a big win. The ultimate source, however, is a variety of draw poker in which only a player dealt a pair of jacks or better can open the betting. Sometimes several hands pass without anyone opening, meaning that the "ante"—the sum each player must chip in before each deal—can mount up to a considerable figure. When the hand is finally opened, the player who wins it hits the jackpot.

Jacob's ladder. In the book of Genesis, we read of how the patriarch Jacob dreamed "that a ladder was set up on the earth, and the top of it reached to heaven; and behold, the angels of God were ascending and descending on it." Aboard ship, a Jacob's ladder is a rope ladder, usually with wooden rungs, dropped over the ship's side for sailors—no angels—to ascend and descend.

jaded. In Chaucer's day, "jade" (its ultimate source is unknown) meant a tired or worn-out horse. If you're jaded, that's rather what you feel like.

jaundiced eye. In medicine, "jaundice" means a yellowish color of the skin and eyeballs, usually caused by excess bile in the bloodstream (it's often a symptom of gallstones). Someone with a jaundiced eye was supposed to see everything yellow; if you look at someone in that way, your vision of them is colored by envy or suspicion.

jaywalk(er). Around 1900, "jay" meant not just the bird but also a rube or **bumpkin.** Back on the farm, "jays" naturally walked across the road anywhere they chose; when they visited the big city, they supposedly did the same on crowded streets, at considerable risk to their necks—and to the tempers of teamsters and drivers.

jeopardy. From French *jeu parti,* a divided game—that is, one with equal chances of winning or losing. If you're in jeopardy, there's a good chance you'll end up a loser.

jerk. In Victorian times, a puritanical (or sex-obsessed) medico "discovered" that masturbation causes physical debility, "softening of the brain," feeblemindedness and even, if persisted in, insanity. (He was, of course, talking about male masturbation—"jerking" or "jerking off"; females never engaged in such unnatural practices.) From this "scientific" legend came the "jerk-off," later just "jerk"—someone showing the supposed symptoms of too-frequent masturbation. (For the record, the idea was pure nonsense. Studies of sexual behavior reveal that if masturbation could cause insanity, at least 90 percent of American males would be **barmy.**)

jerk someone's chain. A relatively new metaphor, meaning to tease or needle someone who is in no position to retaliate ("Quit jerking my chain!"). The image is probably that of a dog with a chain choker collar; if someone jerks its chain, there's little the animal can do about it.

jerkwater town. In the great days of steam railroading, locomotives had to stop from time to time to replenish the water their boilers had turned to steam. Out West, where settlements were few, this meant stopping at some pretty small towns. The great "limiteds," traveling between major cities, couldn't be bothered. Instead of stopping to "tank up," the engineer would "jerk" water at full speed by lowering a scoop into a water-filled trough between the rails. A jerkwater town, then, was one where fast trains never stopped—and few slow ones did either.

jerry-built. Possibly from the name of some unknown British contractor known for shoddy workmanship, but more likely a maritime term. If a ship's mast was broken off in a storm or by enemy fire, the crew would if possible rig a "jury-mast," by lashing a spare yard to the stump of the old mast. This makeshift arrangement was obviously both flimsy and temporary, and during the nineteenth century, "jury" (no connection with the legal term) passed into fairly wide use to describe anything of that sort. Whence, probably "jury-built," which became "jerry-built."

jig is up, the. A jig was originally a lively dance, then a satirical, even scurrilous ballad, and eventually a practical joke or swindle. If the joker or swindler was exposed, the jig was up for him.

Job's comforter. The Book of Job is one of the strangest pieces of religious literature ever written. It recounts how Satan challenged God to test the righteous man Job, to see if he could be forced to abandon his faith. God, simply to prove a point, allowed Satan first to destroy Job's property, then to kill off his family, and finally to afflict him with "loathesome sores."

Three friends gathered round Job in his affliction and reproved him for complaining. At last he snapped, "Miserable comforters are you all!" With a Job's comforter, in short, you don't need enemies—or, I'd say, with a God like that!

jot (or a tittle), not a. Iota (ι) was the smallest letter in the Greek alphabet, as its equivalent, i, is in ours. Since English spelling long confused I and J, "iota" became "jot," meaning the smallest part of anything. A tittle is even smaller than a jot: it's the dot over the i. The phrase, now uncommon, was popularized through the Biblical dictum, "not a jot not a tittle of the Law shall pass away." To jot something down—scribble it very briefly—comes from the same source.

jovial. Jove was another name for the Roman god Jupiter, ruler of the heavens. The planet Jupiter was thought to be highly favorable in one's horoscope, and people under its influence were therefore happy and cheerful—jovial, in fact.

jubilee, jubilant. Surprisingly, the two words come from completely different sources. "Jubilee" comes from the Hebrew *yobel,* the ram's horn that called the Israelites to the "Year of Jubilee," a celebration of their escape from slavery in Egypt. It was held after the passage of seven times seven years—i.e., every 50 years—and was a sort of sabbatical year, in which no one was supposed to do any work.

Slaves in the American South looked forward to their own Year of Jubilee when they too would be liberated; it came with the advance of the Union armies in 1863–65. Whence, the chorus of the famous (in the South, infamous) song, "Marching Through Georgia":

> Hurrah! Hurrah! We bring the Jubilee!
> Hurrah! Hurrah! The flag that makes men free,
> As we went marching from Atlanta to the sea,
> As we went marching through Georgia.

"Jubilant," on the other hand, comes from Latin *iubilare,* shout, which Christian writers (perhaps by confusion with "jubilee") used to mean "shout for joy." If you're feeling jubilant, that's what you feel like doing.

juggernaut From Hindi *Jagannath,* a title of the god Krishna; more specifically, an enormous image of the god, mounted on wheels, that is annually hauled in procession at Puri on the east coast of India. Centuries ago, European travelers reported that devotees of the god hurled themselves under the wheels to be crushed; Hindus indignantly deny this ever happened, saying that the shedding of blood would have polluted the celebration. Be that as it may, a juggernaut is now something irresistible, crushing everything in its path.

junket. Originally, any of various desserts served in a rush basket (French *jonquette*); the curds and whey that Little Miss Muffet dined on was probably a junket. Later it came to mean any delicacy, then a banquet featuring such delicacies, then a picnic. Today, though we still eat junket (sweetened, curdled milk), the word more often refers to the "picnics" enjoyed by legislators and other government officials, financed either by the taxpayers or by corporations hungry for favors.

kangaroo court. As most people know, this court—usually an **K** unofficial one—has very loose rules, and the accused seldom has more than a **Chinaman's chance**. Some say the court, like the kangaroo, came from Australia—specifically, from the convicts who were the first European settlers there. In favor of this theory is that such courts are not uncommon among convicts, who sometimes "try" those of their number who have broken the "rules." Against it is good evidence that the term originated not in Australia but on the U.S. frontier, where regular courts were thin on the ground and justice—or "justice"—was often home-made.

How, then, did the kangaroo get involved? Some say it hopped into the phrase in Gold-Rush California, where such courts were often set up to try "claim *jumpers*"—but the term's first recorded use is not in California but in Texas. The simplest and most likely explanation is that a kangaroo court—well, leaps to conclusions. If you're tried by one, you can expect **short shrift**.

keep a stiff upper lip. Though often considered a Briticism— what upper-class Britishers endeavor to do at all times—the term originated in the U.S. A stiff upper lip doesn't quiver—i.e., the owner isn't about to burst into tears.

keep one's fingers crossed. For centuries, making the sign of the cross was a way of protecting oneself against evil; if you're keeping your fingers crossed, then, you're taking out heavenly insurance against mishaps. The same idea underlies the childhood custom that a lie told with your fingers crossed "doesn't count"— that is, God won't punish you.

keep the ball rolling. The ball is not, as some suggest, a rugby football. The "rugger" ball is an ovoid resembling a U.S. football, and keeping it rolling is virtually impossible. Most likely, it was the ball used in bandy (an early version of field hockey): if you **bandy words** with someone, you're keeping the conversational ball rolling, after a fashion.

keep the wolf from the door. During the Middle Ages, a wolf at the door symbolized a hard, hungry winter, when wolves actually roamed the streets of large towns. In Great Britain, the wolf was wiped out centuries ago, and even in America few of us have ever seen one, but the wolf at the door still symbolizes the hunger that can devour us.

The expression may well go back thousands of years in Europe: as the most dangerous predator around, the wolf was also the "hungriest." If Africans had such an expression (and for all I know, they do), it would be "keep the lion (or leopard) from the hut."

keep your pecker up. A British phrase whose literal meaning was probably "keep your beak (i.e., head) high," hence "keep your courage up." In the U. S., however "pecker" means "penis," so the phrase hasn't caught on. Its most notable use was by Winston Churchill during World War II, at the end of a speech to a joint session of the U.S. Congress. Maybe he used it innocently, but—since he'd traveled widely in the U.S.—maybe not. In any case, his peroration, double entendre and all, brought down the House—and the Senate too.

Keep your shirt on! Most likely from the custom of stripping to the waist before a fight; telling someone to keep his shirt on advises him to stay calm, not start punching.

keister. The literal sense of the word (pronounced KY-ster) comes from German or Yiddish *Kiste,* chest, box, whence the street hawker's keister (suitcase for displaying goods) and the thief's keister (safe, strongbox).

The metaphorical sense—buttocks—is much more widely known; indeed, it has been used by none other than Ronald Reagan. It probably grew out of the convict's and smuggler's custom of using the rectum as a "suitcase"—container for contraband. Significantly, "satchel" has the same double meaning.

kettle of fish. In the eighteenth century, Scottish gentlemen would invite their friends to a "kettle of fish"—a picnic on a river bank with boiled, fresh-caught salmon as the main dish. Used ironically, "A fine kettle of fish!" is equivalent to "A fine stew!" or "A fine mess!"

kibosh, the. Of the many theories about this expression, the least improbable derives it from Irish *cie bas* (pronounced KY-bosh, like the English word), cap of death—the black cap that English judges used to don before pronouncing a death sentence. If you put the kibosh on something, it's "dead."

kick the bucket. A bucket wasn't always just a pail; it was also a beam from which slaughtered pigs were suspended by the heels. If the animal was still twitching, it might be said to be kicking the bucket. However, there's no evidence that anyone ever actually said this. Much more likely, the phrase refers to a suicide, standing on an overturned pail, who adjusts a noose around his neck and then—kicks the bucket.

Kilkenney cats, the. Ben Trovato and his bretheren have devised many legends to explain this phrase. The most plausible comes from the Anglo-Irish writer Jonathan Swift, who derived it from the constant battles between English settlers and native Irish in the small town of Kilkenney.

Be that as it may, the immediate source of the expression is unquestionably a fairly well-known limerick:

> There once were two cats of Kilkenney;
> Each thought there was one cat too many.
>   So they fought and they fit
>   And they scratched and the bit,
> Till instead of two cats there weren't any.

kill the fatted calf. If you know your Bible (specifically, Luke xv), you know the phrase comes from the story of the Prodigal Son, who left home, wasted his substance in riotous living and ended up wallowing in a pigpen, nourishing himself on "the husks that the swine did eat." When he finally pulled himself together and returned home, he naturally expected a chilly welcome. But his parents were so pleased to see him that they killed the fatted calf—that is, brought out the best and tastiest food they had. If you kill the fatted calf for your guests, you're absolutely delighted to see them—or want them to think so.

kill the goose (that lays the golden eggs). Many readers will recognize the source of this one—the old tale of a peasant who found a goose that every day laid a golden egg. I don't know whether the entire egg was gold or just the shell; most of us would settle for either.

The peasant wouldn't. Figuring that if the goose laid golden eggs, it must have a gold mine inside, he killed it—and found that its innards were no different from those of any other goose. If you're involved in a profitable business but try to take too much money out of it too fast, you may end up figuratively killing that goose.

kitchen sink, everything but the. Roughly, everything that isn't fastened down as solidly as a kitchen sink. Some years ago, the papers reported a burglary in upstate New York where the thieves had taken everything *including* the kitchen sink.

kitsch. Said to derive from German dialect *Kitschen,* gutter scrapings; in colloquial German, it means literary or musical junk or near-junk, usually pretty sentimental or **schmaltzy.** Rod McKuen's poetry is kitsch; so, some would say, are Rogers and Hammerstein musicals, though many people, including me, enjoy them anyway.

know beans, not. Beans and similar legumes (peas, lentils) have always been our cheapest source of protein, and as such feature largely in the diets of poor peoples—the Mexican's *frijoles,* the Puerto Rican's rice and beans, the Italian's *past'e fagiole,* a.k.a. *pasta fazool* (pasta and beans).

Beans were so cheap that they soon came to symbolize something almost worthless: an anonymous English poet of the fourteenth century declared that, "No rich man dredeth God the worth of a beane." Of the same provenance are such expressions as "not care a bean" and "not worth a hill of beans." Yiddish *bubkes* means the same thing, literally and figuratively: if you're working for bubkes, you're working for beans—next to nothing.

know the ropes. A full-rigged ship had more than a hundred different ropes for hoisting and controlling its sails and yards; all led down to deck level, with their running (free) ends fastened in groups at the foot of the masts or along the rails. Since loosing the wrong rope could produce anything from confusion to catastrophe, the first thing an apprentice seaman had to learn was which rope did what; until he knew the ropes, he was more a hinderance than a help. If you really know the ropes in your field, you're no longer an apprentice.

knuckle under. To us, the knuckles are the finger joints, but originally the word meant any joint, such as the elbow or knee. If you knuckle under to someone, you're figuratively bending your knees under you, thereby admitting defeat.

kowtow. In old China, anyone approaching the Emperor was expected to *k'o t'ou*—literally, "knock head": kneel and press his forehead to the ground several times. If you kowtow to someone, you're treating them very obsequiously indeed.

L **labyrinth.** In the Greek legend of Theseus and Ariadne (see **clue**), the labyrinth was the dwelling place of the monstrous Minotaur; so intricate were its winding passageways that nobody could find their way out. The word is now used of both buildings and bureaucratic red tape; either way, you'll be lucky to escape.

laconic. In ancient Greece, the Laconians, a.k.a. **Spartans** (from their capital city) were known for not wasting words. A famous example was their reply to Philip, king of Macedon and father of Alexander the Great, who warned them: "If I enter Laconia, I shall level Sparta." The Spartans, laconically, wrote back "If."

lame duck. The term dates from eighteenth-century England, where it meant someone ruined on the stock exchange—a **bear** or bull who had speculated unwisely. How it acquired its American sense—a politician who has failed of reelection but whose successor hasn't yet been sworn in—is unclear; perhaps because the officeholder was a "dead duck" who wasn't quite dead.

In any case, lame-duck congressmen were sometimes a considerable nuisance: elections were held in early November (as they still are), but the new Congress and president didn't take office until early March. In the interval, the old Congress would hold a "lame-duck session," in which the losers might vote themselves all sorts of goodies.

The lame duck problem was largely solved by constitutional amendment: since 1933, the gap between election and taking office is only two months. But "lame duck" is still sometimes applied to a president who is nearing the end of his second term; since he can't run for a third term (thanks to a later constitutional amendment), his political influence is partly crippled.

land-office business. In 1800, land offices were set up in the Ohio territory (later, in other new territories) to sell public lands to settlers—and often to speculators, who by various ruses managed to get hold of thousands of acres, for later resale. Since the lands had been acquired by force or fraud from the Native Americans, they were sold very cheap, and the land offices did a land-office business.

lark (frolic). This metaphor has begotten one of Ben Trovato's best efforts. It supposedly originated in the Middle Ages, when teenagers of both sexes would allegedly go into the fields on a summer's morning before dawn, to catch larks, then considered a delicacy. Presumably they didn't spend *all* their time bird-catching, but engaged in a good deal of larking about.

Alas, history doesn't support this charming tale: the term originated, not in the Middle Ages but in the early nineteenth century. It probably derives directly from the skylark's habits: during the breeding season, the male ascends to a great height, sings his melodious song and then dives almost to the ground, ending with a frolicsome upward swoop.

last ditch. From at least the sixteenth century, soldiers besieging a fortress or walled town would dig a line of trenches (ditches) around it, to protect themselves and their cannon from enemy artillery. If all went well, a second and then a third line would be dug, each closer to the walls; eventually, the beseigers' cannon could be brought close enough to smash a breach in the walls, through which the town could be taken by storm.

If the beseiged forces were strong enough, however, they would mount a sortie against the beseigers, forcing them out of one line of trenches after another until they were defending the last ditch. If they failed, the siege was broken.

laugh in one's sleeve. The only certain thing about this phrase is that it dates from the sixteenth century. By some accounts, gentlemen's sleeves were then so voluminous that one could insert one's head and literally laugh in them. I suspect the actual origin is far more pedestrian: from the gesture of covering the mouth with the sleeve (arm) in an effort to conceal inappropriate mirth.

laurels. In ancient Greece, victors at the Olympic Games and similar contests were crowned with a wreath of laurel (bay) leaves; in English, "laurels" have symbolized victory since the sixteenth century. To rest on one's laurels, then, amounts to quitting while one is still "champion"; to look to one's laurels means to keep a sharp eye on the competition.

lay an egg. The egg in question has nothing to do with the ones you buy at the supermarket; it's short for "duck egg" (Britain) or "goose egg" (U. S.), meaning, in sports, a big, fat zero. The phrase passed into the theater, where a show that laid an egg was a zero—a total failure. In October 1929, *Variety,* the U.S. show-business bible, headlined its account of the catastrophic stock-market crash: WALL STREET LAYS AN EGG.

lease on life. The phrase reminds us that we don't own life in perpetuity but merely "rent" it. Sooner or later, our lease runs out—though if we're lucky we may get a new lease.

leave someone in the lurch. Not the "lurch" that means to sway violently from side to side, but from French *lourche,* an old game resembling backgammon: a player left in the lurch ended up far behind in the scoring. Later, the expression was transferred to several other games (a modern equivalent is a "blitz" or "schneider" in gin rummy). If someone leaves you in the lurch, you're left far behind and—for the moment, at least—a loser.

leftist, left-wing. Beginning in the nineteenth century, European legislatures began seating their conservative members on the right of the presiding officer, their liberal or radical ones on his left. This may have developed out of the old custom of seating an honored guest on the host's right: rightists were obviously more honorable than leftists—or anyway more respectable.

Levant, the. Literally, the lands lying in the direction of the rising (French *levant*) sun; specifically, the lands around the eastern Mediterranean, from Greece to Egypt. It is one of many words in which the sun defines directions. "Orient" comes from Latin *oriens,* rising, while "Occident," naturally, refers to the setting sun—i.e., the Western countries (in German, the latter are *den Abendlandes,* literally, "evening lands"). The regions called the Midi (southern France) and the Mezzogiorno (ditto Italy) take their names from words literally meaning "midday," when the sun lies due south.

level, on the. The level is, of course, a basic tool of the carpenter and mason, used to ensure that a frame or surface is precisely horizontal or vertical. Figuratively, then, "on the level" may mean no more than that the person so described isn't giving you a "tilted" opinion or proposition. But the level and square are also symbols of Freemasonry, and "on the Level and on the Square" describes how one Mason is supposed to treat another: with complete honesty. In any case, someone who's really on the level, Freemason or not, is thoroughly trustworthy.

libertine. In the early sixteenth century, a religious sect called the Libertines sprang up in France and some other countries. Its basic doctrine was that the whole universe, including mankind, was God, and since God obviously can't sin, neither can man—i.e., you're free (Latin *liber*) to do anything you choose.

Anyway, that's what their religious enemies claimed they believed. I take the story with several **grains of salt**; "immorality" of one kind or another is an almost standard charge against heretics, religious or political (see **bugger**). But true or not, the word was quickly transferred to someone wholly given over to wine, women and song. Especially women.

lick into shape. The phrase has nothing to do with the lickings by which English schoolboys were (and sometimes still are) encouraged to shape up; it comes from an ancient bit of unnatural history. At birth, bear cubs, like some other newborn animals, are covered with the amniotic membrane, meaning that to a casual glance—about all their mother would be likely to allow—they seem shapeless. She, like many other animal mothers, licks her babies, removing the membrane and revealing their natural shape. Whence the legend, dating at least from Roman times, that her licking produces the shape.

life of Riley, the. Though nobody knows for sure, the original Riley or Reilly was probably (as William and Mary Morris suggest) the O'Reilly of a song popular during the 1880s. The vaudevillian Pat Rooney Sr. would recount how, when O'Reilly struck it rich, everyone would lead the life of Riley: "a hundred a day will be very small pay" (the average wage in those days was more like $3 a day), railroad trips would be free, and so on. The chorus, in which the audience would join, was

> Are you the O'Reilly who keeps this hotel?
> Are you the O'Reilly they speak of so well?
> If you're the O'Reilly they speak of so highly,
> Gor blime me, O'Reilly, you are looking well!

lily-livered. The seat of human courage has been variously located in the heart, the testicles, the liver or simply the guts; if you don't have the organ in question, or if it's not functioning properly, you're a coward. A lily-white liver was obviously in bad shape, and so was its possessor's fortitude.

limb, out on a. Like **barking up the wrong tree**, it comes from the American frontier. A raccoon, possum or bear that's been treed and forced out on a limb can be shot down at leisure; if you go out on a limb, you risk the same fate.

limbo, in. Limbo resulted from a rather neat theological maneuver by some Christian denominations. They believe that only those who have been saved by Christ, through baptism, can enter heaven. But what about virtuous men, such as Moses, who lived before Christ, or infants who die before they can be baptized? Certainly they can't go to heaven—but it would be terribly unfair to send them to hell. The solution was limbo: a region on the border of hell, but without its torments. If someone or something is "in limbo," then nothing is happening to them or it, either good or bad.

limelight, the. Before electric lights, stages were illuminated by limelight—an intense white light produced by playing a gas-jet against a block of lime (calcium oxide). If someone loves the limelight, (s)he enjoys center stage—and may be a bit of a **ham.**

limey. On long voyages under sail, a frequent hazard was scurvy, a painful and debilitating disease, caused by the lack of fresh fruits and vegetables containing vitamin C. Late in the eighteenth century, a British naval surgeon discovered that a small quantity of lime juice would prevent the disease (as we now know, limes and other citrus fruits are rich in the vitamin).

A daily ration of lime juice was soon made compulsory on British naval vessels, and eventually on merchantmen as well. Americans thereupon began referring to British sailors as "lime-juicers," and eventually, "limeys."

lion's share, the. Everyone knows that this means nearly all of whatever is being shared out, but in the original version (or one

of them) it was even more. As Aesop told the tale, the lion and
three other animals went out to hunt. When it came time to share
out the quarry, the lion divided it into four equal parts. The first
he took as his share; the second, because he was the king of the
beasts; the third, for his mate and cubs—and as for the fourth, "let
him who will dispute it with me!" The moral: don't go hunting with
a lion.

litmus test/paper. Litmus is a sort of dye, obtained from certain
lichens, that turns red in acids, blue in alkalies; chemists use paper
impregnated with litmus as an "indicator" for testing the acidity
of a solution. Figuratively, a litmus test indicates the state or
political "color" of something and a litmus paper is someone
whose reactions do the same thing—sometimes, by implication,
changing his or her color to suit the times.

Many years ago, I heard the phrase used memorably in a
Greenwich Village bar, by a lady who'd obviously had a drink or
two. Discussing the state of the nation, which didn't much please
her, she declared: "I'm a litmus paper! I turn Red when things go
sour!"

little end of the horn. The horn is the mythical cornucopia or
Horn of Plenty, whose large, open end overflows with fruits and
other goodies. At the little end, there's no opening—i.e., it's not
a good place to be.

loaded to the gills. The gills on either side of a fish's "neck"
have been humorously used of the flesh around the human neck,
in such expressions as "pale around the gills" (nervous). If someone is loaded to the gills (with liquor), he's full-up—almost juiced
to the eyeballs.

lobotomized. A metaphor that is happily obsolescent. During
the 1930s, a Spanish surgeon announced that lobotomy—inserting a scalpel into the brain's frontal lobes and cutting them in
various ways—could cure some psychological disorders. Since

there was then no effective treatment for these diseases, surgeons throughout the world latched onto the procedure; by the 1950s, they were profitably performing more than 50,000 lobotomies a year—with no clear notion of what conditions, if any, it could be expected to benefit.

With the discovery of drugs that could ameliorate psychosis, some researchers started checking out the original lobotomies. They found that the procedure often did nothing good for the patient, and that even when it "succeeded" did so by destroying much of the personality: "cured" individuals were emotionally unreactive and sometimes mentally subnormal—lobotomized, in fact.

lock, stock and barrel. Any rifle or shotgun includes a stock and a barrel. In the old muzzleloader, the firing mechanism was known as the lock, presumably because of some fancied resemblance to a door lock. "Lock, stock and barrel," then, means the whole works—or, you should excuse the expression, the whole shooting match.

loggerheads, at. In Shakespeare's day, a loggerhead was a blockhead; a century later, the word had picked up the additional sense of an iron ball, fixed to a long handle, that could be heated and used to melt tar, as for caulking the seams of a ship (see **devil to pay**). Quite possibly quarreling shipyard workers used these formidable tools as weapons, in which case they could be said to be at loggerheads.

logrolling. Another relic of pioneer days, when settlers had to clear their lands of virgin timber. Chopping down trees four and five feet in diameter was hard work, and removing the logs was harder—for a man working alone, virtually impossible. Accordingly, a settler would invite his neighbors to a "logrolling," on the understanding that he would render similar assistance when required.

Neighborly logrolling is long gone—cranes and tractors handle even the biggest timber—but the practice continues in our legislatures. Members routinely help one another roll their pet "logs"— funds for projects beneficial to their state or district, though often pure waste from the standpoint of the nation as a whole. See also **pork barrel**.

long in the tooth. If you're past 50, you've probably noticed that your gums have receded somewhat over the years, so that your teeth look longer than they once did. In short, like me, you're getting a bit long in the tooth.

look a gift horse in the mouth. If you know horses, you can make a pretty accurate estimate of an animal's age by examining its teeth, noting which of the permanent set have come in, how worn the grinding surfaces are, and so on. Obviously, if someone has *given* you the horse, it's bad manners, to say the least, to look into its mouth.

loose cannon. Modern, breech-loading naval guns are mounted immovably in turrets. The muzzle-loading cannon of the old-time warship, however, had to be hauled inboard for loading, then hauled outboard for firing. It was therefore mounted on a wheeled carriage, which between battles was securely lashed to the ship's structure.

Now imagine a warship rolling and pitching in a violent gale. The lashings on a gun break, and it becomes a loose cannon—a ton or so of metal on wheels rolling unpredictably about the deck, crippling or killing any sailor unlucky enough to get in the way and perhaps smashing through the ship's side. Human loose cannons are equally dangerous to their associates and to bystanders—and equally capable, if unrestrained, of sinking the entire "ship." (Worth noting, however, is that some so-called loose cannons have actually been deliberately and surreptitiously loosed by their superiors, who hope to dissociate themselves from any resulting smash-up.)

lose face. For obvious reasons, the face has long symbolized the emotions displayed on it and, by extension, the personality, character or reputation of its owner; "face" metaphors are common in English (see any unabridged dictionary) and in many other languages. In Chinese, *tiu lien* (lose face) means to have one's reputation damaged by public humiliation.

Orientals in general, and Chinese in particular, are supposed to be obsessed with "face," and in cases of conflict will often go to considerable lengths to find a compromise that will save the face of both parties. Occidentals, of course, aren't so childish as to care about losing face—just about losing "credibility."

low water, at—see **tide over.**

lower the boom on. The boom in question was the movable part of a **crane** used to handle cargo aboard ship or on the docks. And on ship or ashore, "accidently" lowering the boom on the head of some disliked person was a good way of getting rid of him.

luddite. In the early 1800s, English textile manufacturers were busily introducing new machinery that allowed them to cut wages drastically. Their workers organized to resist the cuts—secretly, since trade unions were illegal; their leaders often used pseudonyms, notably "King Ludd" or "Captain Ludd." The "Luddite" protests sometimes culminated in the smashing of the hated new machines.

Contemporary commentators (nearly all pro-employer), accused the Luddites of being selfishly opposed to technological progress, and the word is still used in that sense. Modern historians have pointed out, however, that the original luddites were opposed, not to the new machines but to the wage-cuts; employers who didn't reduce wages (there were a few) suffered no damage to their equipment. If you hear someone described as a luddite, it's worth asking whether the "progress" (s)he's allegedly resisting is really beneficial—and if so, to whom.

M *ɛ* **macaroni.** An obsolete metaphor which I include only because it occurs in a famous American patriotic song ("He stuck a feather in his hat and called it macaroni"). The macaroni in question was not the well-known Italian pasta dish, but a foppish young man— originally, a member of the eighteenth-century Macaroni Club in London, whose upper-crust members favored Italian styles in food and raiment.

machiavellian. The Florentine statesman Niccolo Machiavelli (1469–1527) wrote about politics as it is rather than as it should be. In his famous treatise *The Prince,* he described the often unscrupulous things a wise ruler must do if he is to retain power and maintain a stable government—something of great importance to any Italian of the time, given the local political conditions.

Machiavelli did no more than describe what princes, kings and emperors—including English kings—had been doing for centuries. But many of the English, then as now, disliked calling a spade a spade and were—or professed to be—deeply shocked by the Italian's unvarnished account of how politics really worked.

In defense of Machiavelli, he was not discussing what a ruler ought to do but what (s)he *had* to do to continue ruling over a stable and prosperous state. He was, in fact, applying to politics a principle later enunciated by a Scottish churchman who was asked how he reconciled the doctrine of Divine mercy with that of infant damnation. "The Lord God Almighty," he declared, "is sometimes forced to do things in his public and official capacity that in his private and personal capacity he deplores."

The accuracy of Machiavelli's observations is shown by the fact that statemen (and -women) are still using machiavellian methods. This is regrettable, but probably inevitable. When it gets dangerous is when the stateman starts equating the nation's security with his own job security—which happens far too often.

mad as a hatter/March hare. Hats are usually made of felt, in which fibers of wool or fur are pounded (felted) together, rather than woven. The felting process goes more quickly if the wool is treated with mercury—a deadly poison to the nervous system. In the days before governments began imposing meddlesome restrictions on industry, hatters frequently contracted chronic mercury poisoning, developing first the tremors called "hatter's shakes," and eventually outright psychosis—becoming mad as a hatter.

As for the hare, March is its breeding season, at which time the animals (especially the males) are much wilder than at other times. This "madness" was noted long before Lewis Carroll's Mad Tea Party, where Alice met both the March Hare and the Hatter.

maelstrom. Literally, a whirlpool; specifically, a powerful tidal current near the arctic coast of Norway. It sometimes becomes violent and turbulent enough to sink small craft. In folklore, the Maelstrom was said to be one vast whirlpool that could suck down whales and even large ships; it was the scene of "A Descent Into the Maelstrom," one of Edgar Allen Poe's most vivid tales. If you get caught in a political or social maelstrom, you probably won't sink—but will certainly get tossed about.

Maginot line mentality. During the 1930s, the French government spent tens of billions on a formidable line of fortifications along its German border; they were named for André Maginot, the minister of war who conceived them. Of course, the forts failed to save France from the German panzers, which beat the French in a mere six weeks.

Since then, people who prefer to put their trust in defense rather than offense are often accused of having a Maginot Line mentality. The metaphor, however, obfuscates a basic fact: the "impregnable" Maginot Line actually covered only France's frontier with Germany, not that with Belgium. Accordingly, the Germans (as anyone but a French or British general could have guessed) attacked through Belgium. Whether a really comprehensive Maginot Line could have saved France is something we'll never know, but the facts of the case merely prove that, if you're relying on defense, you'd better make sure it really covers the situation.

mainstay. The mainstay was a stout rope extending from the top of a ship's mainmast to the foot of the foremast—an important part of the "standing rigging" that kept the masts from collapsing when the wind pressed against the sails. It was an important rope, but no more so than several others. Landlubbers, however, assumed that the "main stay" must be *the* most important rope on the ship, and began using the word to refer to the chief support of a policy or person.

make the fur fly. See **back up**.

make the grade. Almost certainly a railroading term, in which "grade" means the slope of the roadbed in hilly country. As commerce expanded during the late nineteenth century and freight (goods) trains grew longer and longer, the question of whether a train could make the grade became a very real issue. Sometimes a single locomotive couldn't do the job, in which case the train was converted into a **double header**, with two engines.

manna. The Book of Exodus tells how the Children of Israel, wandering in the wilderness, were on occasion refreshed with manna from heaven—a miraculous, nourishing dew (it is now believed to have been a gummy exudation from a species of tamarisk). Today, manna is any "miraculous" and much-needed windfall.

mare's nest. Finding a mare's nest would be a wonderful feat— and also an impossible one, since no mare ever made a nest. If you think you've discovered something remarkable, make sure, before telling people about it, that it isn't that non-existent nest.

maudlin. Just as "Bethlehem" was mumbled into **"Bedlam,"** so "Magdalene" was garbled into "Maudlin." And because religious pictures often showed St. Mary Magdalene weeping, her mispronounced name came to mean first tearful, then tearfully or mawkishly sentimental.

mazuma. Ultimately from Hebrew, in which it means "the ready necessary." In Yiddish, whence it was borrowed into English, it means that most necessary stuff, ready cash.

mealy-mouthed. Since the sixteenth century the term has been applied to people who avoid plain speaking, but nobody seems to know why. My guess is that they seem to speak as if their mouths were full of meal; I've heard "mashed potatoes in the mouth" used in the same sense.

measly. No connection with human measles; the word originally referred to pigs infested with tapeworm. The animals would likely be ill-nourished and scrawny and their flesh, worthless; thus, the modern sense of "measly": small, of little value.

mecca. To Moslems, the city of Mecca, birthplace of Mohammed, is supremely holy: the Koran instructs them to make a *haj* (pilgrimage) there at least once in their lives. Whence the word's figurative sense: any place supremely holy or desirable. Moscow was once the mecca of many radicals throughout the world, but its "holiness" has diminished drastically.

meet one's Waterloo. As virtually all Britishers and some Americans know, Waterloo (in modern Belgium) was the site of Napoleon's final defeat at the hands of the Allied armies under the Duke of Wellington. If you've met your Waterloo, you've had it—conclusively and permanently.

melancholy. See **bilious.**

mercurial. Swift-footed Mercury was the messenger of the Roman gods (he was also the patron of merchants and thieves). His name was given to the fastest moving of the planets, and also to quicksilver, the mobile (liquid) metal. Mercurial people, born under the sign of the planet, are supposed to share the god's quick-wittedness, but also to undergo quick changes in mood comparable to the metal's quick changes in shape.

meretricious. Latin *meretrix* means "whore." A meretricious painting or piece of writing is tarted up to catch the eye—and extract the maximum price from the purchaser.

Mezzogiorno, see **Levant.**

Midas touch. Midas, son of Gordius (see **cut the Gordian knot**), and his successor as king of Phrygia, loved gold before everything else. Granted a favor by the god Dionysos, he asked that anything he touched be turned into gold. Modern financial manipulators are sometimes described as having the Midas touch.

The metaphor is accurate as far as it goes—but ignores the end of the story: *everything* the king touched turned into gold—food, drink and (by one account) his little daughter. Which, when you think about it, makes the figure even better: financiers with the Midas touch not infrequently destroy everyone around them, and at last themselves, in their obsessive search for riches.

Midi, see **Levant.**

mill around/about. The water-mill, used for grinding grain, was the world's first machine employing non-human, non-animal power on land. Its historic importance is shown by the fact that we now use "mill" as almost a generic term for powered machinery, as well as for places where it is used (sawmill, rolling mill, paper mill, steel mill).

The mill's grinding action inspired the nineteenth-century sportsman's "mill" (prizefight), in which one or both contestants would be "ground up"; the circular motion of the millwheel inspired the milling around of a restless herd of cattle or crowd of people.

mince words. If you mince (chop up) a piece of tough meat, it's easier to chew and swallow. Later, "mince" took on the metaphorical sense of minimize or extenuate (e.g., one's faults—presumably by cutting them into small bits). If you mince words, then, you're using extenuating rather than blunt language—which makes tough statements more palatable.

mind one's P's and Q's. There are some half-dozen explanations of this expression, none of which strike me as very plausible. So here's another; whether it's plausible you'll have to decide for yourself.

The Latin and Greek languages are related, meaning that their vocabularies show certain similarities. But the sounds differ in certain ways: specifically, for example, QU in Latin was sometimes equivalent to P in Greek—e.g., Latin *quo* (where) = Greek *pou,* Latin *quintus* (fifth) = Greek *penta.* Thus someone studying both Greek and Latin (as many educated Britishers did until fairly recently) would have to mind his P's and Q's to avoid making mistakes.

month of Sundays, a. A century ago, many Christian sects considered the Sabbath so sacred that not just work but games, energetic play and even laughter were forbidden. To most children, and many adults, Sundays must have seemed long indeed; a month of them would have been interminable.

moocher. Originally, a loiterer, tramp or professional begger, and still a begger of a sort: he loiters about hoping that someone will buy him a meal or a drink. Minnie the Moocher, of the old song, was no moocher, but the word rhymed with "hootchie-kootcher" (we'd now say "exotic dancer"), which she was.

moonlight, moonshine. Somebody who moonlights works at two jobs, one by daylight, the other by moonlight—at least when there's a moon. Moonshine was originally white French brandy, named partly for its color and partly because it was smuggled into England by night. In the U. S., moonshine became another kind of colorless liquor: the whiskey called "white lightning" ("looks like water, kicks like a mule"), distilled, illicitly, "by moonlight" to evade the revenooers.

moxie (courage). By one account, the original version of the soft drink called Moxie (a kind of cola popular in New England) was so bitter that you had to have plenty of moxie to drink it. More likely, it contained enough caffeine to make the drinker feel full of energy—and moxie.

muckraker. In Bunyan's *Pilgrim's Progress,* the "man with a muck-rake" was so busy raking muck (manure) that he ignored the halo over his head. Early in this century, President Theodore Roosevelt borrowed the image to blast journalists who exposed political and corporate corruption—notably, Lincoln Steffens *(The Shame of the Cities)* and Ida M. Tarbell *(History of the Standard Oil Company).*

T.R.'s image was somewhat muddled, since it was the U. S. ("God's country") that he saw as having the halo which the muckrakers were trying to tarnish. Investigative journalists are still raking up muck—and presidents and other politicians are still denouncing "the media" for doing so, feeling that political muck is best left out of sight and out of mind. From their standpoint, it is; the rest of us may reflect that if nobody rakes out the muck, you end up with an **Augean stables**.

muff (fumble). A muff was a soft, hollow cylinder, usually of fur, into which the hands could be thrust to keep them warm. A cricketer or baseball player who muffs an easy catch is playing as though his hands were in a muff.

mug (face). A mug was and is a drinking vessel, usually cylindrical and often with a handle. In the eighteenth century, mugs were often shaped and painted to represent the heads of pirates, highwaymen and the like (we now call them "Toby jugs"). Whence, presumably, the slang "mug" ("and the sergeant reports on your ugly old mug"—Kipling).

mugwump. In one of the native languages of eastern North America, *mugquomp* means "chief"; Englished to "mugwump," it has for a century and a half been applied ironically to important—or self-important—people. It was widely used in 1884 when James G. Blaine, one of the more corrupt politicians in a notably corrupt era, won the Republican presidential nomination. Some Republicans found this too much to swallow, and refused to support him; the regular Republicans promptly christened them "Pharisees, hypocrites, dudes, mugwumps," and so on.

The word has come to mean a political independent of any sort—someone who, depending on where you're standing, either puts principles before party or puts expediency before party loyalty. It has also inspired one of Ben Trovato's most brilliant efforts: A mugwump, he has suggested, is "a bird that sits on the fence with his mug on one side and his wump on the other."

muscle. Some two thousand years ago, an anonymous Roman, noting the rippling of a muscle beneath the skin, saw a resemblance to the scuttling motion of a little mouse *(musculus)*. The slang word stuck, evolved into Old French *muscle,* and thence passed into English.

musical chairs. If you've ever played this game at school or at a kiddies' party, you won't need my explanation; if you haven't— read on. The players march to music around a double line of chairs, set back to back—but with the number of chairs one less than the number of players. The music is stopped suddenly and the players grab seats; whoever fails to get one is eliminated. Then a chair is removed and the game begins again; at the end, the child who's managed to grab the final chair is the winner.

Corporate takeovers and reorganizations often produce a game of musical chairs, with more players than seats. In the higher echelons, however, the rules are changed so there are no losers: if you're thrown out of the game, you fall to earth gently with a golden parachute. Political musical chairs also often has no losers, as when the president reshuffles his cabinet: the members march around the cabinet table and sit down in different seats.

muster up, pass muster. Originally, to show or display, from Old French *moustrer*. Later, soldiers were "displayed" (mustered) to check on their equipment and on how many were present and "accounted for" (i.e., sick, in the guardhouse or on leave). If they passed muster, they were properly equipped and their commander was pleased—provided he could muster up enough men to execute whatever operation he had in mind.

N **nail, on the.** In the sense of "precisely," the metaphor is clear to any home carpenter, who has learned—often painfully—the importance of hitting the nail on the head. The origin of its other sense, "immediately, on the spot" ("he paid cash on the nail") is obscure; indeed, the nail in question may not be a metal fastener but a fingernail, as in German and Dutch phrases with the same sense. But why "on the fingernail" should mean "immediately," in any language, is a mystery.

navvy. A Briticism, now becoming obsolete. The original navvys were "navigators" who dug "navigations" (canals) during the late eighteenth and early nineteenth centuries. From canals, the navvys moved on to railway construction; eventually the word came to mean any pick-and-shovel laborer.

neat, net. Originally "neat" meant clean, free from impurities—whence "neat" (undiluted) liquor. The "net" of a business is another version of the same word—this time meaning the pure profit that remains after the expenses are cleaned up.

nemesis. Greek *nemein* means "give what is due"; the goddess Nemesis gave people what was coming to them—specifically, the punishment due for *hubris* (presumption). If you find yourself putting on airs because fortune has been good to you, watch out: your nemesis may be around the corner!

nepotism. In theory, the Roman Catholic clergy was and is supposed to be completely celibate. Today, non-celibate priests and bishops are probably the exception; in medieval times, they were the rule. The inevitable consequences were "nephews" (Latin *nepotes*), whose "uncles," if they occupied high church office, made certain that their bastards got good jobs in the business. Modern, corporate nepotism has been extended from sons to daughters, in-laws, even actual nephews.

nest egg. Before the days of scientific egg production, farmers would place a fake egg, made of porcelain or white glass, in the hens' nests, which supposedly encouraged the appearance of more real eggs. A financial nest egg will, hopefully, lead to the appearance of more money.

nick of time. The original nick was just that: a cut made in a piece of wood, often to mark a precise place. By the sixteenth century, something that had occurred at a precise moment—by implication, the last possible moment—was said to have come "in the nick"; "of time" was added later.

nickel dropped, the. In the days when you could make a phone call for a nickel, the coin sometimes got hung up in the slot. With a few bangs it would often drop and you'd get your connection. We still use the expression to describe the sudden, if delayed, mental connection we make between one fact and another—the comic strips' light-bulb over the head.

nit(-)picking. Nits are the tiny eggs of lice, which are normally removed from the hair of an infested person with a fine-toothed nit-comb; picking them out by hand is almost impossible. Figurative nit-picking concerns details as tiny as nits—and a great deal less important.

nitty-gritty. To get down to the nitty-gritty is to get down to the real situation. And reality, alas, is often gritty—and sometimes nitty (see previous entry) as well.

no great shakes. The "shake" is a shake of the dice; if something is no great shakes, nobody will win much from or with it.

nose, on the. This expression ought to have something to do with horse races, which are sometimes decided by a nose (only a photo-finish is closer). But the authorities say no: it came from the world of radio.

Directors of radio shows couldn't, for obvious reasons, speak to performers during a broadcast, so they used sign-language. Among the signs were a sweep of the forefinger across the throat ("Cut!"), holding up one hand with the thumb and forefinger pressed together ("Perfect performance!"), and touching the finger to the nose ("Perfect timing!").

Even though everyone agrees on this story, I still wonder why this particular gesture—whose "literal" meaning is clearly "on the nose"—was selected. Just possibly, the gesture came before the phrase—though that still wouldn't explain where the phrase came from. All contributions gratefully received!

nut, (on/off the). To a carnival worker, the nut is the rent he lays out to the show owner for his pitch; he's "on the nut" until the rent is paid—i.e., he's not making money. In theater, the nut is the money laid out to mount the show, which must be paid back to the "angels" (financial backers) before anyone makes a profit. In either case, the nut is what you have to crack to get at the toothsome kernel.

obvious. Latin *obviare* meant to meet in the road *(via);* something that's obvious is lying right in the middle of the road. ᴏ **O**

Occident—see **Levant.**

Ockham's razor. William of Ockham or Occam, an English scholar of the early fourteenth century, was the first to put forward the notion that "Nature does not multiply entities unnecessarily." What he was getting at, in modern terms, was that when you try to explain a given set of facts you should pick the explanation that involves the fewest assumptions. The principle can't be proved, but has been immensely useful to science as a "razor" for shaving away unnecessary logical complications and eliminating fuzzy theories.

Oedipus complex. If you know your Greek mythology, you can skip this one. If not—Oedipus was the son of king Laius of Thebes. At his birth, an oracle predicted that he would kill his father; Laius prudently had the baby exposed—left in the fields to die. But a shepherd found the infant and brought it up as his own child.

Twenty years pass. Oedipus gets a prophecy of his own, from the famous oracle at Delphi (see **Delphic**): he will "slay the sower of his seed and sow the field he grew in." Thinking this refers to his supposed parents, he doesn't return home but sets off for another city. On the road, he encounters a stranger (Laius, of course), whom he quarrels with and kills. After other adventures, he arrives in Thebes and marries the widowed queen, becoming king of Thebes.

The gods strike the city with a plague; an oracle declares that it will only cease when the slayer of Laius is expelled from the city. Oedipus asks the seer Tiresias for the name of the culprit, and is told "Thou art the man!" Frenzied at having unwittingly killed his father and married his mother, he blinds himself and goes into exile.

Around 1910, Sigmund Freud evolved the theory that every boy at a certain age unconsciously wants to murder his father and sleep with his mother; failure to resolve this "Oedipus complex," he said, was a prime source of neurosis. No doubt people with such a complex *would* become neurotic—but neither Freud nor anyone else ever proved that most or even many people have it.

There is this much truth to the Oedipus complex (which has become a myth in its own right): boys tend to have warmer feelings for their mothers, and girls for their fathers, other things being equal—which they often aren't. But nobody has ever offered any credible evidence that these feelings normally involve sex, as opposed to simple affection.

off(-)color. For centuries, "color" (British "colour") has meant, among other things, the ruddy hue of a healthy complexion. When a Britisher says (s)he's "off color," then, (s)he means merely that (s)he "feels pale"—sickly or out of **sorts.**

In America, the phrase means something quite different: an off-color story is a dirty one. This sense may derive from an off-color piece of cloth—one that has been improperly dyed; however, a dirty piece of cloth would be equally off-color.

oil on troubled waters. A ship in a stormy sea is in little danger from large, smooth waves (swells), which usually do no more than lift and lower it; the real threat is the large, breaking wave, whose weight may smash through the decking or **poop** the vessel. Since ancient times, mariners have known that pouring oil on a stormy sea, though it won't reduce the size of the waves, makes them less likely to break. If someone tries to pour oil on the troubled waters of a quarrel, (s)he's seeking to smooth things over.

Old Man of the Sea. In the *Arabian Nights,* one of Sinbad the Sailor's adventures was an encounter with the Old Man of the Sea, who, having persuaded Sinbad to take him on his shoulders, refused to get down. After carrying him around for several weeks, Sinbad rid himself of his burden by getting the old fellow drunk. Most of us have encountered people who, like Sinbad's burdensome acquaintance, simply won't get off our backs.

olive branch. When the dove that Noah sent forth from the ark returned bearing an olive branch, the old navigator knew that the Flood was over (Genesis viii). For this reason, supposedly, the olive branch symbolizes peace—i.e., a return to normal conditions; at any rate, no one has come up with a better explanation. If one party to a dispute holds out an olive branch, they're offering to end the quarrel.

one hundred and twenty in the water bag. A metaphor not used outside Australia—and, I'd guess, not very common even there; I include it simply because it's such a wonderful image. In the Australian "never never" (desert or near-desert), travelers must carry water with them—often in a semi-porous bag of heavy burlap. Water seeping slowly through the burlap evaporates, keeping the water inside moderately cool. So if the temperature is 120° F (49° C) *in* the water bag, you can imagine what it is outside!

one-horse town. Back when horses were the main means of transport, a one-horse town—one in which a single animal could do all the necessary hauling—was the ultimate small (practically microscopic!) town.

one-night stand. In one-horse towns, and some larger communities, **barnstorming** theatrical companies would often do one-night stands: a single performance, after which they'd move on to another, and hopefully more profitable, engagement. Today's one-night stands are rather different performances, but often no less unprofitable, to both parties.

open season. As any hunter knows, the open season on deer, ducks or whatever is the period in which it's legal to shoot them. If it's open season on a person or institution, (s)he or it is going to draw plenty of fire.

opium of the people. Not exactly a lost metaphor, but its true sense, I believe, has been lost. Indeed, I'd call this famous phrase of Karl Marx (though he wasn't the first to use it) one of the most misunderstood metaphors in history—thanks to both some Marxists and many anti-Marxists.

It's usually taken to mean that religion, like opium, is an addictive drug that should be stamped out. But at the time Marx wrote (ca. 1850), opium was much more than a "recreational" drug: it was the only effective pain-killer—and one of the very few drugs that actually did the patient any good. I myself have been given "opium" (i.e., its modern derivatives, morphine and meperidine) after surgery—and mighty glad I was to have it.

From that standpoint, then, religion is essentially a painkiller—but is that really all Marx meant? Read the phrase in context and decide for yourself. "Religion," he wrote, "is the sigh of the hard-pressed creature, the heart of a heartless world, as it is the soul of souless circumstance. It is the opium of the people."

The defense rests.

orgy. In ancient Greece, orgies were secret ceremonies honoring some god, especially Dionysos, the god of wine. As the *OED* decorously puts it, his orgies included "extravagant dancing, singing, drinking, etc." Modern orgies concentrate on the etc.

Orient—see **Levant.**

oscillate. Roman farmers would sometimes honor their god of wine, Bacchus, by hanging from their vines little masks *(oscilla)* representing him. Naturally, these would swing back and forth—oscillate—in the wind.

ostracize. In ancient Athens, citizens considered threats to the state (in some cases, probably, only pains in the neck) could be banished for five years or more by vote of their fellow citizens, who dropped potsherds *(ostrakoi)* into an urn to signify aye or nay. People who are ostracized nowadays aren't literally banished, but, since nobody will talk to them, it comes to much the same thing.

other side of the tracks—see **wrong side** . . . .

pagan—see **heathen**. ₵**P**

paint oneself into a corner. A wonderfully vivid metaphor, describing the plight of some inept do-it-yourselfer who begins painting the floor of a room at the door and ends up in a corner, surrounded by wet paint. The painter may be mythical, but painting yourself into a corner leaves you where he was: in a situation from which escape will be both messy and embarrassing.

paint the town red. The meaning is clear enough, though the precise type of painting referred to isn't. Cowboys or sailors on a spree would certainly engage in "nose-painting," which Shakespeare cited as one of the three effects of liquor. And nose-painting can lead to bloody noses—even, if things get sufficiently out of hand, to fires, set accidentally or on purpose, whose flames would indeed paint the town red. So the correct answer to "What kind of painting?" is probably "Any of the above."

pale, beyond the. A "double" metaphor. The original pale was a stout stake with a pointed end; then, a fence (paling) made of such stakes. Whence the original metaphor: various "fenced" enclaves under English control—notably, Dublin and its environs ("the Pale"), which for many centuries was the only part of Ireland where England actually ruled.

The modern figurative sense, like that of "without **benefit of clergy**," probably comes from Kipling, one of whose early stories was titled "Beyond the Pale." The British in India, like South African whites today, lived in physical pales where natives, except for servants, were excluded. But the British also lived in a social pale: personal friendships with natives were out of bounds, and that went double for relationships with native women. (In South Africa, until quite recently, such relationships could put the participants in jail.)

The protagonist of Kipling's story went beyond that pale and became involved with a young Indian widow; of course the affair ended tragically. Someone or something beyond the pale, in short, is socially as far out of bounds as you can get.

palm off. A stage magician who palms a card is tricking you; a card-sharper who does it is cheating you. If someone palms off a piece of shoddy merchandise on you, he's doing both.

pan out. Gold is often found in sand bars (placers) in and around streams, as in California of the Forty-niners. The simplest way of extracting the gold is to put a few handfuls of sand into a large, flat pan—something like an oversize pie-pan—and carefully wash the sand away, leaving the heavier gold particles behind.

Gold rush miners exploring the diggings would wash a sample of sand from a particular placer to see how it panned out. If it produced nuggets or "colors" (flakes of gold), they had hit *pay dirt* and would *stake a claim*—literally drive stakes at the corners of the plot they planned to work.

pandemonium. A word coined by the poet Milton to mean "the high Capital of Satan and his peers" (its literal sense is "place of all the demons"). Whence, later, a place or gathering of wild, lawless violence, but now merely any sort of wild uproar.

Pandora's box. When the titan Prometheus stole fire from heaven and gave it to mankind, Zeus decided to revenge himself on the human race. Accordingly, he ordered Hephaestus, the artificer of the gods, to create a woman of surpassing beauty, who was named "Pandora." She was presented with a box containing every human ill and given to Epimetheus, Prometheus' brother, as his wife.

Either Epimetheus or Pandora herself opened the box, thereby releasing evil on the world. The last thing out of the box was hope, though it's not clear whether this was a sort of consolation prize or an extra turn of the screw (hope, after all, is what induces people to put up with repeated ills). Opening Pandora's box is worse than opening a can of worms.

panic. The Greek woodland god Pan was thought to cause the mysterious sounds heard at night in mountains and other remote places; these often induced "panic" fear. Things that go bump in the night can still induce panic; so can catastrophes at any time of day, as in "financial panic."

paper tiger. A contribution to English from Mao Dze Dung, who described the U.S. as one: ferocious in aspect, paper-thin in substance. His purpose was to convince the Chinese people that the U. S. was a much less formidable enemy than it seemed, but an unintended result was to persuade many American leaders that they must at all costs show they were "real" tigers. Indeed, they became so obsessed with maintaining their tigerish image that they failed to consider whether acting like a predator always makes sense.

paradise. An old Persian word, *pairidaeza,* means an enclosed park or garden. Borrowed into other languages of the **Levant**, it was eventually applied to both the earthly paradise (the Garden of Eden) and the heavenly one.

During a trip to Morocco some years ago I discovered just how appropriate the metaphor is. My wife and I had been exploring the *souks* (markets) and smells of Marrakesh for several hours, under a burning afternoon sun. At last our guide led us into the walled courtyard of the local museum, set with trees, flowers and a playing fountain; it was a paradise indeed!

parasite. In ancient Greece, a *parasitos* was literally one who ate at someone else's table—hence, a professional diner-out who sang for his supper by flattering his host. Human parasites are still at it; biological parasites dine on the host rather than at his table.

pariah. Originally, a drummer; its figurative sense requires a fairly lengthy explanation. About 1500 B.C., a wave of invaders, called Aryans, moved into India, where they installed their own social system, based on four classes, from the brahmans (priests) on top to the farmers on the bottom. The conquered natives of India didn't fit into this scheme, and so were classified as casteless and "unclean." This permanent underclass still exists in India as the so-called untouchables.

In southern India, one of the lower, though not untouchable, castes was that of the professional drummers *(pariyar)*. The English, through a misunderstanding, applied the term to the untouchables themselves—whence the modern sense: someone who is socially "untouchable," and therefore to be shunned by all decent people.

partridge. Surprisingly, the word is akin to "fart"; even more surprisingly, its Greek original literally meant "farter." If you've ever heard the whirring wings of a partridge taking off in a hurry, you'll know why.

pass muster—see **muster up.**

pass the buck. The metaphor comes from poker, allegedly from some small object—a buck(horn)-handled knife or a buckshot—passed to the player whose turn it was to bet. The notion seems improbable: every poker player knows without being told that betting passes to the next player on the left.

Much more likely, "buck" is simply an old term for "bet";

"bucking the tiger" was a common term for betting against the bank at faro. In poker, it took on the additional sense of "raise"—perhaps as a bucking broncho "raises" its rider. If a player passed the buck, then, he was declining to raise ("checking"), thus letting the next player decide whether to raise or fold.

Passing the buck—shifting the decision or responsibility to someone else—is still a favorite tactic in large, bureaucratic organizations, notably, the U.S. Army, where it's known as "the old army game."

patrol. From French *patrouiller,* to paddle (with the feet) in the mud, which became French soldiers' slang for the infantryman's interminable tramping. U.S. troops on patrol in Vietnam did a lot of paddling in the mud.

patter (magician's or pitchman's). During the Middle Ages, Christian prayers were in Latin, which nobody but churchmen and scholars understood (in the Roman Catholic church, this remained true until quite recently). Accordingly, people often muttered rapidly through the Paternoster (Our Father) and other prayers, and this "pattering" was quickly transferred to any form of mumbled fast-talk—specifically, that of conjurers and pedlars.

Five centuries later, "patter" remains an essential device of magicians, pitchmen and carnival workers. (Suggestions that the word derives from some Gypsy term contradict the historical facts: "patter" was used figuratively well before the Gypsies arrived in England.)

pawn. From Old French *peon,* foot-soldier. When chess reached Western Europe in the thirteenth century, a pawn became one of the "foot-soldiers" that are the weakest pieces in the game. But chess pawns, skillfully deployed, may prove decisive; on occasion, they can even become queens—the most powerful piece—as Alice did in *Through the Looking Glass.* Human pawns can be equally powerful when manipulated by a master player.

pay dirt—see **pan out**.

pecking order. More than 50 years ago, animal psychologists discovered that flocks of chickens had a fairly rigid social structure: bird A could peck B, but not vice versa; bird C might be pecked by either A or B, but could itself peck only D and others lower down in the "pecking order." The term was soon transferred from avian to human societies, in which some people can "peck" others without being pecked themselves.

peculiar. In Latin, *peculiaris* means "pertaining to private property"; it derived from *pecu,* cattle, once the commonest form of moveable property. Eventually, it was transferred to another kind of "property": someone's peculiar (distinctive) traits, then to his or her personal oddities, and at last, as an adjective, to anything strange—or peculiar. The original cattle have roamed a long way!

pecuniary, impecunious. The same cattle, but of a different color. Before the invention of coinage, cattle were often used as "money"—which is what Latin *pecunia* means. An impecunious person is chronically short of "cattle."

peeping tom. An old English legend tells of Leofric, lord of Coventry, who taxed his subjects unbearably. His wife, Lady Godiva, continually urged him to lower the taxes; eventually, to shut her up, he agreed to do so if she would ride naked through the streets of the town.

To his surprise, she did, first asking the townsfolk to stay indoors and shutter their windows. Since they wanted their taxes reduced, they did so—except for Peeping Tom, who got an eyeful through a crack in the shutter. The townsfolk got their lower taxes—and Tom was struck blind. Modern peeping toms still get their kicks from peering through shutters and windows at naked or half-naked women, but their punishment—when caught—is less appropriate.

person(a), personality. In the Greek and Roman theaters, the actors wore masks appropriate to the characters they played. Thus Latin *persona,* mask, came to mean a character denoted by a mask, then any "character" in the human comedy we all play roles in. Today a persona is the "mask" a person dons before facing the outside world, which may or may not differ radically from his or her true character or personality.

perspicacious. Latin *perspicere* meant to see through; a perspicacious person can see through the outer appearance of things to their true nature.

pest(er). From Latin *pestis,* a plague or epidemic; its French equivalent, *peste,* was borrowed into English to denote *the* plague—bubonic fever, which from the fourteenth to the seventeenth centuries killed tens of millions in periodic epidemics. With the decline of this pest, the word was transferred to the animals and human beings that plague or pester us.

peter out. There are two theories on this, neither of them airtight. The first cites the apostle Peter who, when Christ was arrested, drew his sword and cut off an ear from one of the cops. But his militance quickly petered out; soon afterward, he was denying that he even knew his Master.

If you don't like this one—I don't, much—consider the possible relationship of "peter out" to French *peter,* fart. In the nineteenth century, a "peter" was poacher's slang for a **partridge**— almost certainly referring to the "farting" noise of the bird's wings. "Peter out" would then be equivalent to "fizzle out," since according to the OED the original "fizzle" was a noiseless fart.

petrel. This family of sea-birds pretty certainly *is* related to Saint Peter etymologically. Stormy petrels (a.k.a. Mother Cary's Chickens) often fly close to the sea and, in the words of an early explorer, "pat the Water alternately with their feet, as if they walkt upon it"—which is what St. Peter is said to have done on the Lake of Gennesareth.

phantasmagoria. In 1802, a showman exhibited in London a special kind of magic lantern that could make the figures it projected seem to advance and retreat, fade into each other, or vanish. Wanting a resounding name for his invention, he coined the pseudo-Greek "phantasmagoria." The word was almost immediately applied figuratively, to any shifting series of imaginary figures, as in a dream, and eventually to any intricately shifting scene, imaginary or real.

phlegmatic—see **bilious**.

phony. From Irish *fainne,* ring, which nineteenth-century swindlers transformed into "fawney." "Fawney rigging" was a con involving the sale of a supposedly gold ring—which was, of course, phony.

picayune. In old (French) New Orleans, a *picaillon* was a small coin worth about five cents; something that's picayune is equally trivial. The leading New Orleans paper is still the *Times-Picayune* (reflecting its original price); as to whether the word applies to its editorial content—I pass.

pickle, in a. We think of pickles as foodstuffs preserved in brine and vinegar, but the word originally meant the pickling solution itself. If you found yourself in a vat of pickle, you clearly were in an embarrassing and uncomfortable position.

pie in the sky. In the years before World War I, the International Workers of the World (IWW), a.k.a. Wobblies, was one of the most radical organizations in this country, and probably the most colorful anywhere. Its members were mainly miners, lumberjacks, migratory workers and seamen, whose occupations largely isolated them from the rest of society. Respectable people therefore looked down on them—and they returned the compliment, with double-digit interest.

In particular, the Wobblies were contemptuous of churches

and churchmen. These, they felt (and with some justice), gave handouts to the poor while preaching the virtue of "humility"—meaning not making trouble for one's "betters," the godly, generous men who paid people's wages.

The IWW attitude was summed up in "The Preacher and the Slave," a song written by the Wobbly organizer "Joe Hill" (Joseph Hilstrom); to add insult to injury, it was sung to a popular hymn tune:

> Long-haired preachers come out every night,
> Try to tell you what's wrong and what's right,
> But when asked about something to eat
> They will answer in voices so sweet:
> "You will eat, by and bye,
> In that glorious land above the sky (way up high!);
> Work and pray, live on hay,
> You'll get pie in the sky when you die." (That's a lie!)

Times have changed: today a fair number of preachers urge their flocks not to wait for heaven, but to get themselves organized and carve out a hunk of pie here and now. But other preachers—along with politicians, propagandists and publicists—continue to promise pie in the sky. And it's still a lie.

piecard. This one is of much the same vintage as the last, though much less common. In IWW days—indeed, as recently as the 1930s—lunch wagons and other off-the-arm joints sold meal tickets: cards entitling the purchaser to $5 or $10 worth of food. Along the margin were printed rows of numbers—25s, 10s and 5s; when you settled your check, the cashier, using a punch like a railroad conductor's, would punch out enough of them to cover the bill.

Circa 1910, a slang term for "meal ticket" was "piecard." The IWW transferred the word to the leaders of "respectable" unions, who—as the Wobblies saw it—considered unionism mainly a meal ticket. A more recent term meaning the same thing is *pork-*

chopper—a union official greedy for the pork chops his job yields, and the gravy, too.

Pied Piper. A medieval German legend tells of the Pied Piper of Hamlin (Hameln, a town in western Germany on the river Weser), which was sore beset by a plague of rats. As the poet Browning later told the story, the animals "fought the dogs and killed the cats/ And bit the babies in their cradles/ And ate the soup from the cooks' own ladles." One day there appeared a man in pied (parti-colored) raiment, bearing a musical pipe (a sort of recorder); he offered, for a thousand guilders, to get rid of the **pests.**

The town burghers agreed, and the piper struck up a strange tune. From the houses, the rats emerged in their thousands, and followed him down the street to the river bank, where they plunged in and drowned. But when the piper demanded his fee, the burghers, figuring that "what's drowned won't come to life," offered him a mere fifty guilders.

The piper warned that if they didn't pay the full fee, "I'll tune my pipe to a different note," but they still refused. Again he began piping, but this time it was the town's children who followed him. They marched to a nearby hill, which split open to let them enter, then closed—and neither they nor the Piper were ever seen again. If you hear someone described as a Pied Piper, you'll know that he can make just about anyone march to his tune.

pig iron. When iron is smelted in a blast furnace, it's drawn off in liquid form into molds—originally, merely an array of oblong troughs in a bed of sand. Long ago, some ironworker noted the resemblance of the row of cast ingots to a litter of piglets nursing at their mother—and the name stuck.

pillar to post, from. The ultimate ancestor of modern tennis was a more complicated game called court tennis (it's still played by a few people). This employed an indoor court, which included as hazards various pillars, posts and sloping surfaces along the

walls. If the ball bounced from pillar to post, it was moving erratically, and therefore not getting anywhere useful.

pineapple (bomb)—see **grenade**.

pioneer. The original (sixteenth-century) pioneers were what
we'd call military engineer detachments: soldiers who marched
ahead of the main body, digging ditches, building bridges and
repairing roads. The pioneers who opened up the interior of
North America also moved ahead of the main body of settlers,
blazing trails and—if they were farmers—doing plenty of digging.

Pipe down! Until fairly recently, crews of naval vessels were
often ordered about by the boatswain's pipe: a sort of whistle
which could be blown in various calls. "Pipe down" was the call
immediately preceding the final one of the night (equivalent to
"Taps" on a bugle); it meant "Quiet down and get ready to turn
in." Nowadays, of course, the phrase means merely "Quiet
down!"—or "Shut up!"

pit(ted) against—see **cockpit**.

play fast and loose. The "fast" here has nothing to do with
speed, but rather means "fixed in place," as a ship is made fast
to a pier. "Fast and loose" was originally a trick played at village
fairs by gypsies and other sharpers. A belt was intricately coiled
so that it seemed to have a knotted loop in its center; a yokel was
invited to bet that he could make it fast to a table by stabbing a
knife through the loop. Of course the belt wasn't really fast, but
loose, and the sucker lost his money. Someone who tells you a
canard is playing fast and loose with the facts.

play hardball. This one is strictly for British readers. The
American "national game" of baseball exists in two forms. Soft-
ball, as its name implies, uses a relatively soft ball, somewhat
larger than a cricket ball, which must be thrown underhand—i.e.,
it moves relatively slowly.

In the "standard" game (hardball or simply baseball), the ball is harder, smaller and is thrown overhand; a really fast pitch can travel in excess of 90 miles per hour. The ball is naturally harder to hit—and painful (at best) if it hits you. When someone announces that they're going to play hardball, they're saying that they no longer intend to go easy on the opposition, but be as tough and nasty as necessary.

play it close to the vest. If you hold your cards close to your vest, or the part of you that a vest covers, you're making sure nobody can peek at your hand and deduce how you plan to play. If you're playing something else close to your vest, you're keeping your "cards" a secret.

play possum. The American opossum has changed little for some 60 million years. Its lengthy survival as a species may be due in part to a useful strategem: when threatened, it rolls over on its back and plays dead, its limbs stiff and its mouth open in an agonized grimace. Since few predators care for carrion, the trick works a good deal of the time. If an opponent seems to be "dead," watch out: (s)he may be playing possum!

play second fiddle. Lovers of classical music know that most instrumental ensembles include two violins or groups of violins: first and second. The second-violin part is naturally less noticeable and less showy than that of the first violin. Which is the sort of part you're playing if you play second fiddle to someone.

play to the gallery. For several centuries the cheapest theater seats have been those in the gallery, requiring the holders to climb several flights of stairs. Occupants of cheap seats were presumed to have less taste than those sitting downstairs, and actors who indulged in cheap effects—ranting speeches or crude humor— were therefore playing to the gallery.

In Shakespeare's day, it was the gallery seats that were most expensive—because they were the only seats; the rest of the audience, the "groundlings," stood in the open courtyard around which the galleries were arranged. In *Hamlet* the playwright wrote acidly of actors who ranted or ad-libbed gags, to "split the ears of the groundlings." Some actors, politicians and preachers still play to the gallery, ranting and taking cheap shots at their opponents. Alternatively, like baseball players who engage in showy maneuvers, they're "playing to the grandstand" or simply *grandstanding*.

Plimsoll mark. Nineteenth-century British shipowners who had insured their vessels heavily often loaded them heavily as well; if an overloaded ship was lost in a storm, the owner still collected. In 1876, Parliament passed a bill sponsored by Samuel Plimsoll, requiring all British-flag ships to carry a mark—a circle with a line through it—on their sides showing the maximum depth to which they could be safely loaded. If someone is loaded to the Plimsoll mark, he's taken aboard all the liquor he can safely carry, and perhaps a bit more.

pluck(y). Originally, the viscera of an animal, as used for food. A plucky person has plenty of guts.

poetic justice. The phrase goes back to the seventeenth century, but there's no clear evidence of its source. However, poets as far back as ancient Greece have enjoyed recounting how the gods, or fate, deal out ironically appropriate punishment to the arrogant or wicked. The fate of King Midas (see **Midas touch**) was a good example of poetic justice.

poker face. To bluff successfully in poker, you must guard against facial expressions that reveal the actual strength of your hand. Many good players find that the best way of doing this is to keep a poker face—show no expression whatever.

pokey (jail). Something that's pokey is small and insignificant—hence, confining. If you land in the pokey, you're in a very small and confining place.

poll. Originally, "poll" meant "head." The poll tax, once used in the southern U.S. to prevent blacks and other poor people from voting (it's now outlawed) was assessed "by heads"—every adult had to pay the same sum. An electoral poll amounts to counting heads, and a public opinion poll is a more sophisticated—though less accurate—way of doing the same thing.

pontificate. The pope is also known as the pontiff, from one of his Latin titles, *Pontifex Maximus.* According to Catholic theology, the pope's utterances are infallible on matters of faith and morals; if someone pontificates, (s)he's talking as if (s)he was the infallible pontiff.

pooh-bah. In Gilbert and Sullivan's still-popular *Mikado,* Ko-Ko was the Lord High Executioner, and Pooh-Bah was The Lord High Everything Else. The name is still applied (especially in Britain) to exceptionally self-important people, especially if they hold many offices.

poop (official information). Almost certainly a former naval term, dating from the days of sail. Naval captains then commanded their ships not from the bridge amidships, as they now do, but from the poop deck at the stern. Information from the poop was therefore official and (supposedly) definitive.

pooped. Probably from the same ultimate source. The poop (stern) of a vessel, unlike the bow, was not designed to resist the waves' battering. A ship sailing before the wind in high seas was therefore in danger of being pooped—being overtaken by a large wave that could smash in the poop and hurl tons of water into the vessel. A pooped ship was in danger of sinking; if you're really pooped, that's how you feel.

pork barrel. Pork was long the cheapest meat available. Probably for this reason it has long been applied to government funds appropriated for particular areas, thanks to the **clout** of legislators from those areas—a cheap way of buying the voters' favor.

A pork-barrel bill is one containing a bit of pork for every law-maker—or at least every one that counts.

porkchopper—see **piecard**.

port—see **starboard**.

posh. When Britons traveled to and from the hot, eastern parts of their empire, they preferred the shady side of the ship—the port (left) side, facing north, on the eastward voyage, the **starboard** (right) when homeward bound. According to Ben Trovato, privileged passengers would therefore have their tickets marked POSH (Port Out, Starboard Home).

The true story is not as "neat," but almost as interesting. In Romany (Gypsy), *posh* meant "half," whence *posh-horri* (half-penny) and *posh-koorona* (half-crown). The term was borrowed into criminal slang to mean simply "money," whence, probably, a later sense, a dandy—who presumably had plenty of the stuff. Certainly the dandy is the immediate source of the modern adjective: a posh hotel is the kind that dandies patronize—if they have enough posh.

possess. Ultimately, from Latin *potis,* powerful—the source of "potent," "potentate" and other words dealing with power—and *sedere,* sit. If you possess something, you're sitting powerfully on it—powerfully enough to, hopefully, keep others from grabbing it.

pot calling the kettle black, the. Nowadays, with most kitchen pots made of aluminum or stainless steel, the metaphor is puzzling. But right up to the end of the nineteenth century, pots and kettles were made either of copper or (more often) of the cheaper iron. Iron pots and kettles were covered by a black coating of oxide, and further blackened by soot from the wood fires used for cooking. Some people feel that many modern political debates are a case of a sooty pot criticizing the sooty kettle—and vice versa. See also **blackguard**.

pot luck. If someone invites you over for a pot-luck supper, you can expect to dine on whatever happens to be in the pot—which may or may not be what you'd prefer. Much the same happens if you take any kind of pot luck.

pot-boiler. A writer who turns out a second-rate piece of work to keep food in the pot has written a pot-boiler. Some people look down on such writers, and it's easy to do so—if your own pot has never been empty.

potter's field—see **blood money**.

precarious. The "pre-" here isn't the familiar "pre-" meaning "before" (prehistoric, pre-cooked), but from Latin *precem,* prayer. If you're in a precarious situation—better start praying!

precipice/precipitate/precipitous. The "-cipit-" is a variant of Latin *caput,* head (see **capital**), and *precipitare* meant to fall headlong: what happens if you get too close to the edge of a precipice—which is a precipitous piece of terrain. If you undertake a precipitate or precipitous act, you double the metaphor, by leaping headlong into the situation—or at least not looking before you leap. And the chemist's precipitate is the solid stuff that falls headlong to the bottom of his test-tube solution.

precocious. Originally, in Latin, "precooked"; later, it referred to fruit that was "cooked" (ripened) before its time. Precocious children have ripened, physically or mentally, before their time, but their judgement, alas, is usually still green.

preposterous. The Latin original means, roughly, "the behind coming before"; what happens when you put the cart before the horse. A preposterous statement is ass backwards.

prestige. From a French word meaning "illusion, juggler's tricks," which is just what the prestige of many public figures is:

the product of media manipulation, photo opportunities and what some political operatives call "smoke and mirrors."

pretext. The Latin *praetexta* was a special toga with a purple border (see **born to the purple**), hence an outer display. A pretext is the "toga" displayed to cloak the owner's real motives.

prevaricate. Latin *varicare* means to straddle, and *praevaricare*, to walk crookedly—hence, what a Roman lawyer did when he betrayed his client by making a deal with the opposition. Someone who prevaricates is emulating that lawyer or, at the very least, **straddling** or dodging the issue.

procrustean. The legendary Greek robber Prokrustes (literally, "the stretcher") had a notorious bed in which his "guests" were forced to lie. If they were shorter than the bed, they were stretched to fit; if longer, their legs were lopped off. Eventually, the hero Theseus gave him what he deserved: a course of treatment on his own apparatus. We still speak of a procrustean theory: one that stretches or trims the facts to fit it.

profanity. From Latin *fanum*, temple, whence *profanus*, outside the temple—hence not sacred. Profanity is the kind of language that you definitely don't use in church.

proletariat. The lowest class of citizens in ancient Rome were considered good for nothing but producing offspring *(proles)*; in Rome as in many other places, the rich got richer and the poor got children. Marx transferred the term to the "working class" of modern capitalist society: those who had no capital or other assets—except their offspring.

protean. The Greco-Roman sea god Proteus was known for his ability to assume innumerable shapes. Someone with protean talents (e.g., Leonardo da Vinci) is deemed to be equally versatile.

pull someone's chestnuts out of the fire—see **cat's-paw**.

pull strings/wires. The strings (or wires) are those that control a puppet; someone who gets something by pulling strings does so through behind-the-scenes manipulation—perhaps of a human puppet.

pull the wool over someone's eyes. Two hundred years ago, all gentlemen wore wigs, made of hair but referred to jokingly as wool. A favorite trick was to pull the wool forward over the wearer's face so that he couldn't see what was going on. If somebody has pulled the wool over your eyes, you've been **hoodwinked**.

pull up stakes. Prospectors, trappers and explorers in the Old West normally lived in tents, the edges of which were staked down with wooden pegs. When they wanted to move on, the first step was to pull up stakes and strike the tent.

pupil. Latin *pupilla* meant "little girl"—and also the tiny human figure you see when you look into someone's eye, whence the "pupil" of that organ. A pupil is also, of course, literally a little girl or boy, at school.

pushover. A double metaphor: a prizefighter who can be easily beaten is a pushover—it takes only a push to put him down—and so, for much the same reason, is a woman who can be easily had. Whence the figurative sense of anything easily accomplished.

put a spoke in someone's wheel. Spokes—the shafts that connect the hub of a wheel to its rim—have been known for at least four thousand years. But in the nineteenth century, the word took on the additional sense of a device for braking a vehicle: a stout rod that could be thrust through the spokes of a wheel to prevent it from turning. If somebody has put a spoke in your wheel, (s)he's braking your forward progress, if not stopping it entirely.

put on the Ritz. From the once ultrafashionable Ritz Hotel in London, and the equally classy (but now demolished) Ritz-Carlton of New York. Someone who's putting on the ritz is assuming the airs and graces ascribed to patrons of those establishments.

put one's foot in it. Not, as some think, from putting one's foot in one's mouth; "it" is the stinking, adhesive substance which careless dog-owners allow their pets to leave on the street. If you've stepped in a pile of "it," you've really put your foot in it—landed yourself in an unpleasant and embarrassing predicament.

put the cart before the horse—see **preposterous**.

put the screws on. The screws aren't those used to fasten a piece of woodwork together, but the much larger screws once used to compress such things as cotton bales. If someone's putting the screws on you, they're squeezing you for all you're worth.

quarantine. In Italian, *quarantina* was literally forty days— *Q* specifically, the period in which ships suspected of carrying diseased people were supposed to remain isolated from the shore. (The first recorded use in English refers, confusingly, to "a quarantine of thirty days.") Modern quarantines have more to do with the "disease" of war: governments sometimes talk of quarantining belligerents, meaning to cut off shipments of arms or other supplies. But such quarantines, unfortunately, seldom last even forty days—assuming they're imposed at all.

queue. In the eighteenth century, a queue was a pigtail—then more often worn by men than by women. A century later it had been transferred to a "pigtail" of people lined up to get into a theater or bus. It's given the British a vivid phrase, "Join the queue!", meaning, approximately, "plenty of us share your sentiments." An equivalent used in both Britain and the U.S. is "Join the club!" New Yorkers often say "Get on line!"

quintessence. To medieval alchemists, the essence of something was its purified substance obtained by distillation. The quintessence was the ultimate "fifth essence," from which the heavenly bodies were supposedly made—but no alchemist ever succeeded in extracting it. The word persists as the ultimate essence or most characteristic quality of something.

quixotic. From the central character in Cervantes' great novel, *Don Quixote de la Mancha.* The "knight of the rueful countenance" was constantly deluding himself into performing supposed deeds of chivalry: rescuing damsels who didn't need rescuing, tilting at windmills under the illusion that they were giants, and so on. Someone performing a quixotic action is, like the good Don, acting with the best motives—but pointlessly, not to say foolishly.

R ₹ **rabbi.** A rabbi is, of course, a Jewish clergyman. But in slang he's the counselor and unofficial protector of a cop or other public servant, at headquarters or City Hall—who, like a real rabbi, gives good advice and is thought to have influence with higher powers.

Rabelasian—see **gargantuan.**

rack one's brains. The rack here is the apparatus used in medieval and early modern times, to extract confessions from criminals and religious heretics. The prisoner was stretched on the rack, ropes were attached to wrists and ankles, and then drawn taut with a windlass—sometimes to the point where the joints were dislocated; the infamous bed of Prokrustes (see **procrustean**) was something like a rack. When you rack your brains, you're stretching them as hard as you can—perhaps painfully.

radical. From Latin *radix,* root (the radish, whose crunchy root adds zest to salads, comes from the same source). A political radical pursues a program that supposedly goes to the root of a problem, rather than ameliorating its symptoms—though radical solutions often engender problems of their own, which must be uprooted in turn. Over the last 50 years or so, the word has become an all-purpose political epithet, applied to anyone whose views go "too far"—in the speaker's estimation.

rain cats and dogs/pitchforks. Two centuries ago, few if any cities had arrangements for collecting garbage; instead, junk and wastes of all sorts—including the corpses of dogs and cats—were simply tossed into the streets, where they accumulated in a gutter along the center, called the kennel. A really violent rain, then, would dislodge the dead cats and dogs from their kennel and sweep them along the street.

This, at any rate, is the most plausible explanation I know of for the phrase. Raining pitchforks is easier: in an intense daytime storm, the slanting spears of rain may look not unlike the tines of a pitchfork.

rake (person). An abbreviation of "rakehell"—a person so wicked and licentious that one would have to rake through hell to turn up his like (the term was never applied to women). Or, just possibly, the reference may have been to the supposed ultimate fate of a rakehell: raking cinders in that sultry locality.

ramshackle. Apparently derived from "ransack"; the original sense seems to have been as wrecked as a house that had been thoroughly plundered. For several centuries, however, a ramshackle structure is one that has been "wrecked" by time, or simply by shoddy construction.

rank and file. Soldiers on parade are drawn up in ranks, from side to side, and in files, from back to front; their officers normally stand in front of, or alongside, the rank and file. The rank and file of an organization are its "ordinary" members, as contrasted with its officers.

rapture. Surprisingly, the word is akin to "rape"; the original rapture was a forcible abduction, especially of a woman. Today it refers to the state of being "abducted"—carried away in spite of oneself—by intense emotion, a much pleasanter business than being kidnapped.

rat race. Originally (1930s) a term from the jazz world, meaning a dance, but quickly borrowed into the business world to mean the intensely competitive personal struggle to stay ahead of the competition—even if you have to act like a rat.

read someone the riot act. The original riot act was an actual act of Parliament, passed during the reign of George I. It provided that if twelve or more people assembled riotously or "unlawfully" (no nonsense about freedom of assembly!), the authorities would literally read them the riot act. If they then failed to disperse within an hour, they automatically became criminals. If someone reads you the riot act, you face the same choice as the original rioters: either back down or be treated as a "criminal."

real McCoy, the. Various authorities have recounted tales concerning a barroom encounter with "Kid McCoy," said to have been a welterweight champion; to the discomfort of his challenger, he turned out to be not just a fellow boozer but the real McCoy. But tales is all they are: in the first recorded use of the expression (in Scotland) it was McKay, not McCoy. So, while everyone knows what "the real McCoy" (or McKay, or McKie) means, nobody is really certain who the *real* real McCoy was.

recalcitrant. From a Latin word meaning "kicking backward"—and that's just what a recalcitrant horse or mule does.

record. From Latin *cord-,* heart; to record something was originally to memorize it—get it by heart. By one of those ironies so common in etymology, it now refers to things we can't memorize or don't choose to, and therefore record in writing, or on tape or disc. Compare **creed.**

red carpet, the. By some accounts, when an important visitor was received at a hotel or other public place, a special red carpet was traditionally unrolled at the entrance. But since the term dates only from the 1930s, it may have a more specific source: the red carpet that led passengers to the Twentieth Century Limited, for many years the crack train between New York and Chicago, and probably the best-known train in the U. S.

The Twentieth Century was all Pullman (first class), and both its accomodations and its dining-car menus were considered the height of luxury. If you're lucky enough to get the red-carpet treatment, you'll be traveling—or living—**high on the hog.**

red flag/rag to a bull. As almost everyone knows, in a bullfight the matador waves his red-lined cape to make the animal charge him. Ironically, however, bulls are color-blind; what draws their attention is not the redness of the cape but its motion. But the image has passed into folklore, meaning something that enrages someone as surely as the matador's cape does the bull.

red-handed. In the days before firearms, knives were the normal tools of the **assassin's** trade. And in knifing someone, the killer was likely to get blood on his hands; if someone came along, he was caught red-handed.

red herring. The flesh of a herring that has been cured in salt has a strong reddish color. These fish, though tasty, have a powerful odor before being cooked, and at one time were used to train hunting dogs to follow a scent. Moreover, if a red herring was dragged across the trail of an animal the dogs were pursuing, they'd chase the herring rather than the game. A "red herring across the trail" has therefore long had the sense of a deliberate distraction, as in an argument.

Following World War I, the red herring became an actual Red: politicians began distracting the voters (or smearing their opponents) with talk of the "Red Menace" of communism—which in the Western World, at least, turned out to be one of the most over-rated menaces in history. But politicians still find the Red herring useful for throwing the voters off the scent of official misconduct—or justifying it.

red letter day. In old-fashioned calendars, Sundays and holy days (holidays) were printed in red letters. Nowadays, though some calendars still follow the practice, a red-letter day is considerably more special than a mere holiday.

red tape. Red or reddish tape was long used to tie up bundles of legal or official documents. With the expansion of the British bureaucracy during the nineteenth century, the phrase was transferred to the bureaucratic rules that entangled the citizen confronting officialdom. Nowadays, official documents are more likely to be stored in a computer—but both citizens and officials continue to grapple with red tape.

redneck. Many white inhabitants of the southern U. S. have fair complexions, meaning that those of them who must spend much time in the sun (such as small farmers) are likely to have red necks. These rednecks were (and often still are) both ignorant and violently racist; nowadays, the word is used of any such person, in or out of the South.

remorse. From Latin *mordere,* bite (a morsel is a "bite" of something). If you've done something bad, your conscience may "re-bite" you, again and again.

requiem. The Latin mass for the dead begins with the words *Requiem aeternam dona eis, Domine* (Grant him eternal rest, oh Lord), and has long been called a requiem mass. A figurative requiem marks the "death" of someone or something. Some species of shark are classed as Requiem sharks, and not without reason.

rest on one's laurels—see **laurels**.

retaliate. Ultimately, from Latin *talis,* such-like, whence *talio,* a punishment like the crime. The Biblical *lex talionis* was the famous "eye for eye, tooth for tooth." If you retaliate against someone, you're paying them back in their own coin.

riddled. Not from the puzzling riddles that people sometimes ask, but a quite different word meaning a coarse sieve, used for separating sand from gravel, ashes from cinders and so on. If something is riddled (with holes)—as, by bullets—it's got as many holes as a sieve.

right bower. In the game of euchre, the right bower is the jack (knave) of trumps, one of the most powerful cards in the pack; a "misplaced" right bower played an important role in a famous game described in verse by Bret Harte (see **euchre**). Metaphorically, it means someone's right-hand man—an almost extinct sense nowadays, but you'll find it in Dashiell Hammett's *Red Harvest.*

ring the/a bell. Old-fashioned carnivals and amusement parks featured shooting galleries, in which patrons were invited to test their marksmanship by shooting at a target—often with a bell at the center: if something was right on target, it rang the bell. Similarly, to say that something "doesn't ring any bells" means that it doesn't strike any "target" (evoke any response) in your mind.

ring the changes on. Give a Frenchman a set of bells—a carillon—and he'll play a tune on them. Give a group of Englishmen a set and they'll ring "changes"—long series of sequences in which each bell is rung once, but in constantly shifting order, as 87654321, 87563421, 78653421, and so on. If you ring the changes on something, you're running through every possible permutation or variation.

ringer. Formerly (and occasionally still) important events or holidays were "rung in" with peals of bells. Later, the phrase came to mean merely "bring in," often quietly if not surreptitiously. Crooked stables would "ring in" (enter) a fast racehorse (ringer) under the name of a slow one, to get better odds on the animal. A ringer or dead ringer for someone is his or her near-double—as of course the racetrack ringer must be if the trick is to succeed.

rip(-)off. Allegedly from burglars who rip off the doors of houses or apartments (flats), but I doubt it: crooks prefer to operate quietly, by picking or breaking the lock. More likely, it comes from purse-snatching, in which a pocketbook is ripped off a woman's shoulder or out of her hand, or perhaps simply from "ripping" fruit or other merchandise off a street-peddler's stand.

During the 1960s the term became a sort of euphemism for any kind of stealing—whence its modern figurative sense. If someone rips you off, they're defrauding you, and a rip-off is either a fraud or an exhorbitant price ("Three hundred bucks for that VCR? What a rip-off!").

rival. From Latin *rivalis,* one living on the opposite bank of a stream. Why this should have evolved into one who seeks to outdo another is unclear—perhaps because people on opposite banks easily fell into disputes over who "owned" the water between them.

river, up the. Sing Sing ("the Big House") is perhaps the best-known prison in the U. S.—it was the scene of several 1930s films, including "20,000 Years in Sing Sing." Since it lies up the Hudson River from New York City, New York crooks used "go up the river" to mean "go to prison"; the term, now meaning almost any prison, has passed into general use. Compare **San Quentin quail**.

rob Peter to pay Paul. The one certainty about this expression is that it originally referred to Sts. Peter and Paul. Possibly it refers to some medieval religious legend, but if so no one has identified it; more likely, it meant that robbing a shrine of St. Peter to buy candles for one of St. Paul would do nothing for your salvation.

Or perhaps the point was merely that, since both were exceedingly saintly men, to satisfy one at the expense of the other was a pointless exercise. Nowadays, it's not always pointless: if you're hard-pressed by bills, you may have to "rob" one creditor to pay off another, hoping that Peter can be stalled off longer than Paul.

Robin Hood's barn, all round. The legendary outlaw Robin Hood, who traditionally stole from the rich but gave to the poor, was supposed to have lived in Sherwood Forest. This was his house, barn and entire "estate," and to go all round it was to make a lengthy, circuitous journey. (It's probably no coincidence that the obsolete phrase "Robin Hood's mile" meant a mile of several times the normal length.)

roman à clef. Literally (in French), novel with a key; figuratively, one in which any resemblance to actual persons is by no means coincidental: if you have the "key" to the cast of characters, you can identify the real people behind the author's fictional ones. A famous roman à clef is Somerset Maugham's *Cakes and Ale,* which satirized, under other names, such English literary figures as Thomas Hardy and Hugh Walpole.

room to swing a cat, not enough. To swing a cat by the tail (usually considered the origin of the phrase) would certainly require a fair amount of room. But why on earth would anyone want to do this to a biting, clawing cat? More likely, the "cat" was the cat-o-nine-tails used to punish sailors. The punishment was always given on deck, since below-deck there was indeed not enough room to swing the cat.

root (verb) **hog or die.** Wild pigs, or those let loose to find their own food, get much of their sustenance by rooting—digging up roots with their snouts and tusks—and any pig that failed to do so would starve. When you're in a root-hog-or-die situation, you'd better get to work fast, or else.

Rosetta stone. Europeans knew of the existence of Egyptian hieroglyphic inscriptions for centuries, but no one—not even the Egyptians—could read them. The problem was that the Egyptian language itself was extinct, so that neither the sense of the inscriptions nor the phonetic values of their symbols could be deciphered.

In 1799, during Napoleon's invasion of Egypt, a French soldier near the town of Rosetta stumbled upon a black stone bearing three inscriptions, in hieroglyphic, demotic (a sort of shorthand hieroglyphic) and Greek—which was, of course, a known language. The French scholar Champollion, assuming (correctly) that these were actually the same inscription in three languages, was able to use the Greek inscription as a key to begin decipherment of the others. A figurative "Rosetta stone" is a document or other set of facts that permits the decipherment of some equally intricate mystery.

roué. As late as the eighteenth century, important criminals in France and some other countries were punished by being broken on the wheel *(roue)*—an apparatus which, when turned, broke the culprit's limbs. Around 1720, France was ruled by the Duke of Orleans, as regent for the child Louis XV; he gathered around him a bunch of cronies so dissolute that many Frenchmen felt they deserved to be *roué* ("wheeled"). Modern roués are equally dissolute, but not punished so drastically—if at all.

round-heeled. If the heels of your shoes are so worn that they're rounded off, you may be prone to fall backward. A round-heeled woman is one who falls receptively on her back at the slightest push; in fact, she's a **pushover**. There's no such thing as a "round-toed" man—presumably because all men are assumed to be easily had.

rub someone the wrong way. If you stroke a cat with the "grain" of its fur, it will purr—if it's in the mood. If you rub it in the opposite direction—the wrong way—it will likely stalk off indignantly.

rubber check. A check drawn against insufficient funds, or no funds at all, will, like a rubber ball thrown against a wall, bounce back (return suddenly) from the bank it was drawn on to the bank or person that mistakenly accepted it. Or possibly it was the other way round: the check was "rubber" because it bounced, rather than bouncing because it was rubber.

rubberneck. Tourists on sightseeing busses often stretch their necks to see the sights; passers-by sometimes do the same to see the tourists. Nowadays, the term is more often applied to drivers who, passing the scene of an accident, slow down to rubberneck at it—thereby blocking traffic even more effectively than the accident did.

Rube Goldberg. If I'd written this book 30 years ago, I wouldn't have bothered to include this metaphor: just about everyone, or at least every American, knew the cartoons of Reuben Lucius Goldberg (1883–1970). They depicted contraptions for doing things in the most complicated (and impractical) way possible; those of us who remember his work still speak of a

Rube Goldberg apparatus or scheme—intricate and guaranteed to fail. There've been times lately when Goldberg's ghost seems to have taken charge of American foreign policy.

rule of thumb. The first joint of a man's thumb is about an inch long, meaning that he can use it instead of a carpenter's rule to get a rough measurement of something. Alternatively (by some accounts), brewers of long experience tested the temperatures of their vats by dipping a thumb in. Either way, a rule-of-thumb procedure is one based entirely on experience, and a rule-of-thumb measurement is only approximate.

rule the roost. In the barnyard, the rooster who's at the top of the **pecking order** dominates all the other chickens; he gets first choice of food, hens and, presumably, his preferred place on the pole where the birds roost for the night.

ruminate. Ruminant animals, such as cattle, sheep and goats, ruminate: chew the cud—a mass of partly digested vegetation—so that it can be further digested. If you ruminate over something, you're chewing it over to try and "digest" it.

run amuck. Malays occasionally become (or became) frenzied *(amoq),* due to religious fanaticism, drugs or simply personal rage. At such times they may attack the enemy—political or personal —in a frenzied, do-or-die fashion, and if anyone happens to get in the way, too bad. A Malay or anyone (or anything) else that has run amuck is totally out of control. Compare **berserk**.

run for one's money. If you're betting on a horse and it doesn't win but comes close, you've lost your money, but at least had a run for it.

run of the mill. The mill was probably a textile mill that produced cloth of varying quality, including "seconds." The run of the mill would therefore have been the factory's "average" output, neither very good nor very bad.

run something into the ground. There are two theories on this—neither very convincing. The obvious reference—to "run" a fox or other animal into a hole in the ground—doesn't fit the sense, which is to carry something too far or make too much of it. The alternative—to run a vessel so close to shore that it goes aground—fits the sense but not the wording: such vessels are run aground, not *into* the ground. So take your pick—or come up with a better idea.

sabotage. For centuries, French peasants and industrial workers ₍ **S** wore wooden shoes *(sabots),* which were both durable and cheap. The verb *saboter* originally meant to make an irritating noise by clattering sabots, but toward the end of the nineteenth century was extended to a more serious form of annoyance: deliberately damaging machinery or goods in a factory, as during a strike. How this shift in meaning came about is unclear; I'd guess from a very quick and simple form of sabotage: tossing a *sabot* in the gears.

sack (dismiss). Various theories have been adduced for the origin of this term, including the Roman (and later Turkish) custom of tieing up malefactors in a sack and throwing them into a river or the sea. But since the term originated as "give someone the sack," it probably comes from a more prosaic source: the sack of tools handed a discharged worker.

The U.S. football "sack" (to tackle the quarterback behind the scrimmage line) may go back to the original, literal sack: the sacked player is, in effect, caught in a sack. But the term may have been influenced by another "sack"—to plunder a captured town. Since this one originated as "put to (the) sack," it may hark back to the actual sacks in which soldiers collected their loot.

sacred cow. As most people know, cattle are sacred to Hindus: it's perfectly o.k. to milk them or use them for hauling, but strictly taboo to kill or injure them. Nearly all countries have their own sacred cows—people or institutions that can't be criticized, on pain of the critic's being branded irreligious or unpatriotic.

sailing close to the wind. As you'd expect, this is an old maritime phrase. A ship whose course lay to windward would sail as close to the wind as possible—but sailing too close to the wind would let it be **taken aback,** with serious consequences. Though the phrase is now rare, someone figuratively sailing close to the wind is taking dangerous chances—implicitly, by engaging in near-criminal activity.

salad days. Salad greens are ideally both young and tender; in our salad days, we were too—and green to boot.

salary. Roman soldiers received a *salarium*—a special allowance to buy salt. Nowadays, a salary buys a lot more than salt—though with inflation, you never know. The expression *worth his salt* may be an elaboration of the same idea. But since it seems to be maritime in origin, it may rather refer to the salt meat that, with ship's biscuit, made up nearly all the old-time sailor's diet. A sailor not worth his salt, then, wouldn't have been worth the cost even of the cheap food he ate.

salt, below the. A few centuries ago, a common feature of banquets was an elaborate salt-cellar set midway along the banqueting board. Honored guests sat at the upper end of the table, above the salt; less honored ones, below it. The phrase still crops up occasionally (e.g., in LeCarre's *Tinker, Tailor, Soldier, Spy*), referring to someone put in an inferior position.

San Quentin quail. In eighteenth century England, "quail" meant a harlot or courtesan, from the bird's supposed amorous disposition; among nineteenth-century U.S. college students, it became any girl. San Quentin, as Californians know, is the most famous prison in the state, comparable to Sing Sing in the rest of the country (see **river, up the**). Put them together and you get a girl who can put you in San Quentin or its equivalent if you have sex with her.

Such young women are "jail bait"—below the age of consent (16 in most states)—and sex with them is statutory rape: rape without force or threats, but also without their legally binding consent. The late Errol Flynn, whose taste for underage girls was fairly notorious, was reported (in a famous trial) to have addressed his mini-mistresses affectionately as "my little J.B." and "my little S.Q.Q."

sanguine—see **bilious**.

sarcasm. Greek *sarkazein* meant to tear flesh *(sarx)* or gnash the teeth. A sarcastic remark may indeed lacerate you—and make you feel like gnashing your teeth.

sardonic. The Latin *herba Sardonia* was a plant, found in Sardinia but otherwise unidentified, which when consumed produced facial convulsions resembling horrible laughter—as strong plant poisons often do. Someone who emits a sardonic laugh, like a victim of the Sardinian herb, isn't really amused.

saturnine. In ancient astrological lore, those born under the influence of the planet Saturn were supposed to be of a cold and gloomy temperament. Saturnine people don't even laugh sardonically (see last); they just grimace sourly.

savage. From Latin *silva,* forest; in English, a "forest" person—something or someone in a "state of nature," whence an uncivilized person of wild, unrestrained habits—which people in a state of nature were supposed to be. We now know that primitive peoples are no more "savage" than civilized ones—often much less so.

sawbuck. A sawbuck is a frame resting on two X-shaped supports, on which logs are placed for sawing into firewood. In the nineteenth century, the word was also applied to the U.S. $10 bill, which then displayed two large X's (the Roman numeral ten) on each side.

scapegoat. According to ancient Jewish law (Leviticus xvi), each year a goat was selected by lot and the chief priest laid upon it all the sins of the Children of Israel. The animal was then taken into an uninhabited place and allowed to escape, bearing the sins of the people with it and thereby enabling them to avoid the Lord's punishment.

Modern scapegoats also have other people's misdeeds heaped on them, thereby enabling the culprits to avoid punishment. The word is sometimes used loosely of someone picked as a **fall-guy**, but this is inaccurate: the scapegoat was (and is) completely innocent, and wasn't punished, though (s)he sometimes is now; the fall-guy is seldom innocent, though he resembles the ancient scapegoat in that he carries off the sins of others into the "wilderness"—away from public scrutiny.

scare something up—see **beat the bushes**.

scenario. Literally, a movie script describing in detail all the scenes that must be filmed. Figuratively (in the words of the late Herman Kahn, who invented the metaphor), "an attempt to describe . . . some hypothetical series of events," such as "the escalation of a small war."

Note that "hypothetical" is the operative word: the scenarios evolved by Kahn and other thinkers about the unthinkable often had even less reality than the Hollywood variety. One of them, used in "war gaming" by the U.S. Defense Department, *began* with the assumption that the U. S. had set up a "pro-American" government in Beijing—just like that! Not a few of these scenarios are merely elaborate versions of the silly answer you get when you ask a silly question.

Note also that the word is often overused in the very loose sense of *any* occurrence or sequence of events—a usage that, says the *OED* Supplement, "has attracted much hostile comment."

schmaltz. In German and Yiddish, *Schmaltz* is rendered animal fat (especially chicken fat), which in kosher cookery must be used instead of butter in meals where meat is served. Figuratively, it means sentimental writing, TV or music that's equally smooth and oily.

schmuck. In German, *Schmuck* means a jewel or ornament; in Yiddish, it became a man's distinctive—and most precious—"ornament." Like its English equivalent, it was also applied to an unpleasant male, but in recent years has softened to mean merely someone both stupid and unpleasant. Some elderly Jews still consider it offensive.

score (games). In the Middle Ages, when few people were literate, records were often kept on tallies—sticks notched (scored) in various ways (see **tally**). Later, "score" was applied to marks that tavern keepers scratched on a wall or slate, to keep track of customers' drinks (see **chalk it up to experience**), and finally to tallies of points scored in athletic contests.

scot-free. After the tavern keeper had reckoned up your score (see last), the total was your scot. If you get away scot free, then, you escape without paying your reckoning for some social or other offense.

scratch, up to. In old-time bare-knuckle prize fighting, the contestants had to be "brought to scratch"—an actual line scratched on the earth—at the beginning of each round; a fighter who wasn't up to scratch forfeited the match. If you're not feeling up to scratch, you're in no mood for fighting—or, probably, for much else.

Likewise, in old-time footracing the contestants had to *start from scratch*—a line scratched in the dirt. If you have to start from scratch, you must go back to the very beginning of the "track."

screw. A word with a long and disgraceful pedigree, in which metaphor is piled on metaphor. Its original sense—the mechanical device—derives from two Latin words used figuratively: *scrofa,* sow (presumably because the groove of a screw curls like a pig's tail), and *scrobis,* vagina, female screw.

The noun begot a verb, which by the eighteenth century had taken on its own metaphorical sense: have intercourse with (a woman). Two centuries later, the metaphor had begotten yet another metaphor: deceive or ruin. Which says something about some men's attitude toward sex.

screwball. British readers will have to get their American friends to help interpret this intricate story; though there was once a "screw-ball" in cricket, the metaphor comes from a kind of pitch in baseball. Baseball pitchers have long known how to make the ball curve—"break" to the pitcher's left, if he's a right-hander, right if he's a "southpaw." Early in the century, the great pitcher Christy Mathewson introduced the "screwball," which broke in the opposite direction; since it was a new and unexpected pitch, it was very effective.

This, at any rate, is the "official" story according to the Sports Department of the *New York Times.* But the *OED* Supplement shows that the *Times* itself has at various times used "screwball" to mean several different kinds of pitches—all unexpected for their time. Thus, in the 1920s, it apparently meant a pitch that broke downward rather than sideways.

The human screwball certainly behaves in unexpected and unorthodox ways. In strict logic, however, he should be called a knuckleball, a pitch that is positively erratic: it can break in any direction—right, left, up or down.

scuttlebutt. Originally, "scuttled butt"—a water cask (butt) set on a ship's deck, with a hole in the top through which sailors could dip out drinking water. Like the modern office water cooler, the scuttlebutt became a center for gossip and rumor, which is what the word means now: unofficial information, true or false—what you get from the **grapevine**.

Scylla and Charybdis, between. Experienced Greek skippers knew the perils of Scylla, a large rock on the Italian side of the Straits of Messina, and Charybdis, a whirlpool on the Sicilian side. In mythology—notably, the *Odyssey*—they were personified as two sea monsters: if you were between Scylla and Charybdis, one or the other would almost certainly get you. The modern equivalent is "between a rock and a hard place."

seamy side. No matter how artfully cut and carefully sewed a garment is, if you turn it inside out you see the unattractive seamy side. An inside view of even the most impressive-looking institution will usually reveal similar seams.

second string. This is actually two metaphors, with slightly different meanings. In medieval times, prudent archers carried a second string for their bows in case the first one broke, whence the figurative sense of a handy alternative. The commoner modern sense probably comes from a later "string" (athletic team), whence our second-string teams and players, implicitly inferior to the first string—as the bowman's second string was not.

seedy—see **go to seed**.

sell someone down the river. The river is the Mississippi; "down the river" in the mid-nineteenth century meant the cotton and sugar lands of the lower Mississippi valley. The rapid expansion of agriculture in the area provided a ready market for slaves from farther north. And since many plantations in the upper South were worn out, their owners often sold their slaves "down the river."

For the slaves, being sold down the river would likely mean harder work and the breaking of family ties; Mark Twain, in *Puddenhead Wilson,* cited it as a slaveowner's ultimate threat to servants he thought had been stealing. Slavery is long gone, but people and companies are still sold down the river—disposed of simply to make a quick buck, and never mind human needs. A few years ago an editor of mine, whose firm in downtown New York had been taken over by a larger, uptown publisher, remarked to me wryly that he'd been sold *up* the river.

separate the sheep from the goats. Goats have acquired a bad reputation over the centuries: they were thought to be "goatish" (lecherous), and the Devil himself had the goat's horns and cloven hoof. Which is probably why St. Matthew, describing the Last Judgement, declared that God would separate the nations "as a shepherd divideth his sheep from the goats." He adds that the sheep would be set on the Lord's right (the "good" side—see **adroit**), the goats, on the left. The sheep, in short, were the good guys, the goats, the black hats.

sesquipedalian. Literally, a foot-and-a-half long; if you use sesquipedalian language, you are employing an egregiously elaborated vocabulary—arguably, to obfuscate the intellects of your auditors. Some scholars and literary critics do it habitually.

set one's cap for. Though we think of caps as men's headgear, the word has also meant a woman's headpiece, of a type, says the *OED,* "varying according to taste and fashion." A woman who set her cap for a man was putting on her most fetching hat—or, perhaps, adjusting it to a particularly flirtatious angle.

set one's teeth on edge. If you've ever bitten into a really sour piece of fruit, you should know this one without being told. For the record, it goes back to the prophet Jeremiah, who declared that "the fathers have eaten a sour grape, and the children's teeth are set on edge."

set the Thames on fire, (not). Nobody was ever credited with setting the Thames on fire; it's always "he won't" or "he'll never" do it. We say the same thing, more succinctly, with "He's not so hot!" (Interestingly, somebody or something once *did* set the Cuyahoga River—it flows through Cleveland, Ohio—on fire, thanks to its heavy surface layer of oily industrial wastes.)

seventh heaven. According to the ancient model of the universe (ultimately exploded by Copernicus), the heavens were divided into different celestial spheres, containing the planets, the sun and moon, the fixed stars and so on. Different writers gave different numbers of spheres; one version considered the seventh sphere the abode of God and his most exalted angels. If you're in seventh heaven, you may not be an angel, but are certainly in a most exalted state.

shake(s), in a (couple of). A shake of the hand takes little time; two shakes of a gamboling lamb's tail, even less. Nobody knows whether the original shake referred to one of these or to some other kind of shake, but it clearly meant what it still means—as the Queen of Hearts said in *Alice in Wonderland*, "in something less than no time."

sham. The only thing reasonably certain about this word (it dates from the seventeenth century) is that it has some connection with "shame"—pronounced "sham" in some English dialects. But the circumstantial story of its origins, though perhaps the work of an eighteenth-century Ben Trovato, is too good to pass up.
    The anonymous author (he's quoted at length in the *OED*), tells us that the word derives from "a Town Lady of Diversion, in Country Maid's Cloathes," which attested to her supposed innocence—and therefore to her health. She, "to make good her Disguise, pretends to be so *sham'd.*" But her customer might too

soon discover that the lady was neither innocent nor healthy, whereupon "it became proverbial, whenever a maim'd lover was laid up or looked meager, to say he had met with a *Sham."* It may not be true—but it sure is *ben trovato!*

shambles. Literally, "shambles" means (among other things) a slaughterhouse. A battle may become a figurative shambles; so, more loosely but less bloodily, may a business or political operation: a catastrophic foul-up from which few if any of the participants emerge uninjured.

shamus. In Yiddish, a *shammos* is the caretaker of a synagogue. The word passed into U.S. criminal slang as "shamus," a cop or (especially) a private detective—who, like the *shammos,* looks after someone else's property or business for a fee.

shanghai. The common sailor's life was never anything to write home about; transoceanic voyages, lasting weeks or months, made it worse. Food was mainly salt meat and ship's biscuit, which became increasingly inedible—though some seamen noted sourly that the weevils gnawing away at the biscuit at least provided fresh meat.

Moreover, the captain was absolute monarch of the ship. The discipline he imposed was doubtless necessary, given the hazards of the deep, but the methods used—fists, boots and the "cat" (see **room to swing a cat**)—gave far too much scope to ill-tempered or sadistic skippers.

Inevitably, seamen were often hard to find, and captains and shipowners manned their ships any way they could. The British Navy sometimes resorted to armed press gangs, which could seize any likely lad for naval service. The merchant marine used more informal methods: proprietors of waterfront **dives** were paid to feed knockout drops to their customers. When the unfortunate fellow awoke, he found himself shanghaied—aboard a ship bound for Shanghai or some equally far-off port.

With the rise of sailors' unions and stricter government regulation, the custom died out, but we still sometimes speak jokingly of people being "shanghaied"—pressured, perhaps against their better judgement, into a pub-crawl or similar expedition.

shank's mare. Before the railway and automobile, travelers who could afford it rode or drove horses—mares, geldings or (sometimes) stallions. Poorer journeyers rode or went on a cheaper mare: their own shanks—as they still do.

shell out. Nuts and some other crops (e.g., dried peas and beans, corn) must be removed from (shelled out of) their shells, pods or husks before they can be eaten by man or beast. Similarly, if you owe someone money you must shell out the nourishing dollars from your pocket, purse or wallet.

shibboleth. The Book of Judges tells us of the defeat of the Ephraimites by the Gileadites near a ford of the Jordan. Jephthah, the Gileadite commander, had shrewdly set a guard on the ford, and whoever sought to cross it was asked if he was an Ephraimite. If he said no, he was ordered to say *shibboleth* (flooding river); the Ephraimites, whose dialect didn't include the SH sound, could only say *sibboleth*—and were immediately slaughtered.

Similar shibboleths have cropped up at various times since. In medieval England, textile workers rioted against Flemish immigrants, and suspected Flemings were required to say "bread and cheese"; if they said "brot and cause," they were killed. During World War II, U.S. soldiers in the Pacific were given various shibboleths to distinguish Japanese enemies from Chinese allies, based on the fact that Japanese pronounce L as R ("Rotsa ruck!") and the Chinese do the reverse ("Velly solly!").

More broadly, a shibboleth is some point of political or religious doctrine that every member of a group must embrace, on pain of being "slain." Thus when a conservative Surgeon General of the U. S. came out in favor of making condoms available to teenagers, he'd said the equivalent of *sibboleth,* and rightwingers denounced him as a dangerous radical.

shindig. From "shinny," a simple kind of field hockey often played by children. A game of shinny, like many vigorous games, can sometimes escalate into a brawl. Hence a shindig is anything from a social "brawl" (noisy party) to a **donnybrook.**

shoofly pie. A dish well known in the Pennsylvania Dutch country: an open pie with a filling made of brown sugar and molasses (it somewhat resembles a pecan pie without the pecans). The sweet, sticky filling naturally attracts flies, which must be shooed away before you start eating.

short hairs, by the. My friend Eric Partridge once suggested that to have someone by the short hairs (or "where the hair is short") might mean to have them by the neck, where the hair is indeed often cut short. He also remarked on another occasion that "a dirty mind is a joy forever"; in this case, his wasn't dirty enough. Except among blacks, there's only one part of a man's body where the hair is always short, regardless of barbering; if you grab him there (as the British sometimes say, "by the short and curlies") you've got him at your mercy.

short shrift. Shrift is an obsolete word meaning religious confession, which even criminals were supposed to be permitted before being executed. A criminal or anyone else who got short shrift had barely enough time to confess before being killed.

The shortest shrift on record is described in *Hamlet,* when the king sends the prince off to England with a letter to the English king, ordering that the bearer be put to death, "not shriving time allowed." Fortunately, Hamlet learns of the murderous scheme and escapes, after arranging that his treacherous companions, Rosencrantz and Guildenstern, will deliver the letter—and get the (very) short shrift.

show one's true colors—see **false colors.**

shrew(d). Shrews, the tiniest of all mammals, look rather like mice, though they're not related. They're aggressive, as they must be, given their high rate of metabolism: a shrew must catch and eat something like its own weight daily, simply to keep alive. In folklore, they're also ill-tempered and even dangerous—whence the human shrew (as in *Taming of the*), a woman endowed with the same qualities.

The adjective "shrewd" originally meant dangerous, like a shrew, then sharp, as in Shakespeare's "a shrewd thrust at your belly." Shrewd people are still sharp—and, to their opponents, sometimes dangerous as well. Similarly, a *smart* person can sometimes make you smart.

shucks, aw. Supposedly, this refers to the worthless shucks (outer husks) of an ear of corn; much more likely, it's a euphemism for something even more worthless—unless, of course, it's used as fertilizer.

shyster. Not, as legend has it, from an unscrupulous lawyer named Scheuster (which sounds like the first line of a limerick); it comes from German or Yiddish *Scheisser,* literally shitter, but figuratively equivalent to son-of-a-bitch. Whence the bastardly attorney, and also the Australian "shicer," a worthless person—but also, interestingly, a gold claim that didn't **pan out**, presumably yielding only *Scheiss.*

Siberia—see **back to the salt mines!**.

sidekick. Vaudeville (music-hall) dancers often worked in couples, either mixed or unisex. A partner who kicked (danced) alongside you was naturally your sidekick and, though vaudeville is long gone, a sidekick is still a partner or assistant.

sidetrack (verb). In the early days of railroading, few lines had more than a single track; this naturally raised problems when a train met another going the other way, or was overtaken by a faster one. Accordingly, the railroads constructed sidings—short lengths of track parallel to the main line, onto which one train could be switched and halted while the other went by. If you've been sidetracked, you've been switched off the main line—and for the moment, at least, aren't going anywhere.

sight for sore eyes. An old expression meaning, of course, a very welcome sight. It probably comes from some ancient superstition, to the effect that unpleasant sights could make the eyes sore while pleasant ones could heal them.

simony. In Chapter vii of the Acts of the Apostles, we read of one Simon, a sorcerer, who was baptized a Christian. But seeing how the apostles were able to heal sick and crippled people by laying on of hands, he offered them money to show him how to do it. St. Peter replied (in modern language) "Drop dead—you and your money!" Simon's name survived in simony—the buying and selling of church **sinecures**—a practice all too common during the Middle Ages.

simple—see **complicated**.

sinecure. Originally, a "benefice"—an ecclesiastical office yielding income without (Latin *sine*) the obligation to take care (Latin *cura*) of souls; often benefices were obtained by **simony**. With the gradual decline of benefices, a sinecure became any job requiring little work—often patronage handed out for political services.

sinister—see **adroit**.

sixes and sevens, at. Originally, as in Chaucer, it was "set on six and seven," meaning to risk one's fortune. It comes from some dice game whose rules, including the special significance of six and seven, are lost. (The expression would make sense in craps—betting that a six will come before seven is a losing proposition—but that game dates from long after Chaucer.)

The modern sense—in a total mess—probably refers to gamblers who set too often on six and seven, and found their finances at sixes and sevens.

sixty, like. By one account, from a terrible drought in 1860, but that won't work: the phrase was used, in the sense of "very vigorously," as early as the 1840s. The same date almost certainly rules out an alternative, more plausible theory, that the "sixty" is miles per hour ("going like sixty"), since such speeds were still unheard of in the 1840s. Yet another possibility is a sixty-pounder gun (one throwing a shot of that weight), which in the early nineteenth century was about the most "vigorous" piece of artillery in use—but there's no evidence. The metaphor, in short, is totally and permanently lost.

sixty-four (thousand) dollar question, the. It started in 1941, when CBS presented a radio quiz show called "Take It or Leave It." Participants were asked a question for $2; if they answered correctly they could take the money or leave it, and answer another question, for $4. With each correct answer, the prize doubled, up to the final, $64 question, the toughest of the lot. Almost immediately, "that's the $64 question" passed into American English, in the sense of "that's the really tough (or decisive) question."

Some years later, a similar show went on television, but with the top prize upped to $64,000; the phrase was revised accordingly. But the show ended in scandal: it turned out that some contestants were being primed with the answers beforehand and, to increase the suspense, were even coached on how seem to ponder and hesitate. One contestant admitted his guilt, and went to jail; others, including Dr. Joyce Brothers (later a well known columnist), said nothing—and kept their winnings. For them, the real $64,000 question was the one they didn't choose to answer.

skeleton in the closet. Almost certainly from some lost horror tale, in which the skeleton of a murder victim, or a relative dead in disgraceful circumstances, was concealed in a closet. Most of us have "skeletons" of some kind—relatives or secrets we prefer to keep hidden; as Thackeray remarked, "There is a skeleton in every house."

skin of one's teeth, by the. In the story of Job (see **Job's comforter**), the suffering man, after rehearsing all his misfortunes, declares that "I am escaped with the skin of my teeth"— i.e., with nothing, since teeth have no skin. In the nineteenth century, the phrase was somehow transmuted to "escape *by* the skin"—meaning, of course, by a margin of next to nothing.

slapstick. Literally, a lightweight paddle consisting of two sticks fixed together so as to emit a mighty SMACK when used. Circus clowns and burlesque comedians used slapsticks for laughs; the word was transferred to any sort of crude, physical comedy.

slick as a whistle—see **clean as a whistle**.

slipshod. Originally, wearing slip-shoes—slippers or other loose footgear that could easily be slipped off; the wearer was more likely to shuffle than to walk vigorously. Nowadays, people may operate in a similar shuffling, **sloppy** way in any kind of shoes —or none.

slogan. A borrowing from Scots Gaelic, in which *sluag-ghairm* meant the terrifying war-cry emitted by fierce Highland clansmen. The "wars" have become political and commercial, but campaign and advertising slogans still lacerate the nerves.

sloppy. This metaphor seems to combine two different words: "slop" = liquid mud, which begot a verb meaning to splash or spill something, and "slop" = bag, then a baggy garment, then (in the plural), ill-fitting garments. A sloppy person is likely to spill things, and also to wear baggy, ill-fitting clothes.

slush fund. In the days when ships' cooks boiled up huge kettles of salt pork or beef, the "slush" (fat) that rose to the top was carefully skimmed off and preserved in casks. In port, the slush was sold to makers of soap, tallow candles and the like; the proceeds were the "slush fund," used to buy small luxuries for the crew. Political slush funds also buy unofficial luxuries—though seldom small ones—for the "crews" of legislative bodies and government bureaus.

small beer/potatoes. In England, "small beer" was (and occasionally still is) weak or inferior beer—hence, something trivial or **picayune**. In the U.S., the expression became "small potatoes," presumably because they provided little nourishment. (In fact, freshly-dug small potatoes are delicious, and nourishing to boot if you have enough of them.)

small fry. Originally, "fry" meant young children; later, the just-hatched young of various fishes—which, by sheer coincidence, are sometimes netted and fried. By an odd twist, the piscine small fry have once again become human small fry.

smarmy. To smalm or smarm something once meant to smear it; later, to smooth it, as by smearing it with grease or hair oil. A smarmy person is both smooth and oily—*unctuous,* in fact.

smart—see **shrew(d).**

smell a rat. When household rats were much commoner than they now are, they would sometimes die inside a wall or under the floor; soon the householders would literally smell a rat. The rats we smell nowadays are usually figurative—but smelling them still means that something is rotten.

snow job. When you ask an inconvenient question and are snowed under by a blizzard of plausible nonsense or flattery, you've gotten a snow job.

sodomy. The Bible leaves us in no doubt that Sodom and Gomorrah, the "cities of the plain," were places of exceptional wickedness, but is curiously coy about the precise nature of that wickedness. As an old and valued friend of mine once wrote in a sonnet,

> Who knows what song the sirens sang, what crimes
> Against the state the Bastille hid, what sin
> They did in Sodom? God knows what gay old times
> Gomorrah saw: whose yang enjoyed whose yin.

What's clear is that "sodomy" nowadays means any kind of "unnatural" sex—not just, as many people think, between males but also between male and female (even, in some states, between husband and wife). The Massachusetts criminal code defines it as "the abominable crime against nature"—but since nobody has ever put Nature on the witness stand, we have no first-hand testimony on what that crime might be.

soft soap. Until fairly recently, soft (semi-liquid) soap was the commonest type. Home-made, out of waste fat (see **slush fund**) boiled with wood ashes, it was remarkably slippery and could soften the toughest skin. A slippery person who ladles out the flattery in hopes of softening you up is soft-soaping you. (Compare **smarmy**.)

soldier (verb). In the figurative sense of "goof off," the term comes from (where else?) sailors. Soldiers aboard a military transport were passengers, with no responsibility for working the vessel; if one sailor accused another of soldiering, he was saying that his shipmate was as "busy" as one of the soldiers.

song and dance. A common vaudeville (music-hall) turn by a performer and his **sidekick** was a comic song followed by a dance routine, interspersed with more or less humorous patter. If someone gives you a carefully rehearsed routine intended to divert you rather than inform you, (s)he's giving you a song and dance.

sophistry. From Greek *sophistes,* wise man. Over the generations, however, Greek sophists increasingly applied their wisdom to devising clever but specious arguments that (as one historian put it) could "make the worser cause appear the better." In short, they engaged in sophistry.

sorts, out of. "Sorts" means, among other things, the various kinds of type that printers worked with in the days when type was set by hand. A printer who discovered, in the middle of an urgent job, that he was out of some necessary sorts would be—out of sorts. Admittedly, this explanation doesn't quite square with the historical evidence: "out of sorts" appears in writing some years before printers "sorts." However, trade terms frequently circulate orally for generations before being recorded—and the typographical explanation is the only halfway plausible one I know of.

sour grapes. Aesop tells of a fox who, one hot day, spied a ripe, succulent bunch of grapes hanging from an arbor overhead. He leaped up to seize them but fell short; leaped again and again, but still without success. Finally, hot and out of breath, he walked away muttering that no doubt the grapes were sour anyway. The phrase has persisted because it sums up one of the commonest human reactions to frustration: who among us hasn't at some point tried hard to get something (or someone), failed, and told themselves that it (or they) wasn't really worth having?

souse (noun). The ultimate root of the word is akin to that of "salt," and its original sense was meat pickled in salt brine. A human souse is as pickled as the meat.

sow dragon's teeth. Cadmus, a legendary Phoenecian prince, migrated into Greece, where he slew a dragon. On the advice of Athena, goddess of wisdom, he sowed the dragon's teeth in a field; they sprouted into a crop of armed men who immediately fell to fighting among themselves until only five were left. These five, led by Cadmus, founded the city of Thebes, later one of the great city-states of classical Greece. If you're ever tempted to pursue wise ends by dubious means, be careful that you're not sowing dragon's teeth: preparing a harvest of future conflict.

sow one's wild oats. The oats we eat in oatmeal and that horses eat raw (see **feeling one's oats**) are the species *Avena sativa.* A close relative is the wild oat, *Avena fatua,* a common weed in European grain fields. *Fatua* is Latin for foolish, and deliberately sowing wild oats would indeed be foolish, since they are worthless and, once established, hard to eradicate. Nearly all of us sow at least a few wild oats when we're young, though most of us soon learn to cultivate more profitable crops. But the bad habits we've acquired may, like wild oats, prove hard to eradicate.

spartan. The ancient Greek city-state of Laconia, whose capital was Sparta (see **laconic**), was something like today's South Africa: the native population were virtual slaves of a small ruling group, whose ancestors had conquered the area around 1100 B.C. But being part of the ruling elite had its price: its male members were brought up in barracks on coarse food, taught (sometimes brutally) to endure pain and hardship, and trained in military skills. In short, they led a spartan existence.

spike someone's guns. Muzzle-loading artillery was fired through a "touch hole"—a narrow opening at the breech end through which the powder charge could be touched off with a fuse or smoldering slow-match. If troops captured guns but couldn't hold them, they'd spike the guns—hammer iron spikes into the touch holes so that the weapons couldn't be fired. (Spiked guns could be made serviceable again by drilling out the spikes with a hand-drill, but this was a fairly lengthy business.) If you spike someone's guns, you've stopped them from "firing" at you—at least for the time being.

spill the beans. If you've ever spilled a package of dried beans, you know that they'll scatter all over the floor—often in the most inaccessible places. How spilling the beans came to mean "reveal a secret" is unclear—but the results in either case are messy.

spinster. Until spinning was mechanized in the late eighteenth century, turning wool or flax into yarn or thread was almost always "woman's work" (see **distaff**). A spinster was a woman spinner—often a professional; in the seventeenth century, it came to mean an unmarried woman—presumably because, having neither husband nor children, she could devote herself full time to her spinning.

spit and/spitting image. The "correct" form is "spit and image." The ultimate source is a seventeenth-century expression, "as like him as if spit out of his mouth," which was clipped to "the spit of"; "image" was a later elaboration.

spit and polish. Before the invention of modern shoe polish, boots and shoes had to be laboriously rubbed up by spitting on them and applying blacking or some similar preparation—plus plenty of elbow grease. Soldiers, naturally, had to spend a good deal of their spare time in this and other spit-and-polish activities. A military or other organization that emphasizes spit and polish will look very trim and efficient, but looks may well be deceiving.

spot, on the. Among crooks of the 1920s, to put someone on the spot meant to place them at the scene of a crime, as an eyewitness might do. Almost immediately, however, it came to mean "kill"— probably from news photographs in which "X marks the spot" where some mobster was rubbed out. Nowadays, the spot is seldom fatal, but if someone puts you on it, you're still in a difficult, even dangerous position.

spout, up the. In the nineteenth century, "spout" was a slang term for a sort of lift with which a pawnbroker hoisted pawned article goods upstairs for storage; something one pawned was therefore "up the spout." Nowadays the expression describes something that, like a hocked watch, is gone—often permanently.

square, (on the). A good carpenter makes sure that his work is properly squared up or on the square, with horizontal and vertical parts of the framing at exact right-angles; a dishonest craftsman, doing a hurried, sloppy job, doesn't bother. (The expression may have take on added color from the jargon of freemasonry—see **level.**)

square the circle. One of the famous mathematical problems of antiquity was "squaring the circle": constructing a square of precisely the same area as a given circle, using only ruler and compass. Nobody ever solved it, and centuries later mathematicians proved that nobody ever will. If you're trying to square the circle, you're taking on a task that's impossible on its face.

squared away. When a square-rigger was under way, her yards would be set at an angle that depended on the wind; if the wind was directly from behind (often the fastest point of sailing) they'd be squared away—set at right-angles to the ship's centerline. The yards would also be squared away in port, to give the vessel a neat appearance. When we get things squared away, we get them neatly arranged, so that our "ship" can move along speedily.

stake a claim—see **pan out.**

stalemate. As you may know or guess, this term, like **checkmate,** comes from chess. Occasionally, at the very end of a chess game, the players reach a position in which it's A's move, yet there's no legal move (s)he can make. That is, A's king isn't under attack (as in checkmate), but can't move without putting itself under attack, while A's other pieces are blocked. Since B can't move legally either—it's not his/her turn—the result is stalemate: a draw. And so with a metaphorical stalemate: neither "player" can move, and the contest is drawn.

stalking horse. Sixteenth-century hunters in pursuit of game birds would sometimes use a stalking horse: one trained to amble toward the quarry until the hunter, hidden behind the horse, was within shooting range; later, some hunters stalked their game with portable screens—which might be shaped like horses. It's not hard to see how a stalking horse became a "front"—a person used to conceal the real operators in a situation—and, later, any expedient or pretext for underhand doings.

stamping ground. During the rutting season, some male mammals, including horses, deer and bison, gather in certain grounds where they stamp their feet and butt or bite one another, to determine which one gets access to a particular female. The "stamping ground" thus became the habitual "turf" of an animal and eventually of a person; it's often called "my old stamping ground."

stand the gaff. Not the fisherman's gaff (see **blow the gaff**), though the two are related: this gaff is the sharp metal spur attached to the legs of gamecocks, with which they slash at each other. A bird that can't stand the gaff is obviously bound to lose.

starboard. Centuries ago, before the invention of the modern rudder mounted on a vessel's stern, ships were steered with long oars. By custom, these were mounted on the right side of the stern ("steering place"), which therefore became the steer-board or starboard side. The left side was called the larboard (empty side) and later the port side, whose derivation is obscure. (The notion that vessels in port were moored with their left sides against the quay, to avoid damaging the steering oar, doesn't fit the facts: by the time "port" came into use, steering oars were long gone.)

start from scratch—see **scratch, up to.**

steal someone's thunder. In 1709, a play by one John Dennis bombed in London; the only thing the critics liked about it was its realistic imitation thunder. Soon after the **fiasco**, Dennis attended a new production of *Macbeth.* And at the very first scene, when the three witches appear with the stage direction "thunder and lightning," he recognized the sound of his own thunder apparatus. Choking with rage, he shot to his feet with the cry: "See how the rascals use me! They will not let my play run, and yet they steal my thunder!" If someone steals your thunder—puts forward your idea without credit—you have equal cause to feel enraged.

stentorian. Stentor was the herald of the Greeks during the Trojan War; Homer tells us that his voice was as loud as that of fifty men together. If someone speaks in stentorian tones, he's almost that loud.

step into the breach. The breach was a gap battered in the wall of a besieged town or fortress, through which the beseigers might charge in—unless the defenders stepped into the breach and repelled them; as the king cried out in Shakespeare's *Henry V,* "Once more into the breach, dear friends, once more;/ Or close the wall up with our English dead." If you step into the breach, you're moving quickly to meet an emergency—though seldom at such a personal risk.

stereotype—see **cliché.**

stick one's neck out. If you stick your neck out, you may well get it in the neck—"where the chicken got the ax."

stick to one's last. The last is the foot-shaped block of wood that a shoemaker uses to shape the upper of a shoe. A sensible shoemaker sticks to his last—i.e., to what he knows and understands; the rest of us, if we're wise, do the same.

sticks, the—see **corny**.

sticky wicket. A British metaphor that has recently crossed the Atlantic. The bowler in cricket, unlike the pitcher in baseball, need not throw the ball directly toward the batter; often he bounces it off the ground (the pitch) so that the batter must hit it on the rebound—if he can. If the pitch is "sticky"—somewhat wet—the ball may bounce erratically, and the batter is batting a sticky wicket. If that's what *you're* doing, you've got problems—in a sticky situation, in fact.

stigma. Fugitive Greek and Roman slaves, if recaptured, were customarily branded on the forehead; in Greek the brand was called a *stigma*. People with a stigma bear a similar "brand" of guilt—though they, like the slave, may be guilty of nothing more than trying to live free.

stoic. The Stoic philosophers of ancient Greece practiced and preached a life-style emphasizing what we'd call emotional repression: your true stoic would show himself unmoved by either good or evil fortune. Modern stoics patiently endure bad fortune, but may, like the rest of us, rejoice when things improve.

stool pigeon. The term commemorates a peculiarly nasty detail of one of the great American ecological tragedies: the extinction of the passenger pigeon. In the early nineteenth century, these attractive birds migrated in flocks that literally darkened the sky; the ornithologist John James Audubon estimated that one of them contained several *billion* birds.

The destruction of these enormous flocks stemmed in part from destruction of their habitat—the beech forests on whose nuts they depended in the fall. But their diminishing numbers were further decimated by market gunners, who shot them down by the tens of thousands.

A favorite ploy of these murderous traffickers was the use of decoys: captured pigeons whose eyelids had been sewn shut and whose feet had been nailed to a "stool," a small wooden platform. These stool pigeons, by their cries of distress, attracted their fellows—who were thereupon shot down. To add insult to injury, the stool pigeon that involuntarily "betrayed" its fellows became the human "stoolie" who deliberately betrayed his fellows, by acting as an informer.

stonewall (verb). Like **sticky wicket,** a recently Americanized cricket metaphor: a batter who simply defends his wicket by blocking the ball, without trying to score runs, is stonewalling. During Watergate, President Nixon's henchmen planned to do the equivalent: not try to score "points" but simply block inquiries, by admitting nothing; happily, they were "bowled out"—of office.

straddle. When you straddle a horse, you've got one leg on either side of the animal. When a politician straddles an issue, he's in much the same position.

straight and narrow (path), the. "Path" has long meant not just something you walk on but also a course of conduct. To get to heaven you need to follow a straight course of conduct, and a narrow one, allowing for no deviations on either side.

strapped. If you're short of money, you have to *tighten your belt*—perhaps even literally, to quiet the pangs of hunger. That is, you're strapped (up).

straw man. The Scarecrow in *The Wizard of Oz* was a straw man, made of old clothes stuffed with straw. A straw-filled dummy is easily knocked down—whence the "straw man" of devious debaters. Instead of dealing with the arguments of their opponents, they set up straw men—ridiculous objections to their own position—which they then proceed to knock down triumphantly.

strike while the iron is hot. With modern powered machinery, iron can sometimes be worked cold. The village blacksmith of song and story, however, had to heat the metal red hot before hammering it into shape; if he failed to strike while the iron was hot, it had to be reheated. Nowadays, if we fail to strike the iron in time, we may not get a second chance.

string to one's bow, another—see **second string**.

stringer. Not a common term outside the newspaper and magazine business, but interesting enough to include. Part-time newspaper correspondents used to be paid by the inch. To collect, they'd paste up all their stories that had appeared in print, end-to-end, and send in the resulting string of clippings; the editor would measure the length of the string and pay the stringer accordingly.

stump (politics). On the U.S. frontier, candidates for office would address the voters from any platform they could find—even a stump. Candidates still stump their state, or the whole country, though—thanks to the rise of TV—they now do much of their campaigning under less taxing conditions, before the camera.

subjugate. Latin *iugum* = English "yoke" (both derive from the same ultimate source). When the Romans conquered some neighboring people, as they frequently did, the defeated army was made to march under a yoke *(sub iugum)* to symbolize that thenceforth they were "yoked" like draft oxen—subjugated, in fact. Once or twice the Romans themselves had to pass under the yoke.

supercharged. When a gasoline or diesel engine reaches a certain speed, its cylinders can't suck in enough air to burn the fuel completely, so that it can go no faster. The solution is a supercharger—a pump, driven by the engine, that *forces* air into the cylinders. Steam-driven warships and fast liners used a similar device, in which air was forced into the furnace that heated the boiler; in such cases, the ship was moving under *forced draft* (in Britain, *draught*). A supercharged person, or one under forced draft, is operating at maximum speed.

supercilious. Latin *supercicilum* means the eyebrows; **big-wigs** frequently raise their eyebrows superciliously (scornfully) at less important folk.

supplication. Literally (in Latin), folding (the knees) under, once obligatory if you were petitioning some high-ranking person. Today we don't literally "crook the pregnant hinges of the knee," but supplication remains a very humble way of making a request.

swan song. The common or mute swan (originally European, but now naturalized in parts of the eastern U.S.), has, as its name implies, very little to say for itself apart from what bird manuals call a low grunt. According to ancient legend, however, when a swan was dying it would give forth one final, glorious song. Thus the final, and presumably best, creation or performance of a writer or artist is his or her swan song.

sword of Damocles. Greek legend has it that Damocles, a nobleman of ancient Syracuse, talked rather too freely about what a great life the king led. The king thereupon invited him to a banquet at which the finest foods and wines were served, but when Damocles happened to look up, he saw a sword hanging directly over his head, suspended by a single horsehair—a tangible metaphor of what a king's life was really like. Prominent people, and some not so prominent, not infrequently find themselves beneath the sword of Damocles, with their fate hanging by a hair.

sybarite. The original Sybarites, citizens of ancient Sybaris in southern Italy, were notorious for their luxurious life-style (meaning, of course, the style of the upper classes; there's no evidence that slaves and commoners lived any better in Sybaris than anywhere else). Modern sybarites also devote themselves to fleshly pleasures.

symposium. A *symposion* was a Greek drinking party, at which the (male) participants discussed anything from philosophy to sex—homo or hetero. The most famous symposium was the (fictitious) one portrayed in Plato's work of that name—a session at which the participants, including Socrates, sought to define the nature of love. Modern academic symposiums generally involve less drinking, but just as much talking.

tabloid (paper). The original Tabloid was a trademark used by a British drug company to identify some of its products—mainly, drugs compressed into tablets. Tabloid newspapers have a "compressed" format compared to that of "standard" papers.

take a powder. Originally, perhaps, from the explosiveness of gunpowder; "to powder" has meant "to rush" since the seventeenth century. But more immediately, I suspect, from the powerful laxative of some decades back called a Seidlitz powder. A favorite saloon trick among criminals was to lock the door of the toilet ("slough the donniker"), slip such a powder (the original Mickey Finn) into someone's drink and watch him take a powder out of the joint.

take another tack. As I've noted a couple of times already, sailing ships could not move directly into the wind but had to tack—zigzag back and forth with the wind first on one side, then on the other. If a skipper approaching harbor found that his vessel couldn't make the harbor mouth on (say) the **starboard** tack, he was obviously on the *wrong tack,* and would have to take the other (port) tack.

take someone for a ride. During the 1920s, gangsters often dealt with a competitor by inviting him to take a ride in a large, black limousine, supposedly to discuss the dispute. Like the young lady from Riga, who went for a ride on a tiger, the guest was never seen again alive. Mobsters dispose of their victims less ceremoniously nowadays; if someone takes you for a ride, you'll be deceived or swindled but not killed.

take the bit in one's teeth. Horsemen and -women control their mounts with a bit; the simplest type is a metal bar placed crosswise in the animal's mouth, with the reins attached to either end. Pulling on the reins presses the bit against the flesh at the corners of the animal's mouth, forcing it to stop. Occasionally, however, a horse will learn to grip the bit between its back teeth, so that pulling on the reins will have no effect. A person who takes the bit in his teeth is equally uncontrollable.

take the bull by the horns. There are various circumstantial explanations of this phrase, none very convincing. About all one can say is that to take a charging bull by the horns (presumably in the hope of throwing it, or oneself, sideways) is to cope with it in both a direct and a courageous (or foolhardy) way—which is what the metaphor means.

take the cake. Often linked to the cakewalk, a sort of parade held at a ball, in which the couple doing the fanciest steps was rewarded with a cake. But "take the cake" came into (U.S.) English in the 1840s; "cakewalk," not until the 1860s. Moreover, "cake" has been a metaphor for goodies of all sorts since at least the seventeenth century, so the phrase means merely "carry off the goodies"—presumably as a prize for achievement. Nowadays, the metaphor is often used ironically: "As a dim-wit, he really takes the cake!"

taken aback. A basic sailing maneuver was (and is) tacking—shifting course into the "eye" of the wind and past it, so that the wind comes from the other side, with the ship on a new course roughly at right angles to the old one. On a square rigger, the maneuver required precise handling: the yards had to be quickly swung around, to catch the wind from the new direction at precisely the right moment.

A clumsily handled ship could be taken aback: the wind, instead of striking the backs of the sails would press against their fronts, bringing the vessel to a halt and forcing it backward—at best; in a gale, a ship taken aback risked dismasting. If you find yourself taken aback, then, you've been brought up short—and, like the ship, may take a while to get back on course.

talent. In the ancient world, a talent was a unit of weight ranging from 26 to 40 kg (57 to 88 lb), and also a unit of value, though a gold talent was obviously worth much more than a silver one. The present sense—natural ability—comes from the parable of the talents recounted in the Book of Matthew, Ch. xxv, in which three servants are given various numbers of (monetary) talents. Two of them invested the money profitably and were rewarded by their master; the third buried his talent—and was not.

Thus it became a matter of faith that God endows each of us with a certain number of "talents"; if we fail to put them to good use we can expect, like the servant in the parable, to be cast into "outer darkness," with "weeping and gnashing of teeth." The blind Milton wrote bitterly of "that one talent [his literary gifts] which is death to hide/ Lodg'd with me useless. . . ."

talk turkey. Usually explained by an early nineteenth-century anecdote. A white man and an Indian went out hunting, and shot a meaty wild turkey and a scrawny buzzard (i.e., the American vulture called the turkey buzzard). When it came time to divide the bag, the white man said, "Take your choice: either I take the turkey and you take the buzzard, or you take the buzzard and I take the turkey." "Ugh!," said the Indian. "You never once say turkey to me!"

Nobody has ever proved that this incident—which summarizes all too appropriately white dealings with Native Americans—actually happened. But fact or fiction, it's the best explanation I know of for why "talk turkey" means to get to the meat of the matter.

tally. From Latin *talea,* stick—specifically, one used to keep numerical records of various sorts, by notching it in different ways. In the case of a debt, the notched stick would be split lengthwise, with the debtor keeping one half and the creditor, the other; when it came time to pay the debt, the two tallies would be matched to guard against sharp practice.

The British Exchequer (equivalent to the U.S. Treasury Department) kept tax records in this form as late as 1826. Thereafter, the obsolete tallies were used to heat the Houses of Parliament, until an overenthusiastic janitor crammed so many of them into the stoves that the building caught fire and burned to the ground.

When we tally up a **score**, then, we're figuratively notching it on a stick. And when we check whether one set of figures tallies with another, we are in effect matching the two halves of a split tally stick.

tantalize. In Greek myth, Tantalus was a son of Zeus who became a wealthy king, but committed some grave crime (the myths don't agree on what). Whatever he did, he got what was coming to him: sent to Hades after his death, he was afflicted by a raging thirst and placed in the middle of a pool, whose water receded every time he tried to drink. As if that wasn't enough, the pool was overhung with branches of fruit, which drew back every time he tried to pick one. In short, he was tantalized—in spades, doubled and redoubled.

tapped out. Probably from the poker-player's custom of tapping the table when (s)he doesn't choose to raise. A player who's tapped out *can't* raise, because (s)he's out of money.

teach one's grandmother to suck eggs. In various forms, this phrase is more than four centuries old; the earliest recorded version is "teach our dame to spin." Sucking eggs without breaking the shells is a very delicate business (see **weasel words**), hence a metaphor for any demanding task—which grandmothers can likely do better than their grandchildren. If you're teaching your grandmother to suck eggs, you're telling someone something they've known for years—perhaps before you were born.

tease. The dried seed-pods of the teasel plant are covered with scores of tiny hooks; the pods themselves, set in a wooden or iron frame, were long used to tease up the nap on a piece of newly-woven cloth. Drawing a teasel pod across someone's skin is likely to irritate them; so does any other kind of teasing.

tell it to the marines. Until fairly recently, nearly all medium-to-large naval vessels carried detachments of foot-soldiers, called marine infantry or just marines. Their job was to take part in amphibious operations, as marines still do, but also to keep order on ship, including (if necessary) protecting the ship's officers against obstreperous or mutinous crew members.

For this and other reasons, there was always some tension between sailors and marines. The sailors in particular considered the marines—who spent much of their time going through the rigid, mechanical movements of close-order drill—rather stupid; their own jobs involved much more initiative and improvisation. So if a sailor spun a grossly improbable yarn, he was advised to tell it to the marines; no sailor was dim enough to swallow it!

tell someone where to get off. Nobody seems to have a clue where this expression came from. My guess would be that it referred to a drunk or obstreperous passenger on a streetcar: the conductor would tell him where to get off.

tenterhooks, on. As one step in finishing woolen cloth, it was wetted and then stretched on a tenter—a frame with a row of hooks at either end—so that it would dry without shrinking or wrinkling. If you're on tenterhooks, your nerves are being stretched like the cloth.

testicles. Would you believe this word is akin to "testify"? Well, it almost certainly is. In Latin, *testiculi* meant "little witnesses"— which testified, of course, to the bearer's virility.

thick and thin, through. A very old expression, probably from riding a horse straight across country through both thickets and (thinner) woodland.

three sheets in the wind. The sheets in question aren't the kind you have on your bed: they were ropes attached to the lower corners of a sail to control it. A loose sheet would let the sail flap in the wind, and the ship would lose power; with three loose sheets, the vessel would be barely under control—like a boozer three sheets in the wind.

throw down the gauntlet. A gauntlet was and is a sort of glove, but in this context it's the metal-reinforced glove that some medieval knights wore to protect their hands. If a knight wished to challenge another to single combat, he might throw one of his gauntlets at his opponent's feet; when the latter picked it up, the challenge was accepted. Throwing down the gauntlet still amounts to a challenge, as to a debate—though the results are seldom as bloody as in the good old medieval days.

throw in the sponge/towel. As fight fans know, a sponge and towel are essential tools of a prizefighter's handlers, to cool him off between rounds. And as they also know, throwing the towel (earlier, the sponge) into the ring is the traditional sign that the fighter is too badly hurt to continue. In any context, it means surrender.

throw someone to the wolves. A favorite subject for Victorian printmakers was a horse-drawn sleigh, traveling at full speed across the Russian steppes pursued by a pack of wolves. Traditionally, if the wolves got too close, one of the passengers was thrown out to lighten the sleigh, and in hopes that the rest of the company could **escape** while the animals were devouring the victim.

I don't know whether this ever happened in real life, but the tale has provided us with a durable metaphor for what often happens when a gang of malefactors is being pursued by "ravenous" journalists or cops: one member of the gang is "thrown" to them, in hopes that he'll satisfy their hunger. A **fall guy** is someone who's been thrown to the wolves.

thug. In Hindi, *thag* means "cheat" or "swindler"; the term was applied by the British to the sinister religious sect called P'hasingars (stranglers). These were worshipers of Kali, the Hindu goddess of death; they "swindled" travelers by striking up an acquaintance with them and then murdering them—usually by strangling with a silk cord or scarf. The thugs limited their attentions to prosperous travelers, thereby neatly combining piety and profit.

Though the sect had existed since medieval times, native Indian rulers couldn't or wouldn't suppress it. Finally, in the 1830s, the British effectively wiped out the thugs, hanging some four hundred and imprisoning another thousand. The word was picked up by American writers and applied to hoodlums who, like the P'hasingars, dealt in violence for profit—though from less pious motives.

thumbs down. A mistranslation of the Latin phrase *pollice verso,* thumbs turned. When gladiators fought in the Roman arena, a wounded man unable to continue fighting would appeal to the spectators for mercy. If they thought he'd put up a good fight, the audience might make the gesture *pollice primo* (thumbs pressed);

if not—or if they were just feeling nasty—it would be *pollice verso,* and the wounded man was finished off.

Latinists have argued for generations over precisely what gestures these expressions signified; the popular "translation" comes from a painting by the nineteenth-century French artist, Jean Leon Gerome: it showed the end of a gladiatorial contest, with the scowling spectators holding out their fists with thumbs turned down. Ever since, to turn thumbs down on something figuratively condemns it to death.

thunderstruck—see **astonish**.

tide over. Small navigable rivers often have bars at their mouths—sand or mud swept down by the stream. At low tide, the bar may block the entrance to boats or ships, which must therefore wait until they are tided over the obstacle by the rising waters. Likewise, if we're temporarily short of cash (as the British sometimes say, *at low water*), we hope a friend will lend us enough to tide us over the difficulty.

tighten one's belt—see **strapped**.

tilt at windmills—see **Quixotic**.

tin ear. "Tin" and "tinny" have meant "inferior" for some generations, perhaps (as the *OED* says) because tin is less valuable than the silver it resembles, but more likely because tin(-plated) cans are flimsy and easily dented. Thus we have Kipling's disparaging "little tin gods" (high-up bureaucrats), Henry Ford's "tin Lizzie" (the original, cheap Model T), and so on. And a tin ear is certainly an inferior one: its possessor can't tell good music (or writing) from bad.

tinhorn (gambler). Perhaps from the cheapness and shoddiness of toy tin-trumpets compared with real, brass ones; a tinhorn gambler is a cheap, small-time one. Alternatively, the "tin horn" may refer to a version of the cage that chuck-a-luck operators use to shake the dice. Since chuck-a-luck was a low-stakes game compared with faro, poker or **euchre**, a tin-horn (chuck-a-luck) gambler was a cheapie.

tinker's damn, not worth a. Tinkers were traveling pot-menders. By one account, they used dams—small "fences" of clay or putty—placed around the hole being repaired to prevent the solder from spreading too far; when the job was finished, the worthless dam was tossed away. The notion is ingenious—but almost certainly false.

Much more relevant is the fact that tinkers were typically itinerant tradesmen, traveling from town to town in search of work; like the gypsies (see **gyp**)—which some of them were—they were "persons of no fixed abode," and therefore presumed to be bad characters, given to boozing, fighting and bad language. A tinker, then, said "damn" so often that it became meaningless.

tip of the iceberg. Water is a remarkable substance in many ways—not least because, unlike most things, it expands when transformed from a liquid to a solid. That is, a given volume of water will occupy a slightly greater volume when it is frozen into ice—enough to burst metal pipes, as many suburban householders know too well.

The increased volume is also the reason ice floats in water—but the increase, though enough to wreck plumbing, is still very small, meaning that the ice won't float very high: only about a tenth of an iceberg will show above the sea's surface. Whether you're talking about an actual iceberg or (say) a political scandal, the tip means the bit that's visible; the remaining 90 percent, because it's invisible, is the really dangerous part.

toady. Many people consider toads disgusting; moreover, the creatures were long deemed to be poisonous if eaten (a few species are). Accordingly, a favorite trick of conjurers was to have an assistant eat a toad—and then "cure" him by some secret potion or incantation. A toad-eater or toady, then, is someone who'll do anything, however disgusting or dangerous, to stay on good terms with the boss.

toe the line. The line may have been the one from which foot-racers start; much more likely, it was an actual or figurative line that newly recruited sailors or soldiers had to toe when they lined up for orders. Certainly when you make someone toe the line, you're making sure they obey orders.

tomfoolery. Originally, Tom Fool was merely a nickname for a foolish or demented person; later, it came to mean someone who played the fool—a clown. Tomfoolery may mean simply foolish behavior, but more often implies deliberate clowning.

tongue in cheek. You obviously can't literally say something with your tongue in your cheek. The expression most likely comes from a lost gesture: pushing one cheek out with the tongue, to show that a remark just made was meant ironically—or not at all.

too big for one's boots/breeches. I don't know if anyone ever deliberately donned a pair of boots (or breeches) too small for him, but if he did, he clearly was both arrogant and cocky—and ended up in serious discomfort. The "breeches" version came first; its replacement by "boots" in Victorian times may reflect the fact that "breeches" included the shocking word "breech" (but-tocks). The Victorians often did that sort of "editing."

Some years ago, Claude Cockburn, then a well-known journal-istic **gadfly**, pointed out that being too small for one's boots could be every bit as uncomfortable as being too big for them. He was discussing post-1945 Great Britain, which he saw as foolishly trying to act like the great power it had once been, but clearly no longer was. In politics as in life, it's important to make sure your boots—or breeches—are the right size.

touch and go. Said to date back to the days of stage-coaches, whose drivers were often intensely competitive, seeking to charge past one another, on narrow roads, at grave danger to life and limb. If the vehicles' wheels became entangled, both would be wrecked; if they were lucky, the wheels would only touch and the coaches could still go, so that "touch and go" became equivalent to today's "fender-bender." I don't guarantee that this is true, but it's the only explanation I know of for the modern sense of the phrase—a situation in which it's unclear which "coach" will win the race.

travail, travel. Both come originally from Vulgar Latin *tripaliare,* to torture on a rack, which became Old French *travailler,* to torment or trouble. "Travail" retains these senses, though as a noun not a verb; "travel" harks back to the days when a long journey was indeed a troublesome, tormenting business. Come to think of it, what with today's delayed planes, lost baggage and muddled hotel reservations, "harks back" may not be the right phrase.

treadmill. During the Middle Ages, all sorts of machinery was powered by water mills and windmills. Temporary power, as for hoisting at a building site, could be supplied by a treadmill—an enormous, hollow wheel, inside which horses or men walked to keep it turning.

With the rise of powered machinery, treadmills fell out of use—except in some prisons, where they were used not for power but simply to keep the prisoners "busy," walking hour after hour and not getting anywhere. If your job is a treadmill, that's about what you're doing.

tribulation. The Roman *tribulum* was a sort of sledge with flint or metal teeth like those of a **harrow**; it was drawn across grain on a threshing floor to remove the husks. Tribulations are, of course, harrowing experiences.

trophy. When the ancient Greeks won a battle, they would erect a trophy: arms stripped from enemy corpses, hung on a tree or pillar, and dedicated to some god. Your modern trophy hunter celebrates the "battles" he has won against (unarmed) animals, by hanging their heads on his wall; the "god" to which he dedicates them is presumably himself.

tryst. The metaphor seems to combine two earlier (and possibly related) "trists," one (akin to "trust") meaning confidence, the other, an appointed station in hunting—hence, an appointed place of meeting. Whence the lovers' tryst—their appointed meeting place where they are confident of finding each other. The modern "tryst"—an *illicit* lovers' meeting—owes its vogue to the headline writer's need for short words that say a lot.

tulip. One of the very few English words borrowed from Turkish. To the Turks, *tulbend* originally meant a turban (they had borrowed both the word and the headpiece from the Persians); they later transferred the term to a colorful, turban-shaped flower. Turks long ago gave up turbans, but they and we still cultivate the little "turbans" that brighten our gardens in the spring.

turkey. In show business, a turkey is a show that opens and closes the same night—whence, no doubt, the human turkey: the sort of person who might write or produce such a show. But how a bird that's both toothsome and (in the wild) elusive lent its name to a dud show remains a mystery.

turn a blind eye. The sense is obvious enough: to not "see" something you choose to ignore. The phrase may derive from a tale told of Admiral Horatio Nelson (1758–1805), the great British naval hero of the Napoleonic Wars.

Nelson commanded a squadron at the Battle of Copenhagen, and at one point had his attention called to a signal from his commander in chief, ordering him to break off the engagement. Nelson, who had lost the sight of one eye in an earlier fight, clapped his telescope to his blind eye, announced that he couldn't see the signal, and continued fighting. Thanks in part to his efforts, the Danish fleet was almost totally destroyed; Nelson had turned a blind eye both literally and figuratively.

turn a hair, not. A horse that's been properly groomed will have a smooth coat. When it's been ridden hard, however, it will sweat and its coat will become ruffled. Someone who doesn't turn a hair remains unperturbed or unruffled, however startling or taxing the situation.

turn over a new leaf. The leaf is, of course, not from a tree but a page of a book—figuratively, one in which a person's deeds and misdeeds are recorded. Someone who turns over a new leaf is putting the past behind them and starting fresh on a clean page—hopefully, one on which past errors won't be once more recorded.

turn the tables on. Said to be from a seventeenth-century card game in which a player could choose to turn the table so that he was playing his opponent's cards—presumably substituting a winning hand for a losing one. The story sounds plausible, but the evidence for it is far from watertight.

turn turtle. To sailors of an earlier era, for whom fresh meat was a rarity, the turtles and tortoises found on some tropical shores were highly valued. They could be kept alive for weeks aboard ship, and could also be easily captured on land, simply by turning them upside down: a turtle in this position can neither move nor right itself. When something turns turtle, it's in the same unfortunate position as the animal.

turncoat. By one account, the original turncoat was a Duke of Saxony whose domain lay between French and Spanish possessions. Accordingly, he had made for himself a coat that was white (for France) on one side, and blue (for Spain) on the other. Depending on which power seemed the more formidable, he would turn his coat.

It's a nice story—but any good historical atlas will show that at no time did Saxony lie between French and Spanish territories. And while the French flag was unquestionably white before the Revolution, Spanish banners were never blue. Either the story has lost a lot in translation or (far more likely) Ben Trovato has struck once more.

A more plausible explanation comes from the fact that "coat" has long figuratively meant "kind" or even "party"; if you "turned" it, you changed sides. Or, just possibly, the sense may go back to a knight's coat of arms, often embroidered on a tunic over his armor. Some prudent warrior, finding himself in the midst of an obviously lost battle, may have literally turned his coat inside out, to avoid being recognized and captured. I don't guarantee this story, but—unlike the tale of the Duke of Saxony—it *could* have happened.

turnpike. You think turnpikes are a modern invention? No way! In the seventeenth century, a turnpike was a sort of heavy turnstile set across a road, so that traffic could not pass unless (and here we get to the meat of it) it paid a toll. Turnpike traffic today moves far faster than in the seventeenth century, and the "pikes" are electrically operated poles—but we're still paying the tolls.

two bits. Three hundred years ago, a bit was any of various small Spanish coins that circulated in the West Indies and North America (the name probably comes from earlier thieves' slang, in which "bit" = money). More particularly, the bit was a coin of one real (pronounced ray-AL).

The eight-real coin, or "piece of eight," also known as the Spanish dollar, had approximately the value of one U.S. dollar. A "bit," then, was one-eighth of a dollar (12 ½ cents), and two-bits, a quarter. Similarly, four bits was half a dollar, and six bits, 75 cents, but these two terms were and are little used outside the southern U.S.

two shakes, in—see **shake, in a**.

Uncle Tom. The central character in Harriet Beecher Stowe's *U*
famous anti-slavery novel, *Uncle Tom's Cabin* was an elderly
slave, constantly flogged and otherwise abused by his master, yet
always obedient to the Christian injunction to forgive one's enemies. (His prolonged forbearance was, in fact, a bit too good to
be true.) Blacks have long used "Uncle Tom" (sometimes, just
"Tom") to describe those of their number considered too forbear-
ing and deferential to "whitey."

unctuous—see **smarmy**.

under the table—see **aboveboard**.

uppers, on one's. The uppers here are the upper part of a pair
of shoes, as contrasted with the sole. If you're very short of cash,
your soles may well be worn through; if they're completely worn
away or have dropped off, you're (walking) on your uppers—dead
broke.

upset the apple cart. To a farmer, an upset cart was inconvenient at best. An upset cart loaded with loose apples was a minor
catastrophe: they'd roll all over the landscape and be bruised to
boot. Someone who upsets the apple cart has produced just such
a catastrophic mess.

urbane. Ultimately, from Latin *urbanus,* city-dweller. For centuries, city-dwellers have considered themselves more sophisticated, with more polished manners—in short, more urbane—
than their country cousins. Few country people share this view.

vandal. The Vandals were one of the Germanic tribes whose *V*
incursions into the Roman Empire helped destroy it; in A.D. 455,
a Vandal army sacked Rome. The Vandals' activities were cer-

tainly destructive, but no more so than those of other Germanic groups such as the Visigoths and Franks—nor, so far as I know, did they get any kick out of destruction as such. Nonetheless, their name was much later attached to people who deliberately destroy or trash things.

venereal. The Roman goddess Venus, like her Greek counterpart, Aphrodite (see **aprodisiac**), symbolized sexual love. A venereal disease, evidently, is one acquired by casual, unselective celebration of the rites of Venus.

vestige—see **investigate.**

vet (verb). A vet is a veterinarian; to "vet" someone or something means to examine carefully, as a vet does a sick or injured animal. An editor may sometimes speak of "vetting" a manuscript, and members of John LeCarre's fictitious "Circus" often referred to vetting members of the security services, to uncover possible Communist associations.

W ◠ **waffle** (verb). Any resemblance to the waffle you eat with butter and syrup is purely coincidental; this waffle derives from "waff," an English dialect term akin to "wave" and "waver," meaning to move to and fro. A speaker or writer who waffles is wavering to and fro—**equivocating,** or **straddling** the issue.

wagon, on the. The wagon is (or was) the horse-drawn water-wagon once used to spray city streets, as its gasoline-powered counterpart still is. A heavy drinker who has sworn off liquor has climbed on the water-wagon, or simply on the wagon.

wash (noun). Originally a "wash sale" was a device, too intricate to explain here, used by dishonest stockbrokers to chisel extra money from their clients. A modern "wash sale" is a (legal) scheme for tax avoidance. If you hold stock on which you've taken "paper" losses, you can sell it and deduct the losses from your taxable income; then, 30 days later, you can buy back the same stock—presumably, at or near the same price.

That is, the second transaction has washed out (cancelled) the other: your stock holdings are still the same—though not your taxes. A wash is any similar situation in which two things cancel out. The term, by the way, has nothing to do with "laundering" dirty money, though this is every bit as illegal as the original, stockbroker's "wash sale."

wash one's hands of something. When Jesus was brought for judgment before Pontius Pilate, the Roman governor of Judea, Pilate found no evidence that he'd committed any crime. But the hoodlum element in Jerusalem, stirred up by the Jewish establishment, demanded blood. Finally Pilate, more concerned with preserving public order than with justice, "took water and washed his hands before the multitude, saying, I am innocent of the blood of this just person: see ye to it."

So, at any rate, goes the story as told in Matthew xxvii. Some Biblical commentators believe that the tale was contrived later, to let the Roman government off the hook; Pilate, they note, had excellent reasons for getting rid of any agitator who preached the doctrine that the poor were morally superior to the rich. The story has also been used in support of the notion that "the Jews killed Christ," which even the Vatican has now recognized as a libel. Rich Jews, hand in glove with their Roman overlords, may or may not have helped kill Christ—but Christ himself was every bit as Jewish as they were; so were all his disciples.

watered stock. For generations, cattle have been bought and sold by the pound. Accordingly, cattlemen who'd driven their stock to market would water the animals—encourage them to drink heavily—just before they were weighed. The term was soon transferred to financial stock that had been similarly "watered"—that is, whose value had been diluted by issuing additional shares, though the firm's assets hadn't increased.

The phrase, I think, points to the true origin of *bucket shop*—a disreputable stockbroking establishment. Supposedly, the original bucket shop was a place where whiskey was sold by the bucket, but I don't believe it. Whisky has been sold by the shot, glass and barrel; beer, before Prohibition, was sold by the bucket. But a bucket of whisky? Come on! Much more likely, I think, is that bucket shops were so named because they dealt in watered stock—as many in fact did.

weasel words. Weasels are credited with being able to suck out the contents of an egg without breaking the shell. According to Theodore Roosevelt, a weasel word "sucks all the meaning" out of another word it's combined with. The particular weasel he was speaking of was President Woodrow Wilson's proposal for "universal voluntary" military training; as Roosevelt correctly pointed out, the training might be either universal or voluntary, but not both. Wilson, as we'd now say, had **waffled**.

weather eye, a. The weather side of a sailing ship was the side from which the wind happened to be blowing—either port or **starboard**, depending on what tack the ship was on. Squalls, or giant storm waves, normally came from that side, and so did human dangers. That is, a warship or pirate to windward—on your weather side—could, other things being equal, attack you or not as he chose, but if you were on *his* weather side, you could attack or flee as *you* chose. Thus a ship's officer wanting timely warning of possible perils would keep a weather eye out.

well-heeled. "Heeled" originally referred to a gamecock armed with steel fighting spurs, which were attached to the backs of its feet; in the U. S., the word was transferred to a person armed with a revolver, often carried in a back pocket. Whence—possibly— the well-heeled person with a fat wallet or roll of bills in that pocket. A more likely derivation reflects the fact that poor folk often have shoes with badly worn and run-over heels; rich people, by contrast, are invariably well-heeled.

welsh (verb). English writers suggest that the term may derive from the old nursery rhyme, "Taffy was a Welshman, Taffy was a thief"—whence the dishonest gambler who welshes on a bet. Some Welshmen have countered that the original welshers weren't Welsh but English: bookies owing more than they could pay, who took refuge in the wilds of Wales. Being neither Welsh nor English, I'm neutral.

Welsh rabbit. Often incorrectly called "Welsh rarebit." The word is "rabbit"; the phrase reflects the long-standing poverty of Wales, where even rabbit was something of a luxury. Cheese was much cheaper, so that melted cheese on toast became the only sort of "rabbit" that most Welsh could afford. Similarly, a concoction of hot water flavored with burnt bread was once called "Scotch coffee," and dried codfish, "Cape Cod turkey."

wet behind the ears. All baby mammals are wet when they emerge from their mothers. By some accounts, when a calf or colt is born, the last spot to dry is the small depression behind its ears—which, indeed, may also be true of human babies. Someone who's (still) wet behind the ears is almost as inexperienced as a new-born babe.

wheeler-dealer. This may originally have meant a gambler who bet heavily on both roulette (the wheel) and cards (the deal). More likely, it means simply a big wheel (see **big-shot**) who goes in for big deals—often none too ethical.

whip (legislative). In foxhunting, one of the hunt "servants" is the whipper-in, who keeps the hounds from straying after false scents by whipping them back into the pack. In the British parliament, and later in the U.S. Congress, the whipper-in became the whip, a party leader who keeps party members from "straying": makes sure they show up for votes, and vote right.

whipping boy. Centuries ago, young princes who misbehaved couldn't be whipped as ordinary kids were. Accordingly, the whipping was delivered to the prince's whipping boy—a commoner brought up with him for that purpose. Whipping boys are no longer associated with royalty; instead, they take the "whipping"—blame or reproof—properly due someone else.

whisk(e)y. The word comes from (where else?) Scotland, in whose Gaelic tongue *uisgebeatha* means "water of life." Interestingly, the same idea crops up in many names for spirits: to the French, brandy is *eau de vie,* while Sweden's caraway-flavored vodka is *akavit,* from Latin *aqua vitae.* When you're feeling really down, a shot of whisky may well be a life-saver, but too many of them can turn the water of life into its opposite.

white elephant. White (albino) elephants are rare animals—so rare that in ancient Siam (Thailand) they were considered sacred. According to legend, when the King of Siam took a dislike to a nobleman, he'd give him one of the animals. Being a gift, it couldn't be sold; being sacred, it couldn't be put to work or (even less) killed—yet the new owner had to keep feeding it. If you happen to have (say) a house larger than you need, whose upkeep and mortgage payments are keeping you broke, you've got a real white elephant on your hands. Unlike the unfortunate Siamese, however, you can at least try to sell it.

white feather, the. A white feather in a gamecock's tail was considered a mark of inferior breeding, meaning that the bird could be expected to show no courage in a fight. Someone who shows the white feather is also showing no courage—to put it mildly. During World War I, some ultra-patriotic British civilians made a practice of handing out white feathers to "cowardly" young men who hadn't enlisted. British soldiers who'd been in the trenches, by contrast, knew well enough that you didn't have to be cowardly to be scared of combat—just sane.

white man's burden. Another phrase we owe to Kipling. Around 1900, when the U.S. government had grabbed the Philippines from Spain and was debating whether to keep them, Kipling wrote a poem urging Americans to "take up the White Man's burden"—that is, the onerous task of governing and "civilizing" the darker races.

Kipling, like many devout imperialists, really believed that governing the "lesser breeds" was both a responsibility and a labor of love. The merchants, mining magnates, plantation owners and bankers who made fortunes out of imperialism knew better—but went along with the illusion. Nowadays the metaphor is generally used ironically; since World War II, it has become clear to almost everyone that governing peoples of any color against their will eventually becomes an insupportable burden—as France (and later the U. S.) discovered in Vietnam.

whitewash (verb). Anyone who's ever read *Tom Sawyer* remembers how Tom whitewashed a fence. I must be one of the very few city dwellers who's actually done it—covered a dilapidated fence with a mixture of slaked lime, salt and water. Whitewashing is a quick, cheap way of covering something up, whether it's a fence or a scandal—but the new, clean surface isn't very durable.

whole cloth—see **cut out of . . .**

wild-goose chase. In a horseman's game of Elizabethan times, a rider would take off across country—up hill, down dale, over fences, through hedges and across ditches. His companions were supposed to follow him in line, as wild geese follow their leader—for as long as they could keep up.

The phrase soon became a metaphor for pursuing anything hard to catch. Two centuries later, when the original game was long forgotten, Samuel Johnson defined it as "a pursuit of something as unlikely to be caught as a wild goose." Today's "geese" are even harder to catch, since they're not just wild but imaginary.

win hands down. No one seems to have any information on this phrase; I'd guess that it comes from poker. If one player seems to have an unbeatable hand, the others may simply fold rather than meet his bet. He then wins the pot hands down—without having to show his cards and thus reveal whether he was bluffing.

windfall—see **hook or crook.**

wire, just under the. Probably a racetrack expression: the (imaginary) "wire" is the finish line. A horse that gets in "just under the wire" is one that just manages to finish in the money, having beaten out another horse by a nose.

woolgathering. Actual woolgathering—wandering through the fields collecting tufts of wool left by sheep on bushes and thorns— was an occupation requiring little concentration and yielding little profit. Figurative woolgathering, in which our wits wander like the woolgatherer, also yields little profit.

works, the. The works of a clock or other machine include all its parts; the "works" of an animal humorously meant all its innards. To give someone the works, then, means to give them "everything"—which, depending on context, can mean anything from murder to comprehensive medical treatment.

worth one's salt—see **salary.**

wrong/other side of the tracks, the. Nobody seems to have a clue as to how this American expression got started. The tracks are, of course, railroad tracks, which more often than not ran right through the middle of town—if, indeed, the town hadn't grown up around the railroad. Presumably the upper crust lived on one side of the tracks, their social inferiors on the other side—the wrong side.

At a guess, the "right" and "wrong" sides depended originally on the prevailing winds in the area, which would blow the locomotive's smoke—later, industrial smoke as well—to one side or the other. People who could afford it would live on the cleaner, windward side, those who couldn't, on the other, "wrong" side.

wrong tack, on the—see **take another tack**.

yahoo. One of Jonathan Swift's most acid portraits of humanity ⌐ **Y** occurs in the voyage that Gulliver made to the country of the Houyhnhnms. These were rational, civilized creatures in the shape of horses (their name was supposed to resemble a horse's whinny), served by a degraded, brutal race in human form, which Swift christened Yahoos. The term was quickly applied to any group of ignorant, brutal human beings—the kind we now call **rednecks**.

yellow dog contract. In nineteenth-century America, "yellow dog" became for some reason a metaphor for a cowardly or otherwise worthless person. In the early twentieth century, when employers were bitterly fighting trade unions, one device they used was a "contract" in which newly hired workers pledged never to join a union, on pain of immediate discharge.

Union workers promptly christened it the Yellow Dog contract, implying that only a yellow dog would sign one. Alas, it wasn't that simple: for many workers, the choice was sign or starve. These contracts were outlawed by Congress in 1935.

yoga. Ultimately, from a very old root meaning to yoke (cattle). In India, it came to mean "yoking" oneself to (uniting oneself with) the rest of the universe. In many Western countries, yoga has become merely a form of exercise—though some devotees still feel that it somehow joins them to a higher plane of existence.

your day in the barrel. The punchline of a fairly well-known story, which—in a vigorously laundered version—runs like this:

A young sailor, on a long voyage, complains to his shipmates about his rising frustration. One of them leads him deep into the hold, shows him a barrel, and tells him to insert himself through the bunghole. He does so, and obtains ecstatic relief. "Gee," he says, "I wish I could do this every day!" "You can," says his friend, "every day but Thursday." "So what happens on Thursday?" "That's your day in the barrel!"

To those who know the story, the metaphor is a powerful one because it expresses something fundamental about life: just about all of us can expect our share of bad luck and dirty jobs. Unless you're very lucky or very rich, sooner or later it'll be your day in the barrel.

Z ℓ **zealot.** The great Jewish revolt against Roman rule, in A.D. 72, was led by a Jewish sect called Zealots (from Greek *zelotes*), because of their intense religious and nationalistic zeal. The final battle occurred at the Jewish fortress of Masada, where some 900 Zealots, finding themselves besieged and hopelessly outnumbered, chose to commit mass suicide rather than surrender. Modern zealots may not go quite that far, but are equally fanatical.

How you regard zealots—or Zealots—will depend partly on whether you share their aims, and on what the stakes are. But zealots are in any circumstances uncomfortable companions, not least because their zeal may lead them to sacrifice not only themselves but anyone else who happens to be around. The French statesman Talleyrand had a point when he remarked, *Surtout, pas de zele!* (Above all—no zeal!)

zero in. Before World War I, soldiers "zeroed" their rifles by adjusting the sights on a target at a known distance; with the distance known, rather than estimated, the adjustment error would—or should—be zero. In World War II, guns were zeroed in on previously selected targets—aimed so that the gunners need only fire to hit them. Today a speaker may zero in on a particular point, and mosquitoes may even zero in on a particular person.

zero-sum. A term taken from the branch of mathematics called games theory. The "sum" refers to the summed gains and losses of the participants in a game, real or figurative—i.e., an actual game, a business deal or even a war. If the gains and losses of the players always add up to zero (A's gains equal B's losses or vice versa), it's a zero-sum game, and a strategy based on this assumption is a zero-sum strategy.

Many people look on the "game" between workers and employers as a figurative zero-sum game: labor's gains will inevitably equal employers' losses and vice versa. Some commentators have speculated that this need not be so: it's possible that our economy could be restructured as a non-zero-sum game, in which *both* parties would gain—though perhaps not as much as one side might gain with a zero-sum strategy.

Games theoreticians have demonstrated that in some imaginary "games" a non-zero-sum strategy is the only rational one. That is, if both sides pursue such a strategy, neither can lose; in fact, both will gain something. Also worth noting is that some "games" are non-zero-sum in the opposite sense: whatever the outcome, both sides will lose. This is increasingly true of modern warfare—and triply so for nuclear war.

zest. Literally, orange or lemon rind used as a flavoring—whence any intense savor, of a foodstuff or of an experience.

zombie. A word brought to the West Indies by African slaves. In Haiti, where many African traditions survive, it means a corpse supposedly reanimated by magic, capable of following orders but with no will of its own. If someone calls you a zombie, that's about what they mean.

Some anthropologists believe zombies actually exist: people who've been put into a coma by some vegetable poison, buried alive, and then dug up—to serve as slaves of the poisoner. We find a similar word, "jumbie," in the English-speaking West Indies—where, however, it means merely a malignant spirit.